There's this River...

Grand Canyon Boatman Stories

Looking Upstream from South Canyon

Mary Williams

1993

There's this River...

Grand Canyon Boatman Stories

Second Edition

edited by *Christa Sadler*

foreword by *Scott Thybony*

This Earth Press
Flagstaff, Arizona

SECOND EDITION / FOURTH PRINTING
ISBN 0-9776983-0-0
Library of Congress Control Number 2006900670

Book design and production by Mary Williams Design, Flagstaff, Arizona
Cover artwork "Ammo Can and Carabiners" ©2001 Geoff Gourley,
    Geoff Gourley Photography, Flagstaff, Arizona
Back cover photograph "Alive Below Lava: Scotty Spins a Yarn"
    ©2005 Matt Fahey
Background back cover photograph ©2000 Christa Sadler
"Prickly Pear," "Collared Lizard," "Datura" illustrations ©2005 Lisa Kearsley
Printed in the United States

"Havasu" and "Glory Days" by Lew Steiger; "On Big Boats Without Water"
    by Shane Murphy; "By The Light of the Silvery Moon" by Nancy Coker
    Helin, and "Leaving Eden" by Christa Sadler originally appeared in the
    Boatman's Quarterly Review.
"The Story" by Tim Cooper originally appeared in *The Hibernacle News.*
"An Exploration of the Little Colorado River Gorge" by Tim Cooper and
    "Don't Let Your Children Grow Up To Be Boatmen" by Vince Welch
    originally appeared in the *Mountain Gazette.*
"Faith in the Dry Season" by Rebecca Lawton excerpted from *Reading
    Water: Lessons From the River* ©2002 Rebecca Lawton.
"...And the Last Boat Was Just Right!" by Ellen Tibbetts is owned by and
    appears courtesy of Professional River Outfitters, Inc.
"Crowding in the Canyon," by Ellen Tibbetts originally appeared in the
    Boatman's Quarterly Review.

To the river and her canyon, and all their friends.

And for my parents—I never got to take you down the river,
but you're with me on every trip.

Boatman Working I
Mary Williams
1993

TABLE OF CONTENTS

FOREWORD

Scott Thybony

RIVER STORIES. They start when you're still in the tail waves. I once pulled into an eddy to watch the next boat make its run. As it drifted past, I caught the end of a story,

"... and then he popped out of the boat like toast out of a toaster!"

The rest of it, I knew, would come later that evening in camp. And if the story resurfaced back in town, then it had the potential to become part of the canon of river lore running like a current through the boating community.

This oral tradition begins with a swamper untying the boat at Lees Ferry and pushing off. At first the focus is on the craft of running a river—technique, runs, and practical advice like, "Remember, it takes seven minutes to cool a beer to river temperature." Soon the stories told by veteran boatmen become part of the unofficial training, passing on important lessons such as grace under pressure—or at least having a sense of humor about it. After a few seasons the incidents pile up like driftwood, and every bend in the river triggers a memory. In the bigger rapids, even holes and rocks have their own history. The tales told can range from a groover adventure to a passenger whose life was changed forever by the river. Often a boatman's best story will be about the first river trip taken, the moment the hook was set.

It happened this way to a friend of river guide Roger Henderson. "On his first Colorado River trip," Roger said, "he knew this was it, this was what he wanted to do with his life." Roger's friend was married at the time and working for an oil company out of Calgary. After the boats reached Phantom Ranch, his friend sent two postcards stamped, "Mailed by Mule From the Bottom of the Grand Canyon." The first one went to his wife asking for a divorce. The second went to his boss with a two-word message—"I quit."

If it's not the first trip that gets retold, it's the last. My final trip as a river ranger began as usual with an early start from the South Rim. Scientists from around the country had converged there, and the head of the river unit had put me in charge of the research trip before leaving on a patrol. That made sense since I'd already run several dozen trips, most of them as trip leader. Ken, the other ranger assigned to the trip, was a recent hire without enough trips to qualify as a boatman. Having spent most of my time below the rim, I was unaware of the turf battle brewing between the river unit and the inner canyon unit, which was supervised by another ranger. A rumor going around said he'd only been below the rim once in eighteen years and that was on horseback. This was in 1976 when things like that could happen.

At six in the morning we were preparing to drive the boat to the ferry, when the inner canyon ranger walked up with the new boatman. He told me he wanted the new guy to be trip leader.

"No," I said, "he's not qualified."

The ranger wasn't used to having a subordinate disagree with him, so he stormed off to get the head of the science division. My salary was being funneled through that unit, and the head scientist was nominally my boss. Dragged out of bed, he arrived a bit tousled and began explaining to me how the park service worked.

"Ken has a higher GS rating than you," he said; "he has to be trip leader."

"He isn't qualified."

"This is the park service; competency has nothing to do with it!"

So I told him to find another boatman.

"What?"

"I'm quitting."

After some persuasion, I agreed to run one more trip to keep from having to cancel it and leave the researchers high and dry. It would have been easier to have mailed a postcard from Phantom.

As the days unfolded the new trip leader gained confidence, and the night before Lava Falls Ken told me he wanted to run it. He was ready. The rapid is one of the most dreaded on the river, rated ten on a ten scale, but with a thirty-seven-foot motor rig and good, medium water, the risk of trouble was low. The next day we stopped above the rapid, and Ken climbed the rocks for a preview. He stood there taking a long look when a Fort Lee trip pulled in. A boatman named Jet soon joined us on the scout rock. Having flipped in Lava on his previous two motor trips, he wasn't looking forward to a rematch. A quick check on conditions, and he announced that he was going to try the Slot run. I had never seen this done in a big boat.

At certain water levels a gap opens on the right side of the Ledge Hole. If you hit it just right, you can miss most of the big waves, but it's hard to pull off. With nothing to key on, you have to find a faint bubble line lost among the others. I had rowed the Slot a couple of times, but considered it too narrow for a baloney boat. As Ken and I watched from above, Jet hit it perfectly, slipping past the worst of it and barely getting splashed.

"I'm going to do that!" said Ken, caught up in the excitement of the moment.

"No," I told him, "go right. It's good water, let the current take you, and keep it straight—no problem."

"I want to do the Slot!"

It's hard to argue with a true believer. "You're the trip leader," I said; "it's your decision. But if you're going to run the Slot, here's what you have to do." I pointed out a faint trace of foam and told him to memorize it. "Make sure you get on it and let the current take you. No throttle, just drift in. The current gets squirrelly at the top. Don't fight it. If you're lined up right it will bring you back to where you need to be."

We returned to the boat and pushed off. Ken motored upriver and swung around. To my surprise, he made the approach without a hitch. As the boat drifted to the head of the rapid, the entire world dropped away into a chaos of breaking waves. The roaring abyss. Just then the current swung the bow left, and instinctively Ken tried to correct it. I could only hold on and watch the inevitable unfold. The current immediately swung back, turning us sideways. It was too late to make another correction. The boat suddenly dropped over the ledge with a loud crash. Water exploded everywhere. The boat hung suspended for a moment at the point of flipping before crashing back under an avalanche of whitewater.

Before I realized what was happening, we shot toward the right bank at full speed, hitting everything in our path from V-waves to standing waves, washing up on the Black Rock, almost flipping again before doing a one-eighty, and shooting back across the rapid, hitting whatever we missed on the first pass. I had to stop a passenger who had been ordered to grab the bowline and swim for shore; then I jumped into the motor well and took the tiller. The jolt of dropping over the ledge had jammed the throttle wide open. I spotted a beach on river left and landed near the hot spring. During the entire incident at least forty passengers from various trips were crowded on the rocks. I never learned how many of them decided to walk around Lava after watching our run.

That should have been my last trip. But not wanting to leave the river unit in a bind, I agreed to do one more – as trip leader this time. It went smoothly until the final day when we spotted smoke rising from the mouth of Rampart Cave. Thick layers of desiccated ground sloth dung dating back forty thousand years were on fire, destroying an invaluable record of past environments. My river-running career ended inside a superheated cave choked with acrid smoke and a skin-penetrating stench. A boatman plays every role from doctor to dishwasher on the river. But some roles, like sprinkling water on burning sloth shit for nine days, can't be found in any job description.

River stories. You hear them when tied up at Havasu or outside the warehouse at a Guides Training Seminar, at Dave Edward's studio or Brad Dimock's Christmas party, and sometimes not until a funeral comes around. They tell about tight binds and epic runs, are often wildly improbable and sometimes uncanny. Many are told by boatmen with an incredible depth of experience—a group of "highly maimed impressionables," as one of them put it.

Most stories never get written down, much less published, so they have a tendency to take on a life of their own. They will balloon out of all proportion or shrink to an off-hand remark depending on the mood of the teller, the interest of the listeners, and of course the amount of alcohol consumed. Trips tend to overlap in the retelling, one incident becomes spliced to another, and sometimes an entire tale gets transplanted to another river. At that point you may have a legend in the making.

Since most boatmen are content to tell it rather than write it, many stories never get heard outside a small circle of friends. Christa has been able to do what few others have done. She has convinced the river people to write them down, giving a much wider circle the chance to hear them. In the process her book has become part of the oral tradition itself. One of these tales I first heard on the river, only to discover later it had come from her book. A good story keeps flowing.

So now imagine that dinner is cooked, the dishes washed, and you're sitting on someone's boat as the evening air absorbs the cool of the water. Sit back and listen as the stories begin.

Scott Thybony
Flagstaff, Arizona 2006

Preface to the Second Edition

Christa Sadler

In August of 2005 I was in Page, Arizona, to give a talk for the Glen
Canyon Natural History Association. *There's This River* was out of print
and the book was hard to find. I had the last fourteen copies from Red
Lake Books, and had brought them up for the association to sell. The
response from the audience was astounding. People came up to see me
after the talk, clutching the book close to their chests like a precious thing.
"I've been looking for this for so long, I'm so happy to find it!" "My
boyfriend is going to be so jealous!" "This is a present for my sister, I'm so
glad to be able to give it to her." One group of locals told me that they had
done a reader's theater from some of the stories in the book. It was a wonderful image: this group acting out some of the stories with makeshift
props on a homemade stage. Most of them had never even seen the whole
collection, only the xeroxed copies of the stories with which they worked.

Over the years, people have told me of their favorite pieces in the collection—seems like everyone likes a different story, for different reasons.
Almost every trip I've done since the book was published has at least one
guide reading to our passengers from the book. I myself do it quite often.
I've met people throughout the Southwest, even in the airport in Phoenix,
who have told me how much they enjoy the book, how it made them laugh
and cry and remember their trip with tremendous fondness.

These responses, and all the others I have received over the years since
the book's initial publication, are a testament to the talent and passion of
the Grand Canyon guide community. I am delighted to be able to reprint a
new edition. In rereading the original stories in the process, I am reminded
of how timeless they are. More than a decade later, they are still as funny,
sad, whimsical and entertaining as they ever were. The new stories and artwork added to this collection serve to remind us that this community is a
vibrant and evolving one, and that good stories are never in short supply
here.

For this new edition, all the authors wanted to take a look at their old
stories and make some changes, so even some of the old stories have new

faces as their authors remembered new details or dates or names. Some of the new contributions were written by familiar names: seems like Brad Dimock is never at a loss for a great story. Others add to the already varied facets of this collection: what Grand Canyon storybook is complete without a tale about the importance of learning proper bathroom techniques, or finding a snake in your sleeping bag, after all?

In the twelve years since the publication of the first edition of *There's This River*, a lot has changed. There have been births, deaths of dear friends and colleagues, marriages, divorces, career changes. People have left the river and come back. Some have left for good. Many of the contributors have expanded or begun careers in art or writing and publishing. New boatmen continue to arrive, eager to tackle the hottest trips of the year, while the older guides retreat to the cool and shade of spring and fall. September 11, 2001, intruded into our river lives to remind us that we are still connected to the outside world despite our best efforts to distance ourselves while on the river. That moment made the canyon and the river and what happens on our trips even more precious for many of us.

Some things about the river itself have changed. The water level doesn't fluctuate as much as it used to in the 1980s; environmental legislation requires that Glen Canyon Dam be managed in ways more consistent with protection of the river ecosystem. Endangered species are being studied with increasing intensity, as is our ability to recreate natural processes such as floods, to replenish beaches with precious sediment.

Some things haven't changed. The political battles continue to rage over how to manage the Colorado River, and who is allowed access to the river. Some of these battles have reached epic proportions; this seems oddly out of sync with the very fact of the experience to which we are seeking access. Perhaps a new river management plan that was released in 2005 will help diminish some of these battles.

But the river cares for none of this. Happily for us, she continues flowing through the canyon of her making, creating with every bend and every riffle the stuff of which communities, and legends, are made.

Christa Sadler
Flagstaff, Arizona 2006

The Colorado River Through Grand Canyon

Kanab Creek

Upset Rapid

Sinyala Rapid

Lake Mead

Lava Falls

Whitmore Wash

Matkatamiba Canyon

Olo Canyon

Pearce Ferry

South Cove

Parashant Wash

Havasu Creek

National Canyon

Separation Canyon

Mohawk Canyon

205 Mile Rapid

217 Mile Rapid

Diamond Creek

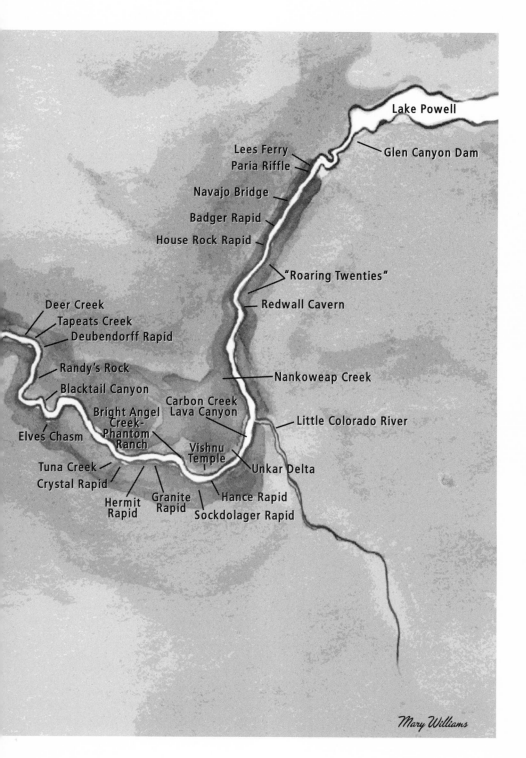

Lake Powell

Lees Ferry
Paria Riffle

Glen Canyon Dam

Navajo Bridge

Badger Rapid

House Rock Rapid

"Roaring Twenties"

Redwall Cavern

Deer Creek
Tapeats Creek
Deubendorff Rapid

Nankoweap Creek

Randy's Rock

Blacktail Canyon

Carbon Creek
Lava Canyon

Bright Angel
Creek-
Phantom
Ranch

Little Colorado River

Elves Chasm

Vishnu
Temple

Tuna Creek

Unkar Delta

Crystal Rapid

Hermit
Rapid

Granite
Rapid

Hance Rapid

Sockdolager Rapid

Mary Williams

INTRODUCTION

Christa Sadler

THE INSPIRATION FOR THIS collection of short stories came from a young passenger on a river trip back in 1991. She was about twenty-five, and she had just hiked in at the halfway point of the trip about three days before. It usually takes several days for people to get "into" the canyon after they've joined a trip, whether from the beginning or halfway through. She wasn't really "there" yet, and was still missing her boyfriend, her hair dryer and hot showers, not necessarily in that order. On my boat one lazy afternoon, floating through the calm water of the Muav Gorge, she asked to read a copy of the Grand Canyon River Guides' newsletter. I guess that was a subtle way of telling me she was tired of hearing about geology. I went on talking with the other three people in my boat, when she began giggling. She continued to giggle until she finished the newsletter, and handed it back to me. "That was a great story." I glanced at it: Lew Steiger's "Glory Days." Hmm. She had only been here three days, didn't know anyone mentioned in the story, had never even *seen* a motor rig. But she enjoyed it nonetheless, enough to remark on it. I started thinking: *There are some great stories and storytellers down here, and people should know about it!*

I began rowing here in 1988, after becoming hooked as a commercial passenger in 1985. When I arrived, wide eyed, wet behind the ears, and terrified, I sat around on the boats with all the boatmen (both men and women call themselves boatmen) at night, and listened to stories of flips, rips, epic hikes, medical emergencies, illicit activity, ghosts, wildlife, full moons and romance. Many of the people I was working with had been down in the Ditch for ten years or more, some for as many as twenty-five or thirty years. They had made a life of this place, and they were telling me, telling each other, about that life.

There are several hundred men and women who presently work, part- or full time, for the fifteen commercial companies in Grand Canyon. There are many who no longer work in the canyon as guides but remain here in their hearts. I have come to respect these people more than any I've ever met. They are a unique bunch, not given to following or joining, yet despite themselves they've become a community. They are raunchy, rowdy and kind. They are some of the most talented people I know. They can take a thirty-seven-foot motor rig through a rocky rapid at low water, or guide a tiny paddleboat through the giant waves of Lava Falls without missing a stroke. They can cook the best food you've ever eaten, bandage a wound, set up a tent during the rain in record time, play the guitar, sing opera, patch a seven-foot rip in the boat while still grinning. In their other lives these people are teachers, doctors, psychologists, ski instructors, carpenters, artists, moviemakers, technicians, photographers, masseurs, scientists. Good people to have on your side.

And they can tell stories! There are a couple of jokes that every passenger hears within the first day or so of a river trip: "How can you tell if a boatman is lying? His lips are moving." "What's the difference between a fairy tale and a boatman story? A fairy tale begins with 'once upon a time' and a boatman story begins with 'no shit, this really happened!'" We joke about it, but stories are the butter for our bread. The river community has a strong storytelling tradition, like the Native Americans and many other cultures. We pass on our lives to the next generation through our tales. Our stories are our way of learning, bragging, hearing about our world. We teach each other with our stories. We find out what hike not to do in mid-July, or where that great hidden camp is that's perfect for a small group. We learn about new runs in rapids, we mourn some of the mistakes of our friends, we laugh at others. Our stories make us a community. And this community is tight knit, for we have a powerful common thread that binds us: the river.

It's why we came. It's what inspires our writing, our photography, our paintings, our lives. It's why we stay. Not just for the rapids or the hikes. Boatmen who show up to conquer the rapids don't usually stay that long. Only five percent of the river is whitewater, and most of this is pretty straightforward once you learn the entry and the one or two moves you might have to make. If you're there for the rapids, you could get bored. There are long flat stretches of water, when the wind is more than likely going to be blowing upstream. There is baking heat and water so cold it's often not even refreshing. There are sand storms that plaster everything in camp with grit. There's the Trip Leader From Hell.

But in the mornings a golden band of light moves down the cliffs towards the river, and in the afternoon that same band moves back up until it is only a sliver at the top, and then it is gone. The canyon wrens are only the size of golf balls, but their songs echo off the walls as you float by. Side canyons here lead to trickling waterfalls with maidenhair ferns and columbine. Raging summer thunderstorms create red-brown waterfalls that plummet eight hundred feet to the river, and turn it brick red in an instant. The stars at night sparkle shamelessly in an uneven narrow band bounded by the black silhouettes of canyon walls. Some of the rapids here make your gut curl beforehand, and afterwards you howl as loud as you possibly can, to no one and to everyone.

Your friends are here. You *make* friends here. When a group starts out together, many of the passengers think they are just "going on a river trip." It doesn't take long to discover they've signed up for a journey. You become a family, all of you together, floating through this wild and inaccessible place. You depend on each other, laugh with each other, come to know each other. As with any family, there are quirks and oddities, good times and bad. But there is no way you can leave this place without being affected somehow by the experience you've just shared. Some of the best friendships I have began on river trips.

River trips. Always there is the river. She rages, she teases and she plays. She keeps all of us on our toes and gives us reason for a life that we find hard to leave. Even boatmen who have left the river can't stay away. They come back for private trips, they bring their kids, they do science that keeps them in the canyon, they become National Park Service rangers.

These are people worth knowing. This is a place worth knowing. Few in our world are lucky enough to find something that they truly love and be able to stick with it long enough to turn it into a life. These men and women have learned how to do just that, and this book is a tribute to them and the place they call home. For every story in this book, there are a hundred others that will remain only campfire tales, or yarns spun out on the boats late at night. There are more that remain untold: not just tales of adventure and excitement, but stories of a favorite passenger, a particularly beautiful sunset, or a quiet time in a side canyon that was somehow special that day. These stories and artwork are part of the history of a unique American community, in an incomparable place.

One of the authors told me that his granddad had lived in a sod house on the plains in the 1800s. The stories were never written down and they're gone now. He said he didn't want that to happen with us. As boatmen at this time in history, we are indebted to some impressive pioneers of the river—people like John Wesley Powell, Robert Stanton, Nathaniel

Galloway, Norm Nevills, Dock Marston, Bert Loper,Georgie Clark and many others. There has been a great deal of change since those early days. Companies have been bought and sold, equipment has improved, food has gotten fancier. Now all the passengers and boatmen wear special shorts and river sandals, where it used to be cut-off jeans and old tennis shoes. But the river flows on. In time, other boatmen will stand on our shoulders and these stories will be their legends. And so it goes.

Welcome to the Grand Canyon and the Colorado River. Welcome to a way of life.

Travertine Waterfall
Larry Stevens
1986

THE UPPER HALF
Lees Ferry to Phantom Ranch

EVERY RIVER TRIP—oar- or motor powered, private or commercial—begins at Lees Ferry, seventeen miles downstream of Glen Canyon Dam and the official boundary between Glen and Grand canyons. Lees Ferry is designated mile 0 on all river guides of the region: the beginning. It operated as a ferry crossing for more than forty years from the 1870s to 1929, the only place to cross the Colorado River in almost five hundred rugged, inaccessible miles. The only place you could even *reach* the river for most of its length across Utah and Arizona. The river flows serenely past the banks here, having just emerged from the confinement of Glen Canyon's narrow sandstone walls, as though it is gearing up for the task ahead of carving the Grand Canyon.

Just a few decades ago at Lees Ferry there was only a dusty dirt road leading to a wide spot on the bank that functioned as a boat ramp. Today, a paved road ends at a broad cement ramp, where all river trips going downstream, and trout fishermen bound upstream, put their boats in the water: this is the put-in.

There are two basic choices in boat types for passengers considering a river trip: oar powered (including paddle boats) and motor powered. About thirty percent of the trips that go downriver use oar rafts, seventeen- to eighteen-foot inflatable rubber rafts with a metal frame strapped on the middle. Gear is tied onto and into this frame; the boatman sits in the middle and rows with a pair of ten- or eleven-foot oars. As many as five passengers sit in the bow and stern of the raft and hang on. A few companies run another type of oar boat called a dory, a sleek and charming hard-shelled wood, aluminum, fiberglass or (believe it or not) styrofoam rowboat with hatches below the surface decks. Several companies also run paddleboats. These fourteen- to eighteen-foot rafts are propelled by several people with canoe paddles, while the guide calls commands and steers. Because these boats usually contain less gear, they ride higher and are great fun in the rapids.

Motor rigs are inflatable rafts that range in size from twenty-two to thirty-nine feet, and exhibit various designs and arrangements of rubber tubes. All use an outboard motor to get them downstream and carry from six to fifteen or so passengers, a guide and a swamper (an assistant, often a boatman in training). On a motor rig, you can run the entire canyon in five to nine days, as compared to a twelve-day or longer trip on an oar boat.

Boatmen and their gear arrive the day before a trip starts to rig the boats. On that day they will spend several hours wrestling with heavy gear and sloppy rubber, cramming hatches and tying knots, sweating under a mid-summer desert sun to put the trip together and get everything ready for their passengers, who will arrive the next morning. Sometimes the ramp can be so crowded with motor and oar rigs, private and commercial trips, that it resembles a swap meet. That night, after all the dirt and grease, the guides spend time visiting, telling tales with their friends from other companies, sitting on boats lined up like cars in a parking lot on the dark quiet river.

The next morning the people arrive, stepping gingerly off the bus and peering uncertainly about them in the bright sun, trying to figure out which of the ragged-looking types standing in front of them belongs to their trip. For a while there is chaos, as bags are tied on or loaded in hatches, lifejackets are fitted and introductions are made. People gasp at the icy river and shudder at the thought of spending several days with water so cold it seems impossible to even drink it, much less be immersed in it. Safety talks about flipping and swimming and rapids only make it worse. But then the boats are loaded, the people are on, you pull away from shore, and drift downstream on the emerald green ribbon of water beneath you. All of a sudden, everything seems right. The quiet takes over, and the madness at Lees Ferry fades like an echo.

Many people choose only to do the upper half of the river. Perhaps time or money constraints dictate that only three to six days can be spent on this vacation, and they opt to run the eighty-eight miles to Phantom Ranch, and hike out to Grand Canyon Village by way of the Bright Angel Trail.

People always ask which half I would suggest for someone who can only do a portion of our two-week trips. After attempting to convince them that the best, the only, way to do it is to go all the way, I try to describe the virtues of the two halves. It's a little like trying to choose a favorite among your children.

The upper half is a stretch of spectacular beauty. The rapids are fun but, with a few notable exceptions, not gut wrenching. Much of the river winds quietly through a narrow, ever-deepening gorge of yellow limestone, red sandstone, gray and pink limestone, brown sandstone. The first sixty-one miles are called Marble Canyon, named by John Wesley Powell for the polished rock of its walls. In the calm stretches, the river mutters and burbles on its way past wide sandy beaches and eight hundred foot sheer cliffs. Sometimes it is the color of polished steel in the late afternoon or the early morning, a blazing sliver of bronze sunlit wall reflected in the calm pools.

Your boats bounce through the energetic rapids of the Roaring Twenties and glide through the calm water of the Thirties. At mile 33, Redwall Cavern looms to your left, a huge overhang floored with soft white sand, perfect for playing frisbee or volleyball and relaxing with your lifejacket for a pillow. Clear, sweet springs gush from the smooth limestone walls, and where they reach the air, a profusion of ferns and red monkey flower grows in startling contrast to the muted reds and browns of the rocks.

The side canyons of Marble Canyon are not numerous, but they are lovely, and a little effort yields many subtle rewards. In North Canyon, the smooth brown sandstone cups around you like a hand. Silver Grotto's grey polished limestone feels as soft as velvet, with cold pools strung like beads on a necklace up the canyon's stairstep bottom.

Nankoweap Creek has carved an immense canyon from the North Rim. The creek spills into Marble Canyon at mile 52, where the main canyon walls have retreated to form an amphitheater of titanic proportions. Most trips stop at Nankoweap to explore the ruins of the Native Americans who lived and farmed here eight hundred years ago. Along the creek there are waterfalls, spectacular views, a perennial bubbling stream, and trout. The water released from Glen Canyon Dam leaves the dam at a chilly forty-eight degrees, a perfect temperature for the trout stocked in the river below. It hasn't taken long for these trout to discover Nankoweap Creek as a winter spawning ground. The bald eagles have discovered the trout. The scientists have discovered the bald eagles. The Colorado River and its ecosystems continue to evolve…

Ten miles downstream from Nankoweap, Marble Canyon ends at the confluence of the Colorado and Little Colorado rivers. The canyon is thirty-five hundred feet deep, carved through over five hundred million years of sedimentary rock, the youngest of which does not yet encompass the earliest dinosaurs. You have begun to gain a sense of the timelessness of the canyon, the patience of the enclosing rocks. You have given up trying to predict the weather from a strip of sky a half a mile wide and three miles long. Every day the canyon has been changing, and it seems like it will go on changing forever. On your river trip, it is day two or four, perhaps five or six, depending on whether you have chosen to travel by motor or oar.

The Little Colorado River, affectionately abbreviated as the LCR, is unusual for a desert river. It is unusual for any river, in that it is both ephemeral and perennial. Until the rains or the spring melt from the high country comes, it is as dry as a bone to thirteen miles from the confluence. There, clear spring water bubbles from the walls of the canyon and the bed of the river, filling the channel with warm, mineral-rich, turquoise blue water. If the river flows with snowmelt or rain above Blue Spring, the powerful water picks up the sediment through which it runs and becomes a swirl the color of coffee with cream, and twice as thick. When this Little Colorado meets the main river, the waters of the larger stream are stained red-brown, and the river flows downstream looking more like its wild namesake than it has since 1963, when Lake Powell began trapping the sediment that flowed out of the canyons to the north.

River trips that encounter a clear LCR may spend hours there, frolicking. The warmth is a welcome respite from the punishing cold of the Colorado. The color is delightful. This is often where a trip begins to bond. Teachers and doctors, CEOs of major corporations and high-powered lawyers may become as silly as children with their lifejackets wrapped around their rear ends, diaper-style, bouncing through the small rapids of the LCR. This is where people begin to understand where they are. Watches disappear deep into waterproof bags. Comments about makeup and mirrors and hot showers diminish. The Groover (a metal box with a toilet seat on top) seems less threatening.

Your trip heads downstream, south, past the sacred Hopi Indian salt mines, and through The Land of a Thousand Eddies, where huge swirls of water suck at your boat and a windy summer day feels like Dante's Inferno. You might hike the loop up Carbon Creek and over to Lava Canyon, stopping along the way to discuss the new geology that keeps changing rapidly now. You have gone back in time more than a billion years since you started. In four miles the canyon opens up, and you see for the first time the North and South rims over a mile above you, stairstepped back in tiers of blue, brown and purple. Desert View Watchtower stares down from five thousand feet above: a tiny, solid finger of humanity. It's tempting to believe that people are watching you right now through the telescope lenses at the overlook. In two more miles the river makes an abrupt right hand turn to the west, and heads into the heart of Grand Canyon, past Lipan Point, Angel's Window, Wotan's Throne and Vishnu Temple. To most guides, these pinnacles and temples are the stuff of which stories are made. Your guide might tell you about the time he once climbed Vishnu Temple in a snowstorm…

At Hance Rapid—mile 77—you may stop to scout your runs through one of the largest and most technically difficult rapids on the river. Rocky debris from Red Canyon has spewed into the river, littering the channel with obstacles ranging in size from toasters to dump trucks. Your guides may not be laughing as much as they were before. If the water level is low, they probably won't be smiling much at all.

Below Hance, as you are celebrating a successful run past the giant holes and waves of the rapid, you notice that the scenery has changed once again. The river is carving through the Kaibab Upwarp, a giant bulge in the earth's crust, shaped not unlike a watermelon sliced in half lengthwise and lying on the flat side. As the river slices into this bulge, it encounters layers of rock deeply buried elsewhere, but here exposed by the arching of the watermelon. The layer at the center, the pink heart of the melon, almost two billion years old, is the schist. Hard, black and unforgiving. No longer is the river lazily meandering through wide sandstone walls, flowing quietly past white beaches. Now it is funneled into a deep, narrow gorge into which it cannot carve sideways, only down. The river becomes deeper, faster and filled with frustrating swirly boils and eddies. At times it can feel like the river isn't moving downstream at all, only sideways. The rapids become larger. This is the Upper Granite Gorge. The rapids in the gorge are numerous, and even the small ones have a kick to them. Scouting is nearly impossible due to the sheer walls, and a flip can mean a long swim in fast water with few places to leave the current or climb out of the river.

On the morning of the gorge, the boatmen will take extra care tying in their loads. They'll check the fit of your lifejacket, which has probably loosened substantially after the Little Colorado. They'll review safety procedures and remind you to hang on. Motor boatmen will show you, once again, exactly where to sit. The paddleboat will be bonded. Tight. And everyone will have a ball. The day of rapids in the gorge above Phantom Ranch is exhilarating, exhausting and a little sad. At the end of the day, some in the group will realize they have to leave tomorrow, and they've started to see why they would like to stay. Your last night on the river is spent telling new tales, laughing at talent show antics, saying goodbye to the river as she gurgles by your camp.

The upper half ends at Phantom Ranch or Pipe Creek, river mile 88 or 89. You are at the bottom of the Grand Canyon, nearly a vertical mile below Bright Angel Lodge on the South Rim, and eight miles down the trail. You say your goodbyes and cry over a few new friends, cool down in the swirling river one last time, shoulder your pack and your water and begin to go up…

FARVANA

Larry Stevens

(Excerpt from *The Book of Lesser Delights*: Chapter 17, preceding the section entitled "Bowling for Sheep")

Whupped. A dozen twelve-day trips from April to November; several sets of back to backs, and this: the swansong launch. We slave like white ants under the blister called sun, amid trucks, diesel fumes, and frames, rigging lines and rubber, through the endless canyon summer heat. Rigging with a speed and surety that comes from months of intimacy with each piece of equipment: what order to load, who gets what, where each piece goes. Our boats are our lives, and each of us knows every scrape, ding, and wear mark. Rigging until dark, which, thank god, comes earlier and cooler in mid-October. Five regulars and the new baggage boatman, Sandy, who works Cataract for Holiday out of Moab. He's good humored, strong, and experienced. Most important, he's fresh and can be called on for help with the rest of us so rag-tired.

By dusk, six Avons are lined up along shore like a small herd of inflatable horses ready for action. The rigging done, we head to dinner. The crew's spirits rise a bit with the realization that the season is almost over. We're almost ready to quit river running for the winter, maybe forever, and let heal that threatening sense of self-hatred that builds up when you give too much for too long. Shooting pool, drinking beer, to hell with the food, jukebox Willie singing "On the Road Again." Afterwards we drag Jomo, our warehouse manager and driver, out to Big Blue, and drive back down to the ferry. Blue is a five-ton stakebed with a tommie lift—the only good vehicle our boss ever bought.

We roar back down to the ferry in the back of Blue through that enormous October night sky: Cassiopeia, Polaris, Ursa Major. Orion later on. Drunk on beer and the bittersweet feeling of the year's last trip, we bust in on the silent darkness of the ferry like the band of hooligans we surely have become. Sorting through the gear pile, backlit though truck lights, we haul essentials to our boats, now slowly stranding by the night's subsiding flow.

We methodically set up bedrolls on cooler tops: me on the *Judy* next to Sandy on the baggage queen. We plunge immediately into oblivious sleep under the sky's blanket of stars: zonked, comatose, dead to the world. Jomo drives Blue up to the parking lot at the top of the ramp and passes out on the driver's seat, as dead tired from the endless season as we all are.

Jomo rolls over in the middle of the night, knocking Blue out of gear. At low water, the eighty yards from the parking lot down to the river is more than enough distance for a truck that size to pick up a lot of speed. I wake to the crunch of tires on gravel and the wind swish as Blue passes inches from my head. A terrible loud crash erupts as it jumps up onto, over, and across Sandy's boat. Wrenched from unconsciousness, I scream, a wail that haunts me still, knowing that our new friend is a bloody mess, crushed beneath the wreckage.

Shouts, air hissing, metal grating. Flashlights play across the bizarre scene. Big Blue humped halfway out into the river across a twisted mass of industrial scrap: hypalon, steel, plastic, and line. The eighteen-foot baggage boat absolutely smashed to bits, Blue's front tires sunk to the axle in the vegetable cooler. But damn if Sandy isn't standing right there beside the wreckage. He'd gotten up a short while before to pee and had only just set-tled back down when he heard the truck coming and leapt off his boat in his sleeping bag.

Jomo climbs out of the cab and works his way along the truck frame into the river and back to shore. "Shit! Now what?"

"Maybe we should call the ranger."

"The law? Right, just the kind of help we need now. Besides, the poor guy doesn't need this late-night disaster any more than we do."

First things first. We set up a lantern and salvage what we can of loose gear. We build a bridge of metal food boxes from the cooler across the span river, and then back Blue out of the cabbage and up onto shore.

"Oh man, we're going to need another boat. But we don't have any left in the warehouse."

"It's 2:30 A.M. If we call the HB at 4:30, he can bring up my boat and cooler and some more rabbit food," I said.

"OK, but who's going to wake up and call?"

The conversation kind of dies out there. The exhausted crew drifts back to their boats. I stay up reading organic chemistry for the course next semester. What a nerd. At 4:30 A.M. I try the phone at the boat ramp.

"Jomo, wake up! The phone's dead. We gotta drive to Marble and get a call through." His first response, a fart, informs me of his enthusiasm for this idea. But he fires up Blue and away we go.

For some unknown reason, there is a long-standing tradition of telecommunications failure in the vicinity of Lees Ferry and the northern Navajo Nation in Arizona. In other words, the phone at Marble is also dead as a dinosaur.

"OK, so where's the next phone?" I try to monitor Jomo's level of consciousness, which varies from mute silence to a sort of glassy-eyed trance.

Long before some kid torched it, the gas station at Bitter Springs had been abandoned, and now all that remains is a small, dysfunctional quadrant of post-industrial decay. The concrete pad is still used for basketball, and its big, white-man windows make good targets for rock-throwing youth. But the place still has a telephone booth. Jomo drives me over to it and I go in to call. The deep silence of the October night is exceeded only by the dull, mechanical deadness of that telephone. Instead of a dial tone, I hear, off to my right, the unmistakable deep-throated growl of an attack dog on the kill. A massive black Doberman leaps out of the darkness and launches itself against the phone booth door, slamming the structure with its whole weight. It recoils and aims itself at me again.

"Shit! Jesus! Jomo!" The dog hurls itself against the door, snarling. Jomo starts up out of his slumbers.

"Oh crap! Jomo! Open the door and get ready!" As the dog leaps again, I bash the phone booth door into its ugly maw with all my might, and dive into Blue's shotgun seat, slamming the door shut behind me.

"Damn!"

"Well, so much for Bitter Springs, how about Cedar Ridge?" Off we drive.

"Jomo, we forgot to put the tailgate on!" The broken coolers and floor pads are sliding out the back of the truck and bouncing along on the highway.

We stop and I climb up, gather up the gear, and hoist the big wooden tailgate into position.

"It's jammed."

"Just slam it in and let's get moving."

The night air is cold, and I am shivering in my shorts, a thin T-shirt, and flips. I'm glad for the cold as the tailgate crashes into place across my right foot. The pain keeps me awake the rest of the drive as I hobble from dead phone to dead phone across the reservation's innumerable backwater settlements.

Finally, almost back to Flagstaff, the Cameron bug station phone works. It's a miracle. I catch the HB just as he is shepherding the passengers out of the motel. He takes them all out to the warehouse for new boxes and a cooler, and stops by my house for *Farvana*, my boat.

Jomo and I drive back to the ferry, barely missing sheep, goats, and a few dawn-feeding roadside horses.

"Swansong or goose farts?" I inquire.

"Guess I should have blocked the truck tires," he replies.

Allah takes care of all things, but tie your camel, I thought.

"Why'd you call your boat, *Farvana*?"

THE ROCKPILE AT MILE 27

Brad Dimock

O
ne winter in the 1970s a tremendous rock fall near mile 27 clogged the river in Marble Canyon with boulders. A research trip run by the Museum of Northern Arizona was the first to see it, name it "MNA" after themselves, and bring stories of it to the rest of the community. Rumors, as always, ran wild, and by the time I heard about it, there was no way a motor rig could get through it. My boss and a few other motor outfitters, a demolitions expert among them, went in before the first spring trips to inspect it. They brought back reassurances that there should be no problem.

And there wasn't, at least not right off the bat. In low water however, which we usually had on Monday morning when we came through, it was mighty tight. And coming immediately after the swirls and boils of 27 Mile Rapid, it was important to be on your toes.

Glen Canyon Dam in those days released water based almost entirely on power demand. Weekend water was low; Sunday water was especially low. On Monday of a three-day Labor Day weekend we entered 27 Mile Rapid on exceedingly low water. Scott was swamping for me and was driving the boat. As we were about to enter the rapid I asked Scott if he felt okay about the rockpile below and he nodded. At the last minute, however, he changed his mind and with a shrug said, "Why don't you take it?"

I hopped down into the cockpit, grabbed the tiller, and slammed through the sharp waves of the rapid into the swirlies above MNA. I must not have been quite on the mark because the bow of the boat began to swing to the right, into an eddy. I steered hard left and gunned the engine in order to get to the left side of the river where the slot through the rocks was. The boat, however, continued to turn to the right as we neared the rockpile. If the boat did not respond soon, the only way out was going to be spinning the boat all the way around to the right, driving upstream a bit and reentering the main current. At a certain point, I had to decide. The point I chose was too late. I got it about half way around when we hit the rockpile. Too shallow to motor any more, I tilted the engine and cast the boat's fate to the river. We slid over one boulder, then another, then stopped dead about half way through the rockpile, about twenty feet from the right bank. It was not quite eight o'clock in the morning.

Around ten an ARTA trip motored through the rock pile and pulled ashore. I had, by that time, tried every means of extrication I knew to no avail. I had swum ashore once, tied off a rope to a boulder and had the entire boatful of people pull. I had them jump up and down while pulling as hard as they could. We tried swearing. But the boat didn't budge, and the water, diabolically, continued to drop. I swam back to the boat.

Stan, the ARTA boatman, and Joe, his swamper, clambered up through the rocks and began shouting to me. Joe, it seemed, was a climber and wanted to set up a Tyrolean traverse with ropes to get us ashore. I was dubious. I suggested we just take off a side tube and build a bridge. But Joe was already stringing ropes. Before long he was happy with the set-up, and Aaron, one of my passengers, volunteered to go first in order to inspire the confidence of Cathy, his fifteen-year-old daughter. We roped him up and he jumped off the boat onto Joe's aerial tramway. The rope stretched and Aaron was immediately sucked beneath the surface, kiting back and forth in the strong current. Only through a supreme effort by those on shore were they able to pull him out. Joe was undaunted and tightened up the rigging. We sent the rest of the passengers across with somewhat less trauma.

With the load of humans off, we tried to pull the boat off the rocks, to no avail. The water was no longer touching the center of the boat, and it was glued solidly to the freshly fractured sandstone boulder.

Stan allowed as how he had to go, and I agreed. We would just have to wait for Tuesday's water. I announced such to the folks. No, there isn't much here but boulders, but yes, this is lunch, dinner, camp, and breakfast. And still the water dropped.

Scott and I busied ourselves with my original idea, which was to take off a side tube and build a bridge. It was surprisingly easy and we soon carried all the camping gear off and began building forts for folks up in the rocks. By four o'clock there was no part of the boat touching the water, and on the upstream edge of the boat you could actually get off and walk back and forth on the boulder. That's when my kayaking buddies showed up. I had paddled with a few of them in California, and one of them, Don, had become a good friend. They were on a private trip, and were recreating in a number of ways when they spotted us and paddled ashore. The *Brontosaurus*-sized boat on the pedestal in the middle of the river was the funniest thing they had ever seen. It was a while before they would stop laughing but I was finally able to convince them to try and help me. I had a plan, but it required several people who hadn't been scared witless of the water during Joe's attempt to drown them that morning. About eight beefy guys and I crossed the pontoon bridge and climbed down onto the precarious boulder ledge on the upstream edge of the boat. We all got a good grip and started heaving with all we had, rhythmically bouncing the boat as we put our shoulders and backs into the push. After a few dozen bounces the thing began to inch downstream. Encouraged, we doubled our efforts until it was bouncing an inch or more with each heave. It finally reached the tipping point and fell off the downriver side of the boulder. It landed on its side and for a long, sickening moment appeared to be about to flip completely over onto its back. But it didn't, and slid down into an upright position as it hit the current. Scott jumped aboard as it drifted into the rest of the rapid and we waited for the lines to shore to tighten. Moments later they did, and promptly snapped as Scott and the boat drifted away into the dusk. My kayak pals started howling again as I dashed downstream to see what was happening. Although I could not see Scott, I breathed relief as I heard the Mercury fire up and get louder as he pressed back upstream. RrrrrRRRRRRRRRRRRRRRR...ruckkkpphhh. Silence. The engine lurched to a stop as it sucked one of the broken lines into the propellor. Scott drifted away again. Kayakers roared. About a minute later the motor fired again. RrrrrrRRRRRRRRRRRRRRRRRRRRRRR...ughphhh. Another line in the prop. The kayakers, still out on the boulder, rolled, kicked, and shrieked. Finally rrrrrrRRRRRRRRRRRRRRRRRRR. Scott made it in this time, the ughhpphhh of a third snarled line coming just as he hit shore. We tied him off, thanked my ever-so-amused friends, and bid them a farewell as they paddled into the gloom. We cooked dinner and spent the evening rebuilding the boat by lantern light.

⟿

We finished the trip without further incident, and for the rest of the season I looked for Stan. I wanted to thank him but we were on different schedules. But early one morning the following year I was motoring for Havasu when I saw the tail end of a motor rig poking out from behind the big Tapeats Sandstone boulders below Doris Rapid. I peered into the camp, as it looked like an ARTA rig. Sure enough it was Stan. I gave a shout and had just begun to wave when my boat lurched to a clattering stop on the only midstream rock within miles. I quit waving.

Marble Canyon
Lisa Kearsley
2005

BY THE LIGHT OF THE SILVERY MOON

Nancy Coker Helin

Heard this one at the Post Office the other day. A woman from Newark, New Jersey—let's call her Edith—dragged downstream by her adventurous younger sister Hazel (of sixty-eight years), appeared down at the boats an hour or so after sunset. A big, beautiful full moon was rising high above the canyon, leaving the camp whitewashed in gorgeous, thick, reflected light.

Edith was seriously annoyed. After a lengthy discussion, she and Hazel had decided to skip the tent and sleep out under the naked starlight. Hazel was planning to search out Cassiopeia, but the full moon was putting out more light than the Vegas strip, wiping the stars from view. And Edith, ready for rest after a full day of fun, could not keep her eyes closed: they kept opening of their own accord, apparently under the mistaken impression that it was already morning.

"Boys! Booooooooheeeeeeeeys! Are you still awake out there?"

Of course they were, knocking back the Old Weller's and telling tall tales from their arsenal of boatboy stories. The "Buzz Brothers"—hard at play after earning an honest day's pay—were suddenly silent. But Edith could see them, sitting there, bathed in the glorious moonlight (which was closer to a bath than one or two of them had been in several days).

"Hellooooooooo, out there?"

"You got a problem, Ma'am?"

"Yes, yes, I most certainly do!"

"I'm on it," Toad volunteered, scoring a few points with his pards. He rose like a tortoise and picked his way over legs and rubber to shore and the wailing woman.

"Son, I am sorry to bother you, but I cannot sleep for that moon. It is far too bright."

"That's a full moon for you, Ma'am: big and bold and far too bright. Now you gotta know you lucked out, Edith; not every trip gets a full moon."

"Well, we don't like it. Hazel can't find her constellations and I can't keep my eyes closed."

"What would you suggest I do about it, Ma'am? UUUghhggghchgg," Toad belched.

Edith waved her hand to clear the air in front of her face and answered "Well, put it out of course. Get rid of the light...*something*. We need our sleep."

A soft wind blew through camp and carried a thought into the dulled yet somehow brilliant mind of the boatman. Toad looked around for an appropriate tool and found the perfect specimen waiting on a ledge not two feet from his cracked toes. He picked up the small chunk of limestone and offered it to Edith.

"Here, honey. Go ahead. You do the honors. This rock here was made to fly. You can wind 'er up and put 'im out of our misery. Poor ole Mr. Moon, put 'im in his place. But before you do, I must say, Ma'am, with all due respect, you look absolutely radiant tonight, standing there in the moon-light, with your hair all mussed up like it is. Absolutely radiant."

"Radiant?" she asked.

"Radiant. That is the only word for it."

She put one hand over her mouth and giggled. Toad reached out, care-fully took her other hand and placed the weapon of destruction in her palm, as though it were a daisy. Edith's fingers closed over the rough edges. She winked at the boatman, came close to kissing him on the cheek but he belched again in the nick of time. Edith laughed out loud.

"Goodnight, Toad" she whispered.

"Sweet dreams, Ma'am."

Edith wiggled a handful of fingers in Toad's direction and set out to find her sleeping bag. Past blooming prickly pears, sparse grasses and sleeping red ants she carried her trophy of limestone and sang a little tune, barely distinguishable from her breathing. When she found her sister, Hazel was already sound asleep, by the light of the silvery moon.

WILD KINGDOM

Teresa Yates Matheson

T he setting: there are fifteen hundred spawning trout in the first six hundred meters of Nankoweap Creek. Twenty-six bald eagles are out and about taking advantage of the opportunity. There are eagles perched along the creek, choosing a fish from pools five layers thick with trout. Some eagles are hanging out away from the creek, having just devoured a trout a little earlier.

Others fly into the creek arena only to cast a shadow over the waters for a split second. This sends the fish into a frenzied panic. Mostly, all that is seen is a shower of water. Some fish, in their reaction, end up surging out of the creek and swimming frantically across the dry cobbles, right between the legs of an eagle, only to be snagged by a single step of a taloned foot.

Nearby, our dark feathered friends the ravens are getting into the action. They hop around the river where the flows have dropped and left fish stranded in these isolated pools. Or they hang out around pools in the creek. An eagle keying into the interest of the ravens drops in to check it out. The eagle drags a fish out of the creek in a successful forage and starts to tear it apart.

The raven and his buddies line up in front of the feeding eagle. One bold raven leaves the five or six others in front of the eagle and goes around behind the feeding bird. Alone, he hops in and tweaks the tail feathers of the eagle, then hops away again. Again and again the raven keeps pulling the eagle's tail. His accomplices in front wait for just the right moment. The eagle, tired of the tug on his tail feathers, turns his head and shows some aggression to the raven behind him. But as soon as he does, the ravens out front seize the split second to hop in and grab some torn tidbits of fish.

After a while the ravens learn that they can tug their own fish out of the creek by its tail. It is especially easy to get the fish that are tired from their spawning effort.

There, hidden at the top of the Redwall Limestone, taking in the spectacle, is the sleek, aggressive golden eagle. He lunges from his perch and comes down in a swoop towards the creek. Everything in the creek arena flushes or jolts from the appearance of the determined golden. He snatches a fish immediately, removes it to the shoreline and quickly eats it. Or he flies off with his captive to an unseen perch.

Unlike the bald eagles, who cautiously check out the creek from a distance before moving in close to forage, the golden means business and gets a fish mostly before you can even see him coming. Your only clue that he's approaching is in the behavior of everyone in the arena: chaos.

There! Running up the shallows of the creek, splashing water droplets in every direction, with trout swimming madly upstream in front of his paws: the coyote. He stretches his neck, and with one snap of his jaws he delights in the dinner he has draping from each side of his mouth. He leaves quickly as the shadow of the golden makes him duck.

Slowly, things learn to take advantage of the trout spawn at Nankoweap. Some learn from others' examples, others learn on their own. It is February, and cold. Welcome to Nankoweap's Wild Kingdom.

A Red-Tailed Friend Tale

Tom Janecek

The first time I met Karen Byerley was a little intimidating. I was in the boat warehouse, looking up to a tornado of activity above me on top of a thirty-seven-foot motor rig. "God dammit! Who took my spare bowline? If I ever..." She then leaped off her rig onto her Ford F-150 (with the straight six), grabbed some "Hot Damn" schnapps tucked in beside her ATV, a couple cans of chewing tobacco, a Hawaiian dress, and some elk jerky she had just made from a hunt. She was wearing a T-shirt with two rubber hands reaching out of the chest area that said "get a grip on yourself," and as she packed some chew into her mouth our boss piped in. "Ah, Karen, this is TJ. He's our new swamper. He'll be on your trip. Oh, and he's an Eagle Scout, so you have nothing to worry about."

That was the beginning of one of the best friendships I have ever had, even though it took years to get over the Eagle Scout comment. Karen's kindness and generosity, her love of adventure, her courage, her mastery of the river, her love of trickery and poems—Karen was one of a kind and my best friend. She once caught a huge trout by diving into the river with a hammer, but that's another story.

Years after we first met, Karen and I were on a river trip together when suddenly she started pulling the boat over to shore on the right side in the flat stretch just above Nankoweap Rapid. "TJ", she said, "Get the leather welding gloves out. There's a red-tailed hawk in that thicket of tammy trees over there. See it?" This always ticked me off about Karen: she could always see the wildlife and I never did. As the boat touched the shore she said, "Here, take this towel too. I want you to go over there and catch that hawk and bring it back to the boat."

The passengers were overjoyed at watching this strange drama unfold. There goes TJ up through the overgrown mass of vegetation like a stealthy bull in the Amazon. In front of me was a fairly small red-tailed hawk now hopping away from the six-foot-, three-inch-man with the blue leather gloves and candy stripe towel. "Can you see him?" Karen yelled from the boat. "Yeah, it looks like he is hurt or something because he can't fly away;

he just keeps hopping away from me." That's when I learned that you can't catch a hawk by just slowly walking towards it. After about fifty feet of painful bushwhacking, I picked up the pace. The bull was now clearing a trail behind him at a half sprint with the hawk jumping as fast as it could through the bushes. Then the hawk came to a thicket that even it couldn't hop through and turned to face me in self defense.

Being face to face with a hawk is an intense experience. They look right through you with eyes so focused that you can practically see yourself in the pupils. I could tell it was tired as I slowly crept towards him. Stumbling, it backed into the last inches of thicket and looked up at me with utter terror as I lunged and packed the towel around its body. It hardly struggled at all when the towel was over its head and I walked back to the boat holding the hawk like a weightless baby, feeling it panting inside the towel.

The passengers were floored—partially because I really caught a hawk and partially because of the scratches on my body and number of twigs in my hair. I held the hawk out just a bit and showed it to the passengers. Karen had already prepared a cage with some milk crates, but it was happier wrapped in the towel.

We decided to camp at Nankoweap, and on the way I started examining the hawk's body while keeping the towel over its head. A passenger on the trip sat down next to me and joined in the examination. The hawk was sort of smelly and had what looked like a serious festering feather-matted wound on its belly behind its legs. "Well I'll be…" the passenger said in a southern accent. "What?" I asked. "Well I've seen this kind of thing with chickens on my farm back in Georgia. Some chickens just don't seem to know how to clean themselves. They get their own shit caught in their feathers and it makes a kind of a mat in front of their butt hole that looks just like this. It gets so bad that they can die 'cause they can't take a dump. I bet if you cut those feathers away that this hawk would really appreciate it." Sometimes you have just the right passenger along.

We got to camp and everyone sped the kitchen set up along to get to the night's main event: the Hawk Surgery. I was appointed the lead surgeon, Karen would run the operating table and talon control, Turtle was in charge of cleaning water and food items, and Dave was the photographer.

Running rapids is low stress compared to surgery, especially when you don't know what you are doing. I started by cutting away at the mass of feathery poop with EMT scissors and tried to break it up with water but this approach didn't work. With every snip into this unknown mass, I cringed at the thought of going too deep and cutting this beautiful animal. So I came in from the side, cutting a small path of feathers away along the skin towards the lump. This was much more successful and I gradually peeled the lump back until I exposed that ole place on a hawk where the sun don't shine. When the lump was finally off and the feathers cleaned up, the hawk lacked a lot of feathers on its backside, but for the most part it was good to go—so to speak. We felt like we should at least give it food. We learned that you can force feed a hawk a piece of steak fat by pouring water in its mouth while it's facing up. "Whoa…he liked the water I think. He's gripping pretty hard with those talons now. Give him some more water," Karen said. The hawk was getting its energy back by the minute, and Karen stood up and walked out to a place near the river with a following of camera-toting passengers.

What followed was river legend—at least in my mind. Karen unveiled the hawk on her arm and it adjusted its balance accordingly. It looked right into my eyes, but there was no fear this time. Then it looked around at Karen and all the passengers, leaned over and started casually cleaning itself, inspecting my trim job. The seconds ticked by and it didn't leave. A minute went by and it let me pet its head with my bare hand. And then Karen reached her arm up in the air and the hawk flew up and over to a branch about fifteen feet away. "What's he doing?" a passenger asked at the sight of the hawk's back feathers rustling. With cameras pointed at our new friend and the hawk's rear pointed away from us, this little bird let go of the big one, while everyone cheered.

Later, I went back to the hawk by myself with a plate of food, but this time it didn't trust me as much and flew off. It only flew about fifty yards to a boulder and I followed. It let me get close and I set the plate down and walked off. In the morning I went back and saw that the hawk was gone but hadn't eaten any of the food. But one of our passengers said he saw a small hawk flying around in the cliffs above.

For the rest of the season, Karen and I saw a red-tailed hawk fly over our heads on every trip at that same spot on the river. It never failed to happen and every time Karen and I would look at each other in disbelief— was this the same one? Later, a hawk expert told me that hawks have very good memory for people and having one check out a particular person is not surprising.

The last time I saw Karen was midway across the Glen Canyon Bridge. I was in my 4x4 and she was in an eighteen-wheeler, training for her CDL. I can still see the beaming smile on her face as she pulled the air horn. Karen and her husband died that winter in an automobile accident with a sleeping driver. The following season was pretty somber for me and I tearfully told the hawk story every trip. And every trip a red-tailed hawk would show up and end the story in silence. The little hawk story was now everything to me. Everywhere I went I began seeing red-tailed hawks.

One day that season I found two red-tailed hawk wings sitting in the middle of a trail in a side canyon. Contrary to my usual habit of letting things be, I packed the wings away in a zip lock in my boat. I felt at the time that I should have them, but when I spoke to my Native American medicine-man-in-training/mechanic friend Jimmy Cat, I had a change of heart. "TJ-in-the-sun! Why'd you do that? You can't take a bird's wings! That's just too much…you gotta go give those back, cat." "Well they reminded me of Karen, I…" "TJ," he went silent for a moment, looking down at the ground. "No, no, no, TJ-in-the-world," he said quietly. "That's too much for you. Those are for a special world," and he walked off. Now I felt guilty, and the wings were packed away in my Blazer, ready to make the trip to Flagstaff to visit Karen's father.

As I drove down the road, Jimmy Cat's words kept ringing in my mind. The pain of losing my friend grew stronger as I approached the roadside memorial that her father and so many friends had constructed for Karen and her husband. I pulled over and looked at all the memorabilia laying around inside a circle of rocks with a wooden cross a friend had made for them. Karen's husband, Tim, had been an Episcopalian priest. I got back into my car and drove off, feeling like a bad friend because I couldn't think of anything meaningful to put into the circle of rocks. Then I slammed on my brakes. The wings! I turned around and drove back to the memorial. I took out the wings and tied them securely to the cross with some string so they would gently flap in the breeze. It just seemed like the right thing to do and it felt really good to leave something in their memory.

When I arrived at Karen's father's house I was anxious to talk to him about the wings. "Where is Jay" I asked his wife Judy. "Oh he'll be here any minute, he was probably right behind you." Twenty minutes later Jay pulled in and we got to talking. "Did you see the hawk wings when you stopped at Karen's memorial?" I asked. "Wings?" he said. "I was there right after you and there weren't any wings anywhere."

Somehow, within minutes after I left, the wings had vanished. Was it a friend of Jimmy Cat? Was it a coyote? Was it a strong wind gust that untied my triple fisherman's knot? I must confess that a part of me likes to suspend a little disbelief to leave room for the possibility that my best friend Karen and her loving husband Tim have the wings.

Northern Flickers

Larry Stevens

1979

An Exploration of the Little Colorado River Gorge

Tim Cooper

Sitting in a courtroom on a hard chair is not my idea of how to spend a pleasant day in March. Particularly when it's the first day in what seems like months that it hasn't snowed or rained. Particularly when the courthouse is located only a few hundred yards from the South Rim of the Grand Canyon. Out there, with snow dusting the walls of the canyon and the air as clear as nothing—well, it looked pretty nice.

This morning in the newly remodeled interior of the courthouse a federal magistrate is arraigning two haggard-looking young men from Flagstaff, Arizona, charged with violation of Federal Regulatory Code 7.4H(3). It's 10:00 A.M. The two men have already hiked up from the bottom of the mile-deep gorge in the slush this morning. They are dirty and worn out. They face a maximum sentence of six months in jail and a five hundred-dollar fine. Considering the circumstances, the two fellows seem to be in pretty good spirits. They are, in fact, happy to be breathing at all.

With the plodding precision of American justice, the magistrate reads the two men their descriptions, then asks for confirmation. Brad Dimock, male, twenty-five, blond hair, blue eyes, six feet, three inches, born in Ithaca, New York, professional river guide. "Is that correct, Mr. Dimock?" It is. Tim Cooper, male, twenty-five, brown hair, brown eyes, five feet, ten inches, born in San Diego, California, professional river guide. That's me, I tell him.

Then, in terms that cannot be misunderstood, he reads us our rights, pausing occasionally to ask if we comprehend what's going on. We reply that we do, but truthfully I don't think that either one of us is paying much attention. We are undeniably guilty of running the Colorado River without a permit. If the judge ever stops talking, that's what we're going to tell him. How and why we found ourselves sixty-one miles and three thousand vertical feet into the Grand Canyon with little choice but to run the Colorado is something of a long story and of no concern to the law.

I check out the magistrate's enormous turquoise bolo tie for a while. Then I try to appraise the cost of the inlaid mahogany desk my elbows are on. Maximum fine might buy half of it.

It's a nice day for a walk. Down in the canyon it would be cool and bright. The Colorado River would be running muddy like it should, a rich, red brown that its name suggests. Most of the time anymore it flows clear green due to the seven hundred and fifty-foot concrete plug upstream that made an immense settling pond out of Glen Canyon.

The red silt in the river that day was being contributed by a flooding tributary downstream of the dam. Called the Little Colorado River, it's the largest tributary to meet the main Colorado within the boundaries of Grand Canyon National Park. Normally, the upper reaches of the Little Colorado River are dry as a bone. Normally, you'd have to walk forty-five rugged, twisting miles to get from Blue Spring to the Standard Oil outpost at Cameron, Arizona. You'd be walking through a canyon that few people have seen from the bottom, a narrow defile that snakes through the flat-lands of the Navajo Reservation at depths up to three thousand feet. Normally, it would be a long, dry hike.

The winter of '77/'78 wasn't a normal one, however. During most of the month of March, there rolled through the Little Colorado Gorge a torrent of snowmelt and rain that stained the mighty Colorado red. It became, for a while, an honest to goodness river: steep, muddy, littered with boulders and congested with driftwood and flotsam. With the naturally erratic flow of a desert river, it was prone to tremendous fluctuations in volume and likely as not to disappear overnight. The Little Colorado runs through one of the most spectacular gorges in the canyon country, every bit as deep as the Colorado's canyon at their confluence, but more than three times narrower. Sheer walls drop hundreds of feet into the river, making the prospect of walking the bank through the gorge a very dim one. If you wanted to get through the Little Colorado Gorge while the river was there, you'd have to do it in a boat.

There are a number of difficulties that immediately present themselves to anyone anticipating a boat trip down the gorge. First off, there is seldom any water in it. Secondly, when the river is there, it is fifty-six miles long and choked with rapids whose difficulty cannot be determined until you are down there. At those few places along the rim where the river is visible, narrow rocky rapids bend out of sight in either direction. Rumors are heard of fifty-foot vertical falls that cannot be avoided. Thirdly, though the entire section of river that we wanted to run was on the Navajo Indian Reservation, the mouth of the river marked the beginning of Grand Canyon National Park. Travel in the park is illegal without a permit. Private boating permits are handed out once a year in a lottery with little better odds than the Irish Sweepstakes.

These are problems that warrant careful consideration. For several weeks while the snow and rain poured down on Arizona, Brad and I studied topographic maps and talked about the gorge. We drove into the desert and peered over the rim. We compiled a list of needed gear. We consulted the Bureau of Reclamation, which maintains a gauging station on the river, about water levels. They were no help. Meanwhile we talked and studied and thought while the rain poured down.

Someone had been down there before. A river guide named Jim Norton and a partner started down the gorge during the last big flood in 1972. They had inflatable open kayaks and three days' worth of food. Norton watched his friend almost drown on the first day. They repeatedly punctured their boats and ran out of patch material. They ran out of food. The fickle river dried up beneath them. In nine days they reached the confluence carrying their boats.

They had made it though. It wasn't impossible. Most of Norton's problems, we thought, could be avoided by using highly maneuverable slalom kayaks.

Our route plan was full of holes: nobody knew how long the water would last; nobody could say how long it would take us. We had a good prospect of having our boats removed from the park by a large motorized raft on a commercial trip, but we didn't know when. It didn't seem as if further study of these matters was going to clear them up, and every day we pondered was another day's water under the bridge.

So, early one morning, we loaded two kayaks and ninety pounds of gear into the truck. It had snowed the night before, and the sky still threatened. Driving against a brisk wind to Cameron, we slid our boats into the water and started into the gorge.

The water of the Little Colorado is absolutely opaque. During its journey across the soft shales and mudstones of the Painted Desert, it picks up as much sand and silt as moving water can hold. The locals say it is too thick to drink and too thin to plow. When it splashes on my glasses, it leaves the lenses looking as if they were ground out of adobe. This is going to be a major headache for the next few days.

If the geologic work of the upper Little Colorado is moving the desert grain by grain into the sea, at Cameron the little river takes on a task that might stymie the most stalwart general in the Corps of Engineers. Uplifting of the earth's crust over a period of millions of years has interposed a rock barrier three-fifths of a mile thick between the sources of the Little Colorado and where it wants to go. The river's response to this obstacle has been to entrench its course, established when it meandered across ancient lowlands, deep into the earth. It hasn't been easy work. The rocks are the same sequence of resistant sandstones, limestones and shales that form the upper walls of the Grand Canyon. To keep pace with uplifting, the Little Colorado has had to maintain a gradient more than three times as steep as the river into which it flows.

The gorge starts slowly, cutting through the top limestone layers without developing any major rapids. The walls rise steadily around us, and the wind continues to blow upstream.

We travel in patchy sunlight and easy water for about five miles before we encounter the third rock stratum called the Coconino Sandstone. It funnels the river into a passageway so narrow that it will not fit my four-meter kayak through sideways. Soon there are sheer sandstone walls on both sides a couple hundred feet high. From this point on, there is no way out but downstream.

Still there are no rapids of consequence, and we paddle cheerily along commenting about the increasing beauty of the canyon and the onsetting numbness in our fingers. My hands are freezing but this isn't so tough. I ask Brad how his boat handles when laden with forty-five pounds of food and contingency gear. "Like paddling a dish rag," he says.

Seven miles into the gorge, the rapids suddenly start in earnest. Rounding a corner, the river can be seen to drop steeply into a forest of angular sandstone blocks. Like most of the rapids we are going to encounter, this one bends around a corner out of sight. The rumble of what would usually be whitewater is deafening. Here the rumble is of brown foam.

Brad leads in, picking his way among the rocks and holes. I catch up to him a short distance downriver sitting in an eddy behind a boulder. There is a huge block below him directly athwart the current. I can't see around it. Brad shouts something I don't catch as I go left around the boulder. A second and third house-sized rock confront me in quick succession. The rapid continues, careening off one wall, then the other, dividing into channels, foaming and gnashing over more boulders than there is time to count. I can't stop to consider which way to turn or what channel to take. For perhaps half a mile there is only time to stroke and turn, paddle and draw. I finally arrive in calm water with my heart pounding like someone is beating on my sternum with a mallet. Brad paddles up and looks me straight in the eye. He says the first dead serious thing I've heard him say in several years: "We could drown."

There's another rapid just downstream, not much different from the first. Then a third and a fourth until they begin to run together in my mind as a continuous stretch of rocks, walls and rushing mud. By mid-afternoon we are exhausted and stiff with cold. Camp.

In a dry wash we build a fire and warm up our hands enough so that we can get the top off the brandy. It's stowed in a plastic bottle and tastes like polyvinyl chloride. Brad christens the brew Xylene. Because of its probable toxicity, we drink only half.

What a camp! The wall at our backs climbs unbroken a thousand feet to the rim. The sun hasn't shone down here since the late Pleistocene. It's cold and windy, remote, magnificent and pristine. There's not a single Vibram track on the beach, no pop-tops or cigarette butts to grumble about and stuff into pockets. We're delightfully alone under the murk of the sky, the sole occupants of this particularly neglected piece of useless territory. If I've had to sprint through the devil's entrails to get here, well the trip has kept the riffraff out and put a little iron in my blood. The brooding walls seem to be recharging us a little. Them and the brandy. The fire goes out. So do we.

By morning the river has dropped six inches. We can't stand for much of that. Hurriedly, we cook up some cereal and mix instant coffee with hot mud. The first rapid is a hundred yards from camp.

Unlike rapids in the Grand Canyon, caused by outwash from flash-flooding tributaries, these hummers are the result of landslides and rock-fall. There is no pattern to them, just confused jumbles of rock and water. We go as slowly as we can, feeling our way.

It's begun to rain and the wind has a new force. In spite of my wetsuit and paddling jacket, mittens and helmet, I'm getting cold. My fingers have lost all feeling. How long can it keep up like this?

After a short breather, the river slides into Hell Hole Bend. That's what it says on the map: Hell Hole Bend. I watch Brad paddling furiously against the current to avoid something I can't see. Then he's gone. I go into Hell right behind him. For an indeterminate amount of time my boat and I are pummeled on all sides by dark water. We're thrashed with unprecedented violence. I use up my adrenaline ration well into the 1990s getting around the Bend.

We clamber out of the boats and build a fire on the bank where the next flood will wash away the ashes. There's a powerful curiosity and apprehension about what waits around the corner, but we're too cold to continue. There may be a dozen more Hell Holes. There may be nothing. Uncertainty thrills the heart and broadens the parameter of fear. We've put ourselves here purposely, somewhere in the wilderness out of touch.

Downstream on the Colorado the crush of people, seventeen thousand of them running the river each year, has forced the park service to become an agency of regulation and control. The Grand Canyon is a "managed resource" in which the Little Colorado is an "attraction site." My mind balks at these designations. There's no room for the absurdities of bureaucracy in the wilderness; it has retreated further and further into the seldom-traveled places. The very seldom-traveled places. The well-nigh inaccessible places where the mass of humanity cannot or will not go, where the bighorn sheep watch their step and the contrived laws of men are as useless as a garbage compactor. There's a big piece of wilderness breathing quietly in the perpetual twilight of the Little Colorado Gorge. Its only rules are the inflexible requirements of the canyon.

Once we're thawed out a little, we slide our boats back into the water and bounce through a few more rapids bound for Blue Spring, the next topographic feature we should recognize. The water relaxes for a moment in a hallway of limestone riddled with caverns. Small springs of clear water pour out of the walls. We must be close to the big spring, but it is hidden under muddy water.

When there is no water in the upper canyon, Blue Spring transforms the last thirteen miles of the gorge in to a series of azure pools and cascades. The color is due, at least in part, to the heavy solution load of calcium carbonate the water picks up on its long journey through the Redwall Limestone. When it flows out into the hot desert sun, water begins to evaporate, super-saturating the solution and causing the precipitation of calcite crystals. The result is a rock called travertine that commonly builds up from the bottom of the river. The walls grow higher as more travertine is deposited on top until a dam is formed. A hundred miles away at Havasu Canyon these dams reach heights of well over a hundred feet. We've heard that this stream too forms dams, and we have spent considerable time worrying about their existence.

Soon after Blue Spring we come to one. It stretches across the entire river and is all of sixteen inches high. Big deal. Just downstream is another one with two tiers of one and three feet. Brad hangs up in some rocks at the top and I flip over at the bottom. We both recover.

Another dam. This one is multi-tiered with a total drop of about fifteen feet. Brad hits the pool at the bottom with such velocity that he does a submarine reverse end-for-end flip and surfaces upside down. I hit the same place so hard I feel like I've been dropped from the rim. Slightly flabbergasted we push on.

The next one is awesome. A steep slope leads to a vertical falls of perhaps eight feet. Water tumbles over into a cauldron of boiling mud that seems to go nowhere. There is no current; if a kayaker didn't develop enough momentum to blast through the mess, he'd be trapped below the cascade and hammered by tons of falling water.

We stare at it for a long time, so cold we are both shivering like a dog passing peach pits. The wind is draining the last ergs of strength from our bodies. Brad decides to try it before he freezes to death. I crouch on the bank with a camera in the faint hope that I'll be able to capture him going through the rapid at thirty miles an hour on a dark day while shaking like a leaf.

Brad is an excellent boater. He hits everything perfectly, paddling ferociously until the water gives way to air and he drops like a stone into the roiling pool. But this time, it's not going to work. He braces in the froth with his paddle, trying to move downstream but the current has him. He's slowly sucked sideways under the falls. It flips him over and the boat disappears. Horrified, I can only watch. His paddle and arm reach into the air, and he tries to roll up. No good. Again. No good. *Oh God Brad, get out of there. Swim for it.* Another attempt to right himself, then he vanishes for a long time.

Under the water Brad has pushed out of his kayak and is searching the rumbling depths for a current that is moving downstream. There must be one or the river would stop at this point. No air or light to see by. Panic is leaning on the doorbell. He's smacked into the jagged travertine bottom and thrashed about like a cat in a Maytag. Several thousand heartbeats later he surfaces thirty yards downstream of the falls and hollers with his first breath, "Don't try it!"

I don't. Blue with cold, Brad helps me carry my boat around the rapid. We've had enough. Brad's intro to drowning erased the last traces of bravado. I'm ready to take a hot shower and climb into bed, but the river will have none of it. Continuing downstream we find another and another falls to descend. We crash through them bracing and turning by instinct. This has to stop soon.

Just before dark it finally does. Like two survivors of a shipwreck, we drag ourselves up on the bank and grope around in the gloom for the remaining Xylene. That night I become convinced that hell is cold.

Brad's gear was thoroughly soaked in the falls and mine is soon in like condition from the pouring rain. Rocks crash down from the cliffs around us and land in the river. We huddle together in the inky blackness waiting for dawn.

When it comes, we pack hurriedly and get on the water. It can't be much farther to the confluence. On the right bank a mile from camp is a carbonate dome twenty feet high. A pit in the center of the dome is filled within a few feet of the top with bubbling pale green water.

This is the Sipapu, a place sacred to the Hopi Indians. According to their mythology, the Sipapu is the entrance to the underworld from which their ancestors emerged and to which the dead return. Feathers dangle from twigs lodged in the side of the pit. The translucent water seems to glow with its own light. It's an eerie spot, as likely a place for man to have birthed as some electrified Precambrian sea. We stare into the pit. It wouldn't surprise us to see the father of all Hopis loom up from the depths of the pit, long black hair streaming behind him. It wouldn't surprise us but it might scare us to death. We hustle back to the boats.

The rapids are difficult but not deadly, and we are soon in familiar territory. On the left bank, built on the site of an Anasazi Indian ruin, is the cabin of Ben Beamer, a would-be prospector and farmer who scratched a living from this area around the turn of the century. It's a regular stop on Grand Canyon tours. Nailed to Ben's door is a yellow sign, telling anyone interested that the cabin and litter of nineteenth-century cans and broken glass around it are protected by the American Antiquities Act, and fines, imprisonment or both are available to those that might feel compelled to mess with them. Familiar ground.

With a whoop and a holler, we paddle the last few strokes to the Colorado. How exhilarating! It's over and we survived. I'm so happy I almost stop shivering.

Now to get out of here. Standing on the bank just inside the perimeter of the park we examine our options. There's the possibility of burning our kayaks and hiking, taking the ashes, out the Salt Trail, a rugged path that rims out in the middle of nowhere. "Nix," says Brad. "Fires are prohibited." Okay, we could stash our boats here, walk to the Tanner Trail by sometime tomorrow and be on the rim in another day. "We don't have a hiking permit," Brad reminds me. Well, we could paddle down the Colorado for twenty-six miles to the bottom of the Kaibab Trail and be out of here by sometime tonight. "That's illegal," says Brad. "In fact, it's illegal to be standing here. Shall we walk over there where standing is legitimate?"

The choice is easy. I'd trade my watch, car and boat for a warm place to sleep; throw in my bachelor's degree for a pair of dry socks. We run down the river and afoul of the law.

At the head of Hance Rapid there are boats tied to the bank. A couple of them have "Park Ranger" written in large green letters on the side. My heart sinks. *Mr. Ranger, you cannot possibly want me to not be in your park half so bad as I wish I weren't.* Shall we wait until they leave? Should we paddle up to them, crawl up on the bank and insist that we are near death, which is not far from the truth? Shall we wave legally and paddle into Hance, one of the worst rapids on the Colorado, blind?

We wave. They wave back. Someone shouts for us to pull in. "This is a big one," they say. You're telling me. It soon becomes apparent that we're not going to stop. Someone in a green hat and shirt scrambles for a camera and points a lens at us as long as my arm.

Hance is a comparative piece of cake. There are several big water rapids between the trail and us, but they don't hold a candle to Hell Hole Bend. We bomb through them without missing a stroke and reach the trailhead long before dark. It's raining hard, and there's a lot of snow on the rim. Shivering our teeth loose, we bury our boats in the sand and try to get some clothes on. "Let's give ourselves up," Brad suggests. "I bet it's warm in jail." A voice from the rocks above us makes the choice for us. "That's it. You're busted." Paddling as fast as we can is nothing compared to the speed of radio waves.

In the morning I find myself pondering the expensive new woodwork in the federal magistrate's place of business. These are serious charges against us. The laws were designed by good men to preserve and protect the canyon. These people aren't kidding, but somehow today my mind is still clouded with the roar of the river and the beating of my heart. I'm having difficulty just paying attention to the decision of my fate. All the rivers still run into the sea, and we're in one piece. What more could anyone ask? Though we violated the law, we didn't violate the canyons and that, at bottom, is what matters, isn't it? If I risked my fool neck, well it's my neck and it was worth it.

I feel like a man who's gotten a speeding ticket after just being passed by a Cadillac doing 109. The federal government, the magistrate's employer, destroyed the riparian environment along the Colorado in 1963 by constructing Glen Canyon Dam. With one clumsy blow they killed the native fish, drastically altered the riverside vegetation and eliminated the periodic scouring action of spring floods. That ill-conceived hunk of concrete has done more damage to the canyon than an army of renegade boaters bent on destruction could do in a lifetime. I have a pang of righteous indignation.

We enter a plea of guilty. The fine is one hundred dollars apiece plus fees for helicopter evacuation of the boats. Could have been worse.

In need of a shower and two days sleep, I've already got my hat on when a man dressed all in green stops me. "We'd like to ask you a few more questions, Mr. Cooper," he says. It seems I look a lot like a man wanted in Florida for parole violations. I can't believe it. Standing beside the green man is a junior ranger I've been acquainted with for years. We started out with the same river outfitter way back when. This is ridiculous and he knows it. Still, Ranger Kojak is serious as cholera, and he wants me to roll up my sleeves to prove I'm not the Tampa Terror who has tattoos all the way up to his shoulders.

~

Lucky there were no tattoos. I'd still be in jail.

GONE!

Allen Wilson

T he rubber raft is well known in today's world for transporting people and supplies. It allows you to travel down a river in a leisurely and safe fashion. In the beginning, thirty or forty years ago, rafts were designated as RB-10 (or Rubber Boat-10) by the Army. As the years passed people found that these heavy rubber rafts were superb for rafting whitewater rivers, so much so that there is a whole industry built up around the original RB-10.

The raft can become a part of you as you respond to its needs, drifting the currents and feeling all its subtle movements. You are always ready to make minor adjustments in its drift. Your raft's flexible rubber protects you from the violent whitewater. You learn to feel its every whim and need. This bundle of rubber, wood and metal really is your lifeblood. At camp the soft spongy rubber can be a meeting place for the whole trip escaping from the heat and enjoying the natural air conditioning of the cold river. It becomes a place of retreat, a protective haven, a place to lie and rest or a place to escape from somebody persistent. You become dependent on it.

There is a great fear, however, and it lies dormant deep inside. This is the fear of waking up one morning and finding that no matter how hard you search, your raft is just not there. *The raft is gone!* Those moments fortunately are few and far between and there is a good reason for this. Because this is one of the worst fears of the sane, semi-sane or absolutely crazed boatman, most guides make sure the craft is securely tied every night or anytime it is to be left alone.

There are instances, however, when things out of the ordinary can happen. These lapses will undoubtedly create a story, such as the one that took place at Carbon Creek sometime during the summer of 1976. Boyce, Scotty, Jim, Bill and myself were running an American River Touring Association oar trip with four snout boats, which are big, ungainly catamaran-type rubber rafts. They are capable of hauling huge amounts of people and equipment. The only limitation is what you, the boatperson, can actually handle. We were carrying six people per boat plus all the gear for twelve days.

This was no big deal, though, until we arrived at Carbon Creek. We camped there in preparation for the hike up Carbon and over the saddle down into Lava Canyon to the river. The plan was for Boyce and myself to take two boats downriver to the mouth of Lava Canyon, then hike back in reverse, get the other two boats and meet everyone back at Lava Canyon.

I made the announcement about the hike that morning and stated that Boyce and I would take our boats downriver first. I knew there would be several people who didn't want to walk and they should know which boats to board. An overzealous passenger, who was one of the hikers, untied those boats in preparation for leaving but didn't coil up the rope. Without looking carefully you would never know they weren't tied.

After the announcement Jim came to me and said that his boat had a broken frame, and he'd like to take it down first so he could make the needed repairs in the daylight. This minor change in plans impacted all of us dramatically for a few hours of our lives.

Scotty and Bill went off with all but two people on the hike. Jim, Boyce and I went downriver in Jim's and my boat. The two people who came with me were approaching eighty years old. Jack had a heart condition and his wife Ruth didn't feel comfortable hiking. We secured the boats in the small eddy above Lava-Chuar Rapid. We helped Ruth and Jack get settled in the shade with some water and food. Jim went to work on his frame.

Hiking back was uneventful. We met Scotty and most everyone about halfway. It was a leisurely time spent enjoying the special beauty of the East Kaibab Monocline with its layers of tilted sandstones and shales in brilliant hues of red, purple and gray. Hiking down Carbon Creek was pleasant and serene; its sheer narrow walls protected us from the hot, late morning sun.

We stepped out of the canyon onto the brilliantly sunlit gravel bar and looked down to the river where our boats were, or I should say, should have been. At least one of the two was still there. It was Boyce's. Scotty's was gone. I'm not sure but I think I heard Boyce emit a sigh of relief (at least if there were to be a boat gone it wasn't *his*)—maybe not. Anyway, we basically yelled at the same time, "AUGH! A BOAT'S GONE!" Running down to the edge of the river and standing in the very spot where Scotty's boat had been we looked to see if the heavy five-eighths-inch nylon rope had been cut. No. We searched the flat water all around the eddy and downriver on both sides wishfully thinking the craft had miraculously untied itself, drifted out in the river, then got caught in an eddy on the other side. No such luck. We pondered for a moment why we were always getting caught in eddies when it was inconvenient. Now, when it was important for an eddy to do its work, not a single one would reach out and grab the raft.

We went rowing down the river looking in every bush for a twenty-two-foot raft. It was useless; it had either gone upstream which we knew it hadn't, but wished for, or downstream to a destination unknown. It hadn't hidden along the shore in some unsuspecting tamarisk bush, which we were wanting in the worst way.

This predicament actually caused us to take pause for a few moments and discuss how we were responding to the situation. The discussion went something like this: "At least we didn't panic or go crazy." "Yeah, that's right, it's probably the first time a boat has disappeared and the guides didn't have fits or something." We considered the possibility that after we had passed Scotty on the hike, he had followed Boyce and me, snuck by us while we were enjoying the view of the canyon from the saddle and had run ahead of us, taking his raft before we arrived, drifing downstream to Lava Canyon. The ultimate practical joke, taking one of the two rafts to give us a start. Talking to each other we discounted the idea, but later I realized that we both still hoped he had.

It's an easy drift to the mouth of Lava Canyon and it left us time to think and consider what we needed to do when we arrived. Lifejackets were of great concern because each raft had its allotted number tied on and now we were short seven. Boyce said he would help finish Jim's repair work and I volunteered to run up the canyon to gather everyone.

We rounded the point above the eddy at Lava Canyon wishfully hoping to see three boats tied up and Scotty standing on his with a big smile and outstretched arms saying, "Where have you been?" Of course he wasn't there and neither was his boat. This was no real surprise. Instead there was only *one* boat tied there! Jim was bent over, still fixing his frame. I screamed, "My boat's gone!" That did it; Boyce and I had had enough! We were reduced from four boats down to two in a matter of a couple hours.

I couldn't talk rationally, but Boyce, being the cool head that he is managed to ask Jim what had happened. Jim said something to this effect: " I went off behind a bush, and on the way back I saw the old couple rowing out of the eddy. They must have panicked when they saw the boat go by, and they just untied and went after it." I don't remember what our responses were. I do remember the rush of adrenaline and a few choice words.

This was serious now. We saw this episode in a whole new light. All I could think of was heart attack. We could just see Jack getting in the current and not being able to catch an eddy. This would be horrible, for in seven miles they would arrive at Unkar, the first really large rapid in the canyon. After Unkar the rapids would get bigger and more formidable. There would be something of concern every couple of miles. Since things had turned so stinky rotten, we figured now that Jack wouldn't have the luck of a boatman and accidentally get stuck in an eddy.

We forged ahead. Boyce helped Jim, and I ran up the creek carrying the word: "Get to the boats quickly!" Finally I spotted Scotty, he was with the last of the group. There in Lava Canyon was a group of innocent people who, when given the word, shifted from leisure to what could be called controlled panic.

The whole situation was terrible. Jack had a bad heart, and his wife Ruth was probably *going* to have a heart attack when she saw the rapids yet to come. The lifejacket problem was bad; we were short fourteen. We had two rafts for twenty-eight people. Who was going to go without the jackets?

Everyone cooperated really well, and after more than an hour passed we were loaded and on our way. Scotty and Jim were the lucky guys to row two rafts with fourteen people each. To give some perspective to this situation, there were almost as many people on each one of these rafts as there are on one big, thirty-three-foot motor rig. The boatmen and other volunteers who were confident swimmers went without jackets, even though we knew being a strong swimmer didn't help much in the fast currents and strong hydraulics of the forty-nine degree Colorado River. We also knew the added weight would make the rafts difficult to control but they would be extremely stable.

Lava-Chuar Rapid was easily run and without a word all fifty-six eyes were glued on the river ahead and to each side. Hardly a word was spoken; you could feel the intensity. Then someone shouted, "There's a raft!" Sure enough, downstream about a mile below the rapid, stopped in mid-riffle near the island, was a raft. Another voice erupted: "Jack and Ruth aren't on it!" All eyes were on the search again.

Within seconds I think we all saw them at the same time. They were in an eddy (Jack *did* have the luck of a boatman!) behind a small point of cliff jutting out into the river, hidden from our view till that moment. Cheering erupted for Jack and Ruth and I believe they were the happiest of the whole group.

Vishnu Temple

George Bain

The hundreds of summits within Arizona's Grand Canyon National Park come in all sizes and shapes. Some are small, naked rock pinnacles, often dwarfed or hidden by their neighbors. Others are giant, flat-topped islands in the sky, completely surrounded by cliffs, with miles of tall pine forests on top. Between these extremes are all sorts of lofty crags and lowly dirt piles. Some interest me more than others. For a few, I feel a special attraction. It's actually a delightful form of lust.

Vishnu Temple stands above a great bend to the west in the Grand Canyon. Unlike blockier neighbors, Vishnu's massive base tapers up five thousand feet to a very pointed summit, like a peak in the Himalayas, or at least the Tetons.

One clear October day, I sat across the Colorado River, looking up at all of this. My friends and I were on a long, leisurely river trip, with lots of food and lots of time. Their interests for the next two days were in the prehistoric ruins on our hilltop vantage and on the delta across the river below.

With binoculars, I pieced together a route up the temple. The rock layers are more or less horizontal in this part of the canyon, and form alternating cliffs and slopes. From several miles away, I was uncertain about a few places. I decided to try it anyway.

In camp that night, there was only meek enthusiasm among my possible climbing partners. When dawn revealed a chilling drizzle, my companions busied themselves in their tents with a deck of cards and various intoxicants. So much for the crack-o-dawn start. I lay in bed and grumbled, changing my mind again and again, madder and madder until, finally, cursing the loafers I left my tent, raided the soggy kitchen, and was off at 9:00 A.M.

I climbed up the first slopes above the river and saw that clouds hid the higher peaks and buttresses, including Vishnu. Even at my best run-walk pace, I wouldn't be able to reach the summit and return to camp by dark. *So what?* I said to the tiny flashlight in my pack. I comforted myself as I gained the higher elevations where juniper trees grow, stashing dead branches under dry rock overhangs, ignoring the fact that on my return I hoped to be far below these elevations by dark. The moon would rise to my rescue several hours after dark—if the clouds thinned out by then.

The drizzle continued. I scurried on, panting, savoring the smells of the wet desert plants and rocks, and pausing now and then for whatever view the clouds permitted. The obstacles I'd seen with binoculars the day before were going by with surprising ease. Even the troublesome Redwall Limestone, normally a smooth, continuous, five hundred-foot cliff, yielded a hidden gully with little climbing difficulty. This gully lay behind (and also bypassed) a very difficult-looking ridge that hadn't appeared so bad through the binoculars.

Above the Redwall, I found my second underestimate to be the length of a convoluted talus slope traverse around the base of a big rock feature called Rama Shrine. Though longer and rougher than expected, I sped by without incident, and I then faced the northeast side of Vishnu itself, where the Supai Group of rocks presented three red sandstone cliff bands. As luck would have it, I was only able to scale these by going to the far left, then far right, then far left again. During each traverse to the foot of the next face, I'd zigzagged well over a mile to move up a few hundred feet.

Above me was my favorite, the Coconino Sandstone. Once a large desert of wind-blown sand dunes, it is now well solidified into a beautiful, light tan sandstone, and in most places is a continuous vertical cliff. Here, though, was a face less than vertical, and broken enough to allow climbing without a rope. I was able to move almost straight up a four hundred-foot line of chimneys, ramps, short faces and hand cracks. The vertical exposure was frightening. Luckily, the harder moves all seemed to be just above nice soft sandy ledges.

This delightful section led me up into the clouds, which still hid the summit. Moving a little higher, I stepped onto a ridge to discover that I'd been climbing in the lee of a stiff wind. The drizzle was now a driving snow. My thin rain suit, and tennis shoes, shorts and light wool sweatshirt had been soggy, aromatic comfort below. I suddenly felt very cold and exposed. I made haste up the Toroweap ridges toward the limestone summit blocks. Without gloves, my hands were getting numb. I knew that I was in textbook hypothermia conditions, but I felt warm enough as long as I kept moving.

The view I'd hoped would be a canyon classic was now in a white-out, hiding even the summit, which could only be a few hundred feet above. At a precarious mantle move over a wet limestone ledge, I thought briefly about retreating. But with the top so near there was little argument, and lust prevailed.

The visibility from the summit was about a hundred yards. I shivered as I drank the icy water and ate the mangled sandwich from my pack. I made the ninth entry in the summit register, lingered for a few moments, bid a hasty farewell to the rock and the view that wasn't, and began to retrace my route. Every few years, I hear from someone that my sunglasses are still on the summit, corroding away.

I quickly got off route descending the summit blocks, and thought about jumping down a ledge that I didn't think I could re-climb if the ledge below was a dead end. I scooted down, facing out, to a good place to jump, and hesitated. The alternative was to spend more time backtracking in the freezing wind. The jump-down would save time and energy, but what if it cliffed out and didn't reconnect to my route? This time reason prevailed, and I backtracked and found the way I'd come up.

Down-climbing the Coconino face, I thought I saw a rock climber's anchor bolt set in the rock below me. This didn't make sense, since as far as I knew nobody had ever been up this side of Vishnu before. What I found was an old fifty-caliber, copper jacketed tracer slug—a machine gun bullet! I laughed with the pilot in his irreverence, strafing temples.

Zigzagging back down and contouring around in the Supai was a grind. It was quite dark when I got through the Redwall. With my flashlight I followed my tracks down the softer slopes below. I thought I'd lost my way, wading through a field of prickly pear cactus on a Tapeats Sandstone plateau. I tried to doze, shivering, waiting in the lee of a small boulder for the moonrise. Bits of black and gray clouds raced on the wind above. When the moon came up, the broken clouds shot immense rays of blue-white light that filled the canyon with moving shapes. I saw the familiar silhouettes of two stone friends, canyon's pinnacle and man's watchtower, a mile above me to the southeast. The rain had stopped.

With the moonlight I could see that I was in the right gully to descend the Tapeats cliff. The last fifteen hundred vertical feet to the river were of soft red dirt, welcome footing to tired feet, so I skipped, with my hands in my pockets, surrounded by an awesome beauty.

A friend was awake in camp, reading with a carbide lamp. There were leftovers in a pot on the stove.

Lees Ferry Reflections

Joel Russell

2004

Anna and Mustang Sally
Raechel M. Running
2006

The Skagit
Kate Thompson
2005

Imbricated Boulders
Nathan Jones
1986

Redwall Cavern
Tom Hansen
2004

Dave Edwards
Raechel M. Running
2006

Noonday Rest in Marble Canyon

Coby Jordan

1983

Split Twig
Kyle George
2005

BEING FRANK

Brad Dimock

In an attempt to survive the evening we had strung a tarp between two oars stuck in the beach and were sitting between the tarp and the fire, our faces alternately full of smoke, sand, sparks and snow. The wind had blown away any hope of using the stove, along with any desire for the finer points of cuisine. Dinner was whiskey and scorched meat, cooked hobo style on a stick in the fire. Dessert was whiskey in more liberal portions, which, as it often does, began to transform adversity into mild amusement. Funny old blizzard.

Conversation had trailed away and Tom had been gazing off into the blackness when he said, "Brad, does that look like a dog to you?" I looked where Tom was pointing to see if it was a rock, a bush or a dancing shadow from the firelight that had caught his imagination. The likelihood of seeing a dog on a beach in Grand Canyon in November was pretty dim. After a long pause I said, "Yeah...I think that *is* a dog."

Indeed, at the edge of the circle of light stood cowering, trembling, shivering—a dog. An Irish setter. Well, sort of an Irish setter. He looked more like a radiator with hair. He acted and appeared to be very near death, and smelled even nearer. But there, nonetheless, he was.

Being good and drunken Samaritans, we offered him some scorched meat. He seemed terrified, but desperation and starvation won out and he choked down a few pieces. His shrunken stomach could not hold much, though, and he slumped down on the far side of the fire to keep an eye on us.

The next morning he was still there. He could barely walk; his attempts to go to the bathroom were somewhere between hilarious and pathetic. We weighed our options. Hike him out? "He's too weak." Pack him out? "*We're* too weak." Leave him here? "He'll starve." Tell the park service? "They won't care." "Guess we'll have to take him with us." That was quite illegal, but what choice did we have?

We fitted him with a lifejacket, made him a leash, and named him Frank Brown, after the unlucky railroad surveyor who drowned nearby some hundred years prior.

There were eight of us: Tom and I rowing the rafts, Lauren cooking, and the other five biologizing. Our assignment: spend the next two weeks studying the habits of old mesquite trees along the banks of the Colorado. If we didn't freeze to death first.

Getting Frank on the raft was surprisingly easy. He just hopped on. *I'm with you guys.* Being on board the boat was no problem for him either—that is, until we got to a rapid. Then Frank would go completely limp. The first wave would send him sliding across the deck, like a pile of furry Jello, and into the bilge. Initially this had the benefit of washing the stench off him, but we soon had to appoint one person whose sole responsibility in the rapids was to hold on to Frank.

A few days of robust meals, frequent snacks of whipped cream and cold cuts, and a warm fire to sleep by, and Frank began to regain his strength and a little of his dignity. Soon he was romping clumsily about in the bushes while we did our surveys, and could even lift a leg to pee without tipping over.

He was fairly well behaved in camp but occasionally would succumb to temptation and get into the garbage or try to raid the dinner table. A scolding would send Frank slinking for security down to the boats, where he would curl up on the icy cold aluminum decks. At times like this it occurred to us that Frank, in his brush with starvation, had digested his brain.

The only other folks on the river were two more research trips, and we all had to camp just above Phantom Ranch on one particular evening to rendezvous with Dave Wegener, the research coordinator, who was hiking in for the night. The river was low and quiet and our camps were all within earshot of each other and Phantom Ranch. It was here that Frank, his recovery complete, remembered how to bark. And bark, and bark, each bark echoing off the canyon walls and downstream toward the other camps and rangers.

Dave took charge. He took Frank over to the campfire and sat him down for a long talk. A very long talk. Someone who got up to pee during the wee hours later reported seeing Frank and Dave, still sitting side by side staring into the embers, bonding.

In the morning Dave announced Frank would be hiking out the Kaibab Trail with him. This seemed to be an excellent, really the only, logical solution of what to do with Frank. It was a few hours later as were saying our goodbyes at the foot of the trail that the ranger showed up.

There *are* friendly, nature-oriented interpretive rangers in the park service. But there are also by-the-book, enforcement-oriented Gestapo rangers. Ranger Charlie, unfortunately, seemed to be one of the latter. "Whose dog is that?" he barked.

A hasty (and we thought charming) rendition of our story did nothing to placate Charlie, and in a perfect B-movie sinister sneer he said, "I guess he's *my* responsibility now...isn't he?" As he held out his hand for the leash, thoughts of a cold iron cell and lonely death in the gas chamber came to our minds.

Dave's face turned steely. "Charlie," he said, "we'd better go have a little talk." The severity of his tone precluded any further conversation. They left for the ranger station and we waited, with Frank, for the verdict. The sky blackened. The temperature dropped. Grey clouds swallowed up the canyon rim. The wind started to pick up and Frank ripped off a bark.

It was snowing pretty hard when Dave returned. "Frank and I are hiking out now," he said, with a barely perceptible trace of a grin. Which they did. Shivering, grimacing and cursing, we climbed into the boats to go run Horn Creek Rapid in a blizzard. As we pulled into the current we could see Frank and Dave slowly climbing into the clouds, Frank's ears flapping in the wind. We headed downstream.

～

Dave said he and Frank took turns dragging each other out through the snows that night. At McDonald's in Tusayan they each wolfed down two Big Macs and headed back to Flagstaff. For a while Frank lived in Dave's office, Dave's backpack taking the place of our rafts as Frank's security blanket. A few weeks later a local Flagstaff family, better suited to canine needs, adopted Frank Brown.

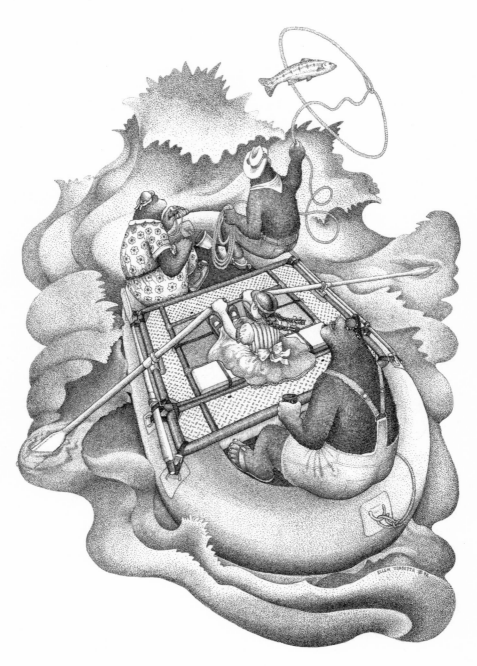

...And the Last Boat Was Just Right!

Ellen Tibbetts

1992

THE LOWER HALF
Phantom Ranch to Diamond Creek or Lake Mead

IF YOU'VE DECIDED TO TAKE the lower half of a Grand Canyon trip, you need to make sure your hiking boots fit. The first part of your trip involves climbing down a five thousand-foot flight of stairs. People begin their hike to the river from the South Rim, Grand Canyon Village. Early in the morning, while the river camps far below are just beginning to stir, the hike begins. For eight miles, you go down. The walls of the canyon tower overhead, and the heat begins to wrap around you. Dust from the mule-kicked trail tickles your nose, and blisters begin to appear in all the wrong places. After what seems like days you arrive at the river, writhing past the banks with an intimidating speed and power. The guides force you to sit, drink and cool your feet in the cold water. The obligatory safety talk begins. You take note of such terms as "flip," "swim," "hypothermia" and "high side," and you sense that your guides are pretty serious about all these issues.

They have their reasons. A mile downstream a series of rapids begins, larger than all but one or two encountered in the upper reaches of the canyon. When people ask me which half of a trip to choose, and they tell me they want big, challenging whitewater, I tell them to book the lower half. More than two-thirds of the river's hundred and sixty rapids are on this stretch, and most of them come fast and furious for the first two or three days of the lower half trip.

The rafts float downstream. Around the corner, a mile or two from where you started, is Horn Creek Rapid, at low water one of the most challenging stretches of whitewater on the river. Then the wild, uncontrolled waves of Granite and the roller coaster of Hermit. All these rapids are relatively short, steep drops formed by debris from side streams damming the river. The level of difficulty and challenge changes with the fluctuating water levels of the river. Sometimes the rapids change on their own.

Crystal. The Sleeping Dragon. Crystal Rapid is notorious for its difficulty and the consequences of a bad run. The rapid is relatively new, however. John Wesley Powell's journal of his 1869 river expedition barely mentions Crystal; only as an inconsequential riffle they navigated with little difficulty.

That changed in 1966, when several inches of rain fell in the Crystal Creek drainage on the North Rim during a three-day flooding event. The rain loosened the soft shales of the canyon walls, which came tumbling down the creek in a mud and water torrent that spilled into the river, narrowing the channel and sending debris over a hundred yards downstream. In minutes, Crystal became one of the hardest rapids on the river. It changed again in 1983, with the high releases from the Glen Canyon Dam, some boatmen think for the better, some say for the worse. In that high-water year, Crystal flipped boats indiscriminately, spectacularly, passionately. There's a saying among the boatmen of the Grand Canyon: "You're always above Crystal."

Below Crystal the rapids continue through the Jewels, and then the river swirls into the calmer water of the Aisles. In Stephen and Conquistador aisles, the river slides easily through the same soft sedimentary layers of the upper half. At mile 116, your trip may stop and lounge at Elves Chasm, a musical little trickle of water surrounded by maidenhair ferns and deep, green pools. You may stop at Blacktail Canyon for a short hike, a geology talk, music and magic. Perhaps you'll see ghosts lingering in the hushed recesses of the canyon.

On the lower half, hiking becomes the off-river focus of the trip. The choice of hikes determines the pace and course of the trip. At Tapeats Creek, a three-and-a-half-mile walk along a rushing stream leads to the refrigerated wonderland of Thunder Falls. Here, an entire river bursts from the limestone walls and tumbles a short, hectic mile to its confluence with Tapeats Creek. Farther downstream, Deer Creek terminates in a sheer hundred and forty-foot drop to the river. Above this waterfall, people gather and sleep on the Patio, where the flat sun-baked rocks are cooled by the waters of the creek and by the shade of overhanging cottonwood trees.

On you go, farther downstream through the recesses of the Muav Gorge, where the silver-gray limestone drops sheer to the water. You might stop and hike at Kanab, climb at Olo, make a butt dam across the warm creek at Matkatamiba Canyon. And you'll probably stop at Havasu.

Havasu is one of the places people look forward to the most. Some trips arrive early and stay all day. Everyone packs bag lunches and plenty of water, and after a warning about the ravens, flash floods and drinking the creek water, heads upstream. Some may hike along the blue-green stream up to Beaver Falls or farther to Mooney Falls. Some folks may just find a pool and some shade and drift peacefully off to sleep, while the ravens proceed to systematically tear apart and carry off everything in their carefully packed lunch. Some of the boatmen will hang out in the mouth of the creek, resting, listening to or playing music, waiting for their pards from other companies to show up so they can restock on beer, ice or cookies. It's the Harbormaster's job to guard the ship.

Havasu Canyon has changed dramatically in the last few years. Every so often a tremendous flush of a flood comes through and cleans things out. In the past few decades, several such floods have wiped the canyon clean, changed the creek bed, removed some travertine dams. But the grapevines still grow in a chest-high jungle, and the downed trees have sprouted new branches, growing vertically from their toppled parents. Only the piles of driftwood crammed into ledges and caves indicate the presence of these periodic floods.

The canyon below the exhausting day spent relaxing at Havasu seems slow and sleepy. The water is calm, the flat broken only briefly by the mutter of riffles. Sometimes an oar trip will tie all its boats together here and tell stories, or read. You begin to hear the boatmen casually tossing around the word "Lava" a lot. If you ask, they'll tell you stories. Maybe you shouldn't have asked...

The next morning your boatmen might be tightening their lines especially well, asking for the heavier people to ride up front, competing for the weighty gear. As you round the corner at mile 179, you understand why. Rumbling up from the depths of the canyon is a sound unlike anything you've yet heard.

Lava Falls is a ten on the Grand Canyon rapid rating scale of one to ten. Hance and Crystal are usually considered tens also, but Lava Falls *feels* like a ten. From the scout rock, forty feet above the river, it *still* looks big, a torrent of angry water cascading over ledges and rocks and building into waves that continuously break in relentless crashing walls of water. In the middle is the Ledge Hole—don't go there. At higher water levels you run left. At just the right water level you can run the Slot, a hair-raising path just shy of the gaping Ledge Hole, and requiring a hefty slice of imagination to find. The right side is still the most fun. Hey diddle diddle, right down the right. It can be a crapshoot. Make the entry, push hard, hold on to your oars and keep her straight. Keep your head down. Don't lose your motor. This is the fastest navigable whitewater in the world, or so they say. It's moving at about twenty-five miles an hour, and feels more like ninety.

Lava's a paradox. It's big and you can't really say you have much control at all. But it is a blast. Everyone gets hammered, and no one cares. A swim in Lava is scary, but not as dangerous as swimming someplace like Crystal or Hance. This big, wild, boisterous river has you by the lapels, and you just have to laugh and go with it.

Below Lava Falls something about the river changes, and your trip changes with it, mellows and slows down. Some people would have you believe it's because nothing interesting happens below that last big adrenaline rush, but they're not looking around. Ancient black lava flows spill over the walls, frozen in place after their eruptions eons ago. Desert bighorn sheep are common here; sometimes you'll catch a glimpse of them moving delicately across the talus slopes, big ram in the lead. The rocks are shattered by faults that cut across the canyon. It's hot here, as the river makes its way into the Mojave Desert.

The trip might end just downstream of Lava Falls, at mile 187. At Whitmore Wash, a helicopter carries you up and out of the canyon, bound ultimately for the bright lights of Las Vegas. Or you may continue farther, down to mile 225. At Diamond Creek a road waits, to take you and all your gear out to the tiny Hualapai Indian town of Peach Springs, and from there back to the green pines of Flagstaff.

Some trips choose to travel as far as they can on the river. These people experience the last rapids of the Colorado River at mile 238. At Separation Canyon, mile 240, the living waters of the Colorado River are officially drowned by the pool of Lake Mead. You are still in the canyon, and the river is still in a channel, but it flows with hesitation, and silt banks garnish the rocks at riverside, remnants of past high lake levels. Your guides may tell you stories of the rapids long buried under silt and lake water, the two most fearsome rapids on the river, sleeping, waiting for the day…

If you travel all the way to Lake Mead, you'll see the end of the Grand Canyon. At mile 277, the river breaks through an imposing line of cliffs stretching away to the north and south. These are the Grand Wash Cliffs, the western boundary of the Grand Canyon. Looking back, you see a massive wall of red and purple, and the river's shadowed canyon like a door, which rapidly becomes a crack, then a line, and finally just a contour in the cliffs. The door has closed. It's time to go home.

MIX-UP IN THE DITCH

Tyler Williams

I've heard it said that all the greatest adventures begin with a mistake. As I ran through the middle of Grand Canyon into a setting sun, wearing nothing more than shorts and flip-flops, this dictum seemed painfully true. *And if a single error brings adventure,* I thought, *what do multiple errors bring?* I decided that I was in for a long night, and left it at that.

I shuffled along through the desert with brief energy-conserving strides. Occasionally my steady plodding rhythm would be broken with darting steps as I dodged an encroaching cactus. The rocky path demanded my full attention, but the scenery was a spectacular distraction. Deep green growth dripped off the South Rim high to my left and the sun sank before me as an orange fireball in the west. I was on the Tonto Platform, with half the canyon above me and half below.

My mind drifted off into a distance-runner's trance. But just as I would get lost in the unbelievable panorama, I would shake off the trance and force my focus on the trail in front of me. I scrutinized the terrain and made sure of every foot placement. I had come too far to let a sprained ankle stop me now.

During the rocky and steep sections of trail I would give my legs a rest, and slow to a walk. The slower pace gave me time to reflect on the convoluted set of circumstances that got me into this impromptu evening jog.

It had all started weeks earlier as a bold plan. My fiancé Lisa was to hike the South Kaibab Trail to Phantom Ranch, where she would rendezvous with my river trip. We would travel downriver for a dozen miles and camp. The next morning we would say our goodbyes, and Lisa would hike back out of the canyon on another trail. It would be a river reunion done in grand style.

Everything about our plan seemed to be in order—until the put-in. It was here that I learned my river trip would depart Phantom Ranch several hours earlier than originally planned. Foolishly, I paid this time change little attention. The bustle of the put-in kept my mind more on rigging rafts than on making the rendezvous at Phantom Ranch seven days into the future.

I launched on the river and the days rolled by. Marble Gorge melted away thoughts of responsibility back home and river time took over. As the rendezvous at Phantom Ranch neared, however, the five-hour time discrepancy loomed larger. Luckily, a solution seemed to be at hand.

My cousin Mary, who happened to be on another river trip at the time, was scheduled to reach Phantom one day earlier than my trip. I took the opportunity to ask if she would call my house back in Flagstaff and leave a message that the meeting time had changed. She agreed. I was going to be saved by the telephone. Again, everything seemed to be in order.

Modern technology and I have never gotten along. It once took me two days to send a fax to Japan. I still use a Walkman instead of an iPod, and I'm not even close to having a cell phone. So I guess it is no surprise that my telephone answering machine failed to deliver the message that my cousin left it. Lisa heard nothing about the change in plans, and she proceeded with our original schedule.

On the morning of May 12th, I was freshly bathed and ready to see my sweetheart. I pulled into Phantom Ranch early in the morning and proceeded with the standard Phantom chores: checking the mail, filling water jugs, gawking at tourists. I stalled the progress of the group as much as possible, and stole frequent glances up at the trail, hoping to see a familiar form hiking down. We dawdled at the ranch for most of the morning. Still no Lisa. Finally, we could stay no longer. With a nauseating sense of regret, I shoved my raft from shore and drifted under the bridge, leaving my hopes for a reunion behind.

We ran Horn Creek Rapid and I somberly drifted between the vertical walls. At Granite Camp several miles downstream, we tied up and unloaded the boats early in the afternoon.

Although I was in the ultimate outdoor playground, I felt joyless. Our plan had not worked, and I needed to know why. I studied the map, scrutinizing for a route that would get me back to Phantom. The trail from Granite to Phantom Ranch led upward one thousand vertical feet before reaching the Tonto Platform, where it began a winding course in and out of every drainage en route to the Bright Angel Trail. From here, the Bright Angel Trail dropped a thousand feet back into the Inner Gorge before following the river one mile upstream to the bridge and Phantom Ranch. Total distance one-way: eleven miles. Out of the question. I wasn't getting back to Phantom Ranch today, not on foot anyway.

I looked at the map again, hoping for a miracle. I noticed it was only six river miles to Phantom. Hope! If I found just enough slow water and the right combination of eddies, I could possibly paddle upstream to Phantom.

Seconds later, I was shoving handfuls of trail mix in my mouth and crawling into a kayak. I fell into a steady rhythm as I plied the gentle swirling water next to polished black walls. I portaged some small rapids, and I continued racing upstream with single-minded determination. Two rafts approached through the tail waves of a rapid, and I shouted, "What rapid is that?" They answered, "Horn Creek." I was surprised and energized to have made such easy progress. If I could make it to Horn Creek, I could easily make it to Phantom Ranch, and I'd only been paddling for ninety minutes! I portaged over the rocks beside the rapid and then stroked smoothly on towards Phantom. River-wide current blocked my progress shortly thereafter, so I pulled the kayak onto a small beach and set out on foot.

Soon I hit the Bright Angel Trail and began jogging down its trodden surface. A river trip floated by hundreds of feet below me. I looked down and could make out the orange life jackets of the passengers.

I arrived at the Phantom Ranch pay phone sweat-soaked but cheerful. I hoped Lisa would be at home, and would be able to explain why she hadn't made our proposed meeting.

Lisa's sister answered, startled to hear my voice. "Where are you?" she queried. I replied, "Phantom Ranch." "Lisa just called from Phantom Ranch an hour ago. She said you weren't there, so she caught a ride downstream with another trip." Lisa was evidently one of those orange life jackets that had just drifted below me. We had missed each other by less than twenty minutes.

Relatively certain that she would recognize my trip at Granite, I hung up the phone with a sense of relief. All I had to do now was paddle back downstream to camp. She would be waiting for me when I came kayaking in later that evening. Everything seemed to be in order.

I gleefully jogged back down the trail toward my kayak. A few hundred feet short of the beach where I had left the boat, I scanned the bank for the bright blue kayak. It wasn't there. What? My glee melted into bewilderment and despair. I hurried to the beach for a closer look, hoping that the boat would be behind a rock, just out of view. Gone, everything was gone. The only thing left was a scar in the sand where someone had dragged the boat into the river.

I swore mercilessly a couple of times, but my hollow shouts echoing through the canyon only highlighted the desperate situation. My only choice was to settle down and think clearly through my options.

It was already four o'clock in the afternoon—no trips would be coming by until tomorrow. I thought about swimming back to camp, but without a lifejacket, I realized that would only bring a cold death by drowning, so I quickly dispelled the idea for the lunacy that it was. I couldn't hike along the river back to camp either, because the shoreline was mostly vertical cliff. The logical thing to do was to catch a night's sleep at Phantom Ranch and hitch a ride to camp with another trip tomorrow. Or I could run the eleven miles of trail back to Granite Camp. The choice was obvious.

I began a plodding marathoner's gait up the Bright Angel Trail toward the flatter terrain above the Inner Gorge. I knew the steep switchbacks would bring me to Indian Gardens, where I would set off downstream on the Tonto Trail—my pathway back to camp.

I passed a concerned park ranger near the bottom of the switchbacks. He eyed me dubiously: flip-flops, shorts, nylon paddle jacket, no shirt, no pack, no water bottle. Before he could lecture me on the perils of Grand Canyon, I dispatched him with a quick and decisive lie. "I'm camped at Indian Gardens just up the hill." He let me pass.

I jogged the flatter sections of trail, and walked through the steep rocky parts. At the head of Horn Creek Canyon, I startled a family from Texas that was just sitting down for a meal of freeze-dried backpacking food. I asked to see their map. The mother kept her distance from me. The girls giggled. The father sternly admonished, "You be careful out there." With a quick scan of the map and a few gulps of water that the father insisted I drink, I was on my way. I'm sure that as soon as I was out of earshot I was berated for being foolish and unprepared, which of course I was.

My mental state was as transient as the Tonto's meandering course. The trail would run straight across expanses of desert near the rim of the Inner Gorge, allowing glimpses of the river and expansive views of the canyon. During these stretches, I would find myself elated and full of energy. But just as my strides would lengthen with euphoria, the trail would approach another side canyon and turn back toward the rim; away from the river, the light, my destination. Daunting Redwall cliffs darkened my world, and suddenly I was in a seemingly desperate situation: tired, alone, and miles from home.

The sun had set and I was resigned to the fact that I would be finishing my trek in the dark, if at all. Just then, in the fading twilight, a figure appeared coming across the desert toward me. I heard a shout, and I returned the gesture. It was Jeff, sent from camp as my one-man rescue party. We promptly partook in a celebration while gobbling granola bars, guzzling water, and lacing running shoes for the journey back to camp.

So where had my kayak gone? To camp, of course, having been paddled there by Lisa. She, along with the rest of her adopted river trip, saw the seemingly abandoned craft on the beach. Since I hadn't waited or left any notes for her at Phantom Ranch, they figured the kayak had been left as a means for Lisa to get to our camp. Imagine her confusion when, upon paddling into camp expecting to see me, she was greeted with nothing but strange stares and my obvious absence.

Upon my nighttime return to Granite, my sweetheart and I crawled into an especially comfortable sleeping bag and, at last, everything seemed to be in order.

COFFEE AT CRYSTAL

Lowell Braxton and Pete Winn

When you start off from Lees Ferry for a sixteen-day river trip through the Grand Canyon, it's extremely important that you pack enough coffee. *Mutiny on the Bounty* would be tame compared to the problems you'd have if you ran short. You'd think a bunch of old river guides on a private trip who, all told, have over three hundred trips under their belts would know this and plan accordingly, but we didn't. It's so hard to admit this that each of us blames someone else. If we were all correct, it would be the fault of someone who wasn't on the trip, but then this wouldn't be a true story.

The trip started off on a perfect note. It was mid-June; the first scorcher was the fourth day out. The river was so high that we could row up into the stunning blue water of the Little Colorado to land. There was another private river trip there, a bunch of yuppies from Oregon. Scotty parked his ragged twenty-year-old raft next to one of their fancy self-bailers, the kind of boat with a special beer can holder built into the frame next to the rowing seat that would keep your beer from spilling even if you flipped the raft. We took a picture of Scott sitting on his garbage scow in his faded, mismatched river garb, next to one of the Oregonians perched on his padded rowing seat wearing color-coded Patagonia quick-dry shorts with a special belt that held his high-tech, quick-release sheath knife. We called the picture "Twenty Years of Experience Meets Five Years of Money."

The trip was going really well. We had good runs in the rapids, the food was great and we all got along, a small miracle on a private trip. We'd just run Unkar, Nevills, Hance, Sockdolager and Grapevine, and planned to camp just above the Kaibab Trail bridge over the river. Unfortunately, a single motor rig beat us to the camp, but the guide let us double camp because we had an exchange the next day at Phantom. It wasn't until we set up camp that night that one unusually intelligent coffee drinker realized we had a problem. Uh-Oh.

The next morning several of us went up to the store at Phantom Ranch to buy coffee. We struck out. The lack of cooperation on the coffee issue was a nasty surprise. What happened to capitalism? We had good old U.S. currency, and we knew they had coffee. Maybe we were supposed to bribe them. Our next hope was the Havasupai Indians, eighty miles downstream. Things didn't look good.

While we were up at Phantom, the motor trip we had shared camp with landed and sent its entire group of passengers off on the trail up to the South Rim. It was one of those total interchanges that boatmen learn to hate. Just when the group is beginning to gel, they leave and you have to start all over. The first group gets a gentle introduction to the canyon because the big rapids are spaced out, and the biggest ones don't come until the day before you reach Phantom. The group hiking in has just walked five thousand feet down eight miles of steep, hot, dusty trail, probably following an incontinent mule train. They're all losing toenails from fashionably uncomfortable hiking boots purchased the week before in downtown Chicago or from an L.L. Bean catalog, and they're desperate for several Tylenol with codeine and a cold beer or three to wash them down. Their first day is full of big, big rapids: Horn Creek, Granite, Hermit and Crystal. One cold douche after another, and no chance to ease into the canyon. It's really tough on the guide. It's tough on everyone.

While waiting for the Phantom expedition, Pete was sitting on the beach commiserating about total interchanges with the motor boatman over a cold one after his group left. They played the old game of one-upmanship, telling stories about their previous experiences with interchanges. Both admitted to occasionally giving the new group the ride of their life by purposefully taking the more challenging runs in the big rapids, rather than cheating them. This particular day the river was really high, and they discussed whether that would be a good idea. Crystal at high water is pretty nasty: lots of flips for small oar boats. Our boats looked so small compared to the motor rig (Cindy's raft was less than fourteen feet long, the motor rig, thirty-eight) that Pete began to worry. He was especially concerned about the boat he was rowing, an aluminum kettle-drum sometimes called a dory.

We floated on down to Pipe Creek where Cindy left us, and Lowell joined us as an extra guide. From Lees to Phantom, Cindy had been training Melinda to row her little boat, and Melinda had done so well she wanted to run the big ones below Phantom. So Lowell joined Pete on the kettle-drum, and off we went. The river was still rising, so the waves were huge. They were so big in Granite that Pete flipped the dory, giving Lowell an award-winning nasal enema. Hermit was the usual gas, big roller coaster waves that went on forever. We were all really jazzed, but Crystal was next and the thought of high water at Crystal was pretty sobering. So we stopped at a beach at mile 96, two miles above Crystal, for a beer and strategy session.

The river had stopped rising, but refused to drop. While we were waiting to see if it would drop, a helicopter flew over, real low. Then another one, and another, and another. They just kept coming. After his flip in Granite, Pete was pretty nervous about Crystal, and was a good victim for Scotty and Allen's irreverent humor. He got so nervous and irritated that he began to think that they were conspiring to make him panic. He just had to do something, so he scrounged around and found a big piece of driftwood that looked like a bazooka. After propping it up, he began to shoot down helicopters. He wasn't a very good shot.

After what seemed like forty helicopter flights, we decided that the motor rig and all of the Oregonians ahead of us must have wrapped their boats on the same rock. Since we couldn't do anything about it from where we were, we decided to tell stories about flipping boats and just hope everyone was OK.

Oar boats flip much more frequently than motor rigs, but they're so much smaller that catching and righting them is usually not a problem. After picking up the swimmers, flotsam and jetsam, and righting the boat, everyone stands around and retells the story a dozen or maybe fifty times. Motor rigs don't flip very often and when they do it's almost always at high water. As far as we knew none of the famous motor rig flips in Grand Canyon had ended up evacuating anyone. After de-rigging, righting the boat and re-rigging, they all managed to finish the trip, a little worse for wear, but basically happy. But it appeared something worse had happened at Crystal that afternoon.

We finally decided to camp on the beach where we were waiting, and made plans to run Crystal at lower water before breakfast the next morning. So after dinner, we loaded all the commissary gear on the boats and sat down to relieve some tension with a bottle of Jose Cuervo's fermented cactus. It was a half-gallon, meant to last several days, but the tension was so great that we finished it that evening. After the bottle had made a few rounds of the entire group, it ended up being passed between Lowell and Pete. Dara was between them, so for each hit they got, she got two.

Allen took it upon himself to wake us up before it got even remotely light. His idea of an effective alarm clock was to stuff a tamarisk branch up everyone's noses —it even worked on Dara, although we had to pour her into his boat. We could just barely distinguish between the river and the bank when Allen and Scotty shoved off. Scotty's last words were something about the river beginning to rise, fast! Pete was still on the verge of panicking, and wasn't that far behind them. Will tactfully waited for Melinda, who was taking a little longer at the Unit that morning. There was just enough whitecap on the waves in Boucher to see them. They were surprisingly big—the river hadn't dropped much overnight. Brrr.

When Allen and Scotty landed on the beach above Crystal, there were ten oar rafts parked there: the Oregonians and another private party, the Tie-dyes. With the exception of one guy on the potty listening to a Walkman (must not have been a coffee drinker) everyone was still asleep. The tromping of our group woke up a few of them, who were immediately grouchy. "Those pricks must know something that we don't!" one yelled as we ran up the hill to check out the rapid.

It was just getting light enough to see the water. Out on the rock island, in the middle of the river near the end of the rapid, a dark, elongated mass was beginning to take shape. It was the motor rig, hung up on the rocks, upside down. We quickly found out what all of the helicopters were about, and that with the exception of a couple of injuries, everyone was OK and on the South Rim. They probably had the ride of their lives.

Before Pete and Melinda could catch their breath, Scotty and Allen ran back to their boats and shoved off, no passengers. If they were conspiring to panic Pete, it was working and Melinda was beginning to think she should panic, too. Dara's sister Terry was trying to get Dara up the hill to watch their run. "Patience sister, I'm barfing as fast as I can!" gulped Dara. Fortunately, both Scotty and Allen made it look easy. Melinda, Pete and Will each took one passenger and tried to match their runs. Will succeeded, but the top wave threw Pete and Melinda so far out into the middle of the river that they had to make a major decision quickly: left or right of the pile of rubber. It would be a big mistake to hit it. Both made it to the left, but it was spooky floating past that soggy hulk in the early dawn light.

Now here's the punch line. Pete pulled into the first eddy on the right below the wrecked raft, and found, floating in the calm water, an unopened three-pound can of coffee, just the right amount, just the right flavor. Yes, coffee floats. And now we didn't have to make the twenty-mile hike up to Supai Village to get coffee.

Scotty had found a boot floating in the eddy with the coffee. One of the Oregonians, Dave (the only one we could relate to because he had a mustache and an old boat), had found another boot floating in the river below Crystal, a perfect match for Scotty's find. Dave and Scotty began negotiations for each other's boot. Scotty was willing to trade just about anything, including someone else's wife (but not including our new-found coffee) to get both boots. Then someone else's wife demanded to know if the boots fit him. They didn't, so while sipping a cup of the coffee we rescued from Crystal, Scotty gave Dave the boot. That was the last we ever saw of Dave. It was obvious the river gave us the best deal!

ELEANOR

Brad Dimock

C rystal Rapid had changed dreadfully when we first saw it in the spring of '84. Although we'd been pretty successful running it throughout the extreme high water of '83, it was just enough lower now that all the worst effects of the flood were staring us in the face.

If you could get right and stay right, there'd be no problem. Simple concept. But there was this giant lateral wave that began mere inches from the right shore and angled out into the middle of the river. The farther out it went, the bigger it got, until it was just huge—too huge. But what was really scary about the wave was that no water seemed to move through it— none at all—it all stopped, collapsed and went sideways to the middle of the river. That's what all the boats were probably going to do.

If you somehow managed not to flip in that first wave, you were probably going to go into a bigger one—we called it the New Wave: a bottomless, frothing cauldron. If you somehow survived that, chances were you'd be full of water and heading down the land of the giants and into the Old Hole, which was positively magnormous. Bigger than all the others. Bigger and more impenetrable than anything we'd ever seen. It didn't look survivable. From there, whatever side up you were, you'd probably wash out dead center into the Rock Island. The only good news this trip was that the water was still high enough to cover the rocks in the island. It was more a series of waves and ugly holes, so maybe you wouldn't wreck your boat— maybe just flip it—or maybe it would flip back up. What I'm saying is that it didn't look all that rosy when we arrived, and we couldn't figure out quite what to do.

Now this wasn't a regular dory trip. This was an all women's charter— a group of ladies of all ages from Ohio who had requested an all-female crew. But in 1984, the company didn't have that many woman boatmen. The trip leader, three other boatmen, the cook, and her helper were all women. But Bego and I were rowing the other two dories. We wore wigs and skirts much of the trip to try and fit in, though it wasn't very convincing. The beards really spoiled the illusion.

We stared at Crystal for a long, long time, seeing no viable run but occasionally spotting a new hazard. Back before the flood when things would look ugly, we'd often have passengers walk around and meet us below at Thank God Eddy. The problem now was that we were none too sure we'd be right side up, and we didn't want to sail on by Thank God Eddy on the bottom of our boats, waving farewell to all our passengers. We thought some more.

We finally decided to ask for volunteers. If anyone really thought they wanted to go, and thought they could help in a crisis, we sure could use their assistance. Maybe then we could get enough boats through right side up and ashore below to pick up the walkers. The ladies mulled it over a while and after a bit of hand wringing, about half of them decided to walk. The rest of us loaded up, tightened our lifejackets, and pushed off. I had a doctor, a lawyer, and a nun aboard. Bases covered.

Chaos reigned. All the places we suspected were nasty—were. All the places we feared were unavoidable—were. We had boats everywhere, dropping into holes and splattered against the faces of waves; side-surfing along the laterals, losing one, two, even three oars; scrambling for one high side, then the other; sometimes just a row of heads showing where there should have been a boat. Out of six boats we had six, maybe seven, different runs. But miraculously—maybe the nun helped—we all came out right-side up and enough of us made it into the eddy to retrieve our hikers.

But that's not what the story is about. This is a story about Eleanor, one of the women who had walked around. She was maybe sixty years old, tall, and stocky—not fat, just heavily built. She used a walking stick. She said she really wanted to go through Crystal, was fully willing to accept the obvious risks, but just didn't feel like she had the strength to be of much use in a flip. She didn't want to be a hindrance or a liability, so she walked around.

She climbed back aboard Ellen's boat and we headed downstream, all of us ecstatic to have survived Crystal. And about a mile later, right in front of me, in a little rapid called Agate that is normally not much of anything, Ellen's boat flipped right over.

Now, it takes a bit of height and weight to right a flipped dory and Ellen is not all that large. Riding with Ellen and Eleanor were three other gals—an eleven-year-old girl, a paramedic in her mid-twenties, and one other woman. The paramedic washed directly into the eddy, unable to help. From where I was I could see that the eleven-year-old and the other woman had washed well ahead of the dory. Ellen, like most boatmen, had reacted quickly enough that she had crawled right up the flip-line and onto the bottom of the boat. I jammed into the eddy and picked up the swimmer, and watched Ellen's inverted boat sailing downstream.

But not for long. Following Ellen up the flip-line was Eleanor, hand over hand onto the bottom of the boat. A moment later they were leaning back on the flip-lines, Ellen giving it all she had and Eleanor using the height and weight she knew she had, and the strength she didn't believe she had, heaving back as the boat rolled back up right. In another moment they were back in the boat, Ellen back on the oars and Eleanor grabbing the remaining swimmers and hauling them aboard like flounders. All in all, a pretty spectacular self-rescue.

As I said before, this was a spring trip, and as it had been a wet winter, all the side streams were in flood. The hikes we did up wet side canyons had some pretty tricky crossings and we would station guides anywhere we could lend a hand in swift water. Before long we noticed something pretty cool. At each crossing, smack in the middle of the raging stream stood one Rock of Gibraltar: Eleanor. Giving a hand to each of the other ladies and the boatmen as well. Strong. Solid. Confident. And no one could remember when they last saw her walking stick. A while ago—maybe on the hike around Crystal.

Blacktail
Ote Dale
2002

BLACKTAIL

Christa Sadler

This is a ghost story. I don't really believe in ghosts. At least, none have ever given me any reason to believe in them. I've heard stories from other boatmen, about seeing strange shapes and hearing voices in the wind off the canyon walls. Some even swear that they were chased out of some of the canyon's ruins by nameless shadows and shapeless figures with ancient voices. Yeah, right. Put the tequila down, guys. I've always been way too practical a person anyway.

It was a dark and stormy night. No kidding. It was 1992, and we were about halfway through a month-long December trip in the canyon. This was the last third of a three-month river trip we were doing with Prescott College, as part of a field-based natural history class. Andre, Julie and I were instructors traveling with eleven college students, and we'd already been on the river since October 8—five hundred and seventy miles and about sixty-five days ago. But that's another story.

We were camped at Blacktail Canyon for the night, mile 120. Blacktail is my favorite place in the canyon. It's like a church to me. It has always been a welcoming place, if a little aloof. For years now, my river company has made a practice of doing a silent hike up the narrow, twisting side canyon. I like this, because if you spend your time talking, before you know it you've walked the quarter mile to the end and you haven't really seen anything all that unusual. But if you're quiet, the walls close in and surround you. They're plum-colored Tapeats Sandstone, and they bend in over your head, so that only a narrow strip of sky remains. It's absolutely still in that place, and drops of water fall with a resounding noise into the pools that you pick your way over and around. Sometimes a canyon wren sings, or thunder rumbles over the North Rim, and it sounds like it's coming right out of the walls. This is where I sing, where the String Quartet plays, where any boatman with a guitar or a flute comes to make special music.

It was raining pretty hard by the time we finished dinner, and the students all retreated to their tents in the patches of soft sand scattered among the boulders of the debris fan at Blacktail's entrance. Andre and I were feeling lazy, and we knew that there was a deep overhanging ledge of sandstone at the entrance to the canyon where we could lay out our bags and sleep unmolested by rain and snow. As we settled into our niche, we could hear the sound of Blacktail Rapid reverberating off the walls behind us. The canyon's mouth at my side yawned wide and so black I couldn't see my hand in front of my face.

"Listen." Andre said, "I hear drumming." I listened. If you stretched your imagination, the deep booming waves of the rapid did sound like drumming when they echoed off the walls. I looked over to my right. The canyon mouth got a little darker. "It's just the rapid, Andre. Let's get some sleep." He chuckled and we settled down for the night. I probably just should have stayed awake and convinced myself that the noises I heard all had a sensible explanation. It took a long time to get to sleep…

*An old man comes to me, holding a stone knife. He has long, white hair and wears something on a thong around his neck. I can't see his face. He says nothing, but somehow I know that he wants to show me something. Something horrible. I feel death, but not for me. Something has happened in this place, a long time ago. Maybe even before the people who lived here a thousand years ago. Something has happened to someone, and it lives in these walls. I'm not supposed to be here. I should leave. Now. "They" want us out of here. The old man is telling me this, only without words. I am so scared I'm rigid. I am in that in-between sleep, where I feel like I'm awake, only I can't move, I can't talk. The only things that work are my eyes, watching the darkness of the canyon mouth, waiting to see something come out of it. I feel myself trying to move, to break the paralysis. I can't wake up. I'm awake, but I'm not. **I can't wake up.** I try again, and again until I literally drag myself out of sleep. I feel like I've come back from someplace very deep and far away…*

I lay there, heart pounding. The first thing I heard was the deep, resonant drumming of the rapid off the walls. I couldn't even look at the mouth of the canyon; it was too dark and bottomless, threatening. Finally, I got up enough guts to speak. God, I hoped Andre wasn't asleep. "Andre, are you awake?" I whispered anxiously. "Yes," he said, in a tense voice that told me he had been awake for a while. "I had a terrible nightmare," I told him. "So did I." I felt the hairs on the back of my neck prickle. "What was yours about?" I asked him. "I don't know. I just know it was something horrible." My stomach turned over. "We're not supposed to be here,

Andre." "I know." I looked over at the darkness of the canyon mouth. "We should leave right now," he said.

Without another word, we gathered our bags and went out into a driving rain to set up a tent near our sleeping companions. The drumming was gone.

———～———

I go to Blacktail Canyon every chance I get. It is still my favorite place in the canyon, and it still welcomes me. In the daytime. I will never sleep there at night; I know I'm not supposed to. I've camped there since, on the debris fan. I've sat under the overhang at the entrance while our hikers were walking up the canyon. I've never heard the drumming again.

RANDY'S ROCK

Pete Winn

L ook, we've known each other for almost ten years!" exclaimed Rob in exasperation. "Let's quit playing games. The truck is almost loaded and ready to go. Where's the third boat?"

"Rob, I'm telling you the truth. Randy left his boat at mile 127. We didn't hide it just upstream so we could tell the other guides how we pulled your leg!" I don't think he believed me until we left the beach at Diamond Creek. It was hard for me to believe it, too. A twenty-two-foot-long by nine-foot-wide snout boat with three-foot-diameter tubes and eight air chambers just couldn't sink. Its heavy steel frame just couldn't turn into a pretzel in a few minutes.

But it really happened once upon a time, and for a few days it was a real nightmare. Fortunately, we didn't lose anyone. We never guessed that the entire Grand Canyon river guide community would come to call it Randy's Rock, or that the rock would later be given that official name in Lorenzo's mile-by-mile river map.

It was my last commercial trip in the canyon. It was early June 1976, and I had planned to be in Moab, Utah, for a Cataract Canyon trip. I had worked on and off for the American River Touring Association since 1967. I was ARTA's area manager for their Canyonlands operation that year. My first Cat trip had been canceled and Louise, the lead guide on the fateful Grand Canyon trip, was unable to make it. I was available, so I took her position.

It was a small trip, just seventeen passengers. We had three oar-powered snout boats plus a ten-foot paddleboat to liven up the easy stretches. We weren't supposed to run any big water with it. Marilyn, a good friend of Louise's, was the third guide. I hadn't run the canyon with either Randy or Marilyn, but I knew them both.

Randy was about five years younger than Marilyn and I, so we called him "the Kid" (we didn't question his ability to row; we'd started when we were just kids, too). Moley hiked in at Phantom to be the assistant guide. We took turns captaining the paddleboat when it was safe to run the rapids.

It was a twelve-day trip to Diamond, and it started off really well. Everyone liked Marilyn, especially a couple of young bucks. One of the young bucks, Josh, was a wild man, marginally controllable, but still likable. Walt was an older passenger with just one arm, and his wife helped him hold on in the rapids. Hal was making a movie about rafting in the Grand Canyon. He'd been on several previous trips, and thought he knew everything.

We encouraged our passengers to switch boats every day. On the fourth day, everyone waited on shore in the morning to see which boat Hal got on, and then rushed to the other boats. Hal chose my boat that morning; it was a big mistake. After a few hours with me, Hal learned to keep his mouth shut. Every time he'd open it I'd throw a bucket of frigid river water on him. After a while he was too cold to talk.

The nightmare began after lunch on the seventh day. We'd stopped at Blacktail Canyon for lunch, and Randy's boat was the first to leave. Marilyn and I stopped to gather some firewood, and were a little ways behind him. It was a hot, lazy afternoon, and everyone was in the mood for a nap.

Marilyn and I first saw people from our trip waving at us from the right bank above the riffle at mile 127. Then we realized someone was standing on the huge block of Tapeats Sandstone that had fallen out of the cliff on the left side of the riffle. Finally we noticed the almost completely submerged raft plastered on the sandstone block.

Randy had been nodding off while reading as one of his passengers rowed. The collision of his raft with the rock gave new meaning to the phrase "rude awakening." By the time Marilyn and I landed above the riffle, Randy and his passengers had already done a head count, and other than being cold and scared, everyone was OK and accounted for. Some had swum to the left bank quite a ways downstream.

We had two immediate problems to deal with. First was how to get Jim, the guy on the rock, to shore. He had the presence of mind to climb onto the rock as the boat wrapped. He was terrified, however, and not about to be convinced to jump in the river and swim to shore. Second, since only the upper part of one snout was above water, we couldn't see a way to get the raft off the rock. The rock was undercut, and the current was slowly pushing the raft farther under. The boat had one-third of our food and gear; we were only halfway down the river and we just had to get it back.

I was the only one who had ever been down the narrow channel on the left side of the boulder, so I knew it was about fifteen feet wide. I was pretty sure it would be possible to get to the boulder from the nearby cliff. So Marilyn gave me a ride over to the eddy behind the boulder. I jumped in and swam to a crack in the cliff. I managed to climb up to a ledge about twenty feet above the water and shinnied along until I was adjacent to a big crack in the boulder.

I couldn't stand on the ledge, but I was able to push myself far enough across the narrow channel so that I landed in the water below the crack in the boulder. Then Jim helped me climb onto the boulder. It was really spooky out there, watching the huge snout tube slowly disappear into the foamy water. The six straps holding the top snout to the frame were just barely visible. I talked Jim into holding my feet while I reached into the water and cut them.

Suddenly, the snout floated free and took off down the riffle. I had hoped the other snout, with the frame and one-third of our food and gear would come free too, but the river still had a lesson to teach us. Jim pulled me back and when we went over to the edge of the boulder to watch the snout float away, I quickly pulled him into the riffle with me. We reached the far shore about two hundred yards downstream, near where Marilyn had pulled in with the snout. Jim was too happy to be pissed at me.

We had no choice but to load up on the remaining two boats and look for the first camp we could find. We found one near mile 127 behind a big eddy on the left. The first order of business was to inventory food and gear. We were short six sleeping bags, but managed to scrounge enough blankets and sheets for everyone. We were short two days' worth of food, resulting in a large group discussion about whether or not to shorten or even abort the trip. The river was high, and we expected it to drop significantly by morning. Everyone agreed to postpone any decision until morning, hoping the raft would come loose and we could salvage the food and gear.

Hal's only concern was that his spare camera batteries and most of his film were on the wrecked boat, and the trip would be a waste if he didn't get them back. Needless to say, this attitude didn't sit well with the folks who had lost everything they had brought with them. Wild man Josh, who had lost his gear, decided to express his feelings by dumping a bucket of cold river water on Hal. This caused Hal to attack Josh with his Buck knife. We'd have had a murder on our hands for sure if Moley hadn't tackled Hal just in time. At that moment I knew exactly what the old saying "you could cut the tension with a knife" really meant.

That night the river dropped as predicted. Marilyn, Randy, Moley and I had taken turns sitting up all night, watching to see if the raft would come loose. Just as dawn broke, I woke to one of Josh's Tarzan calls and a big splash. Marilyn was already untying her boat when Josh came along, straddling the other snout, with frame still attached. We got our boat back!

Or so we thought. The frame hung deep in the water by two straps. As we began to de-rig it, taking turns swimming down into the cold water, it became apparent that the frame was not salvageable. It was twisted and broken beyond hope. We managed to cut the food boxes loose, but there weren't any personal gear bags to salvage. The river had claimed them.

We couldn't get the frame near enough to shore to drag it out; it kept catching on boulders. Finally, a motor rig passed by and the guide volunteered to drag the frame out into the middle of the eddy and drop it. Randy asked if he could join their trip for the day to help look for gear bags that might have gotten stuck in eddies. So far, the group had accepted the wreck as an accident, and had not ostracized him. I agreed that it was a good idea, and he took off. We had plans to meet him at Deer Creek Falls.

We left both snout tubes deflated and rolled up in the rocks. I later arranged for a motor rig to pick them up. We loaded up on the remaining two rafts plus paddleboat, and headed downriver. The boats were heavy but manageable. Between camp and Deer Creek we found three gear bags. One was in the eddy on the left next to the island at Bedrock. I rowed into the eddy with Moley and got it, making an old favorite run of mine down the narrow shoot below the eddy. Another bag was on the beach below Deubendorff. We had to stop there anyway, because Walt had dislocated his good arm in the rapid and we had to reset it. Now he couldn't hold on by himself at all. The third bag was in Helicopter Eddy. We hauled the paddleboat along the bank and paddled out to retrieve that one.

When we got to Deer Creek, we found out that Randy had hiked up Tapeats Creek to Thunder River and across Surprise Valley to Deer Creek. It was the same hike our trip had planned to do until the wreck. People were furious, especially Hal, whose camera gear was still missing. The group was starting to unravel again, so I told Randy to camp with another party that night if he valued his life.

It's funny how word travels along the river. Sometimes it seems like it actually travels upstream. Every river party we encountered seemed to know about our disaster, and many offered us food and gear, especially the motor trips. Unfortunately, I couldn't convince them to take Hal. I was really impressed with the community spirit. It definitely helped me convince our group that we could end the trip on a positive note.

We had arranged with several other river parties that we would be camping the next night at Ledges Camp. We desperately needed a long relaxing day at Havasu to get back on track. All the other camps between Upset Rapid and Havasu were spoken for. Unfortunately, while we were hiking Matkatamiba Canyon, another party passed us and set up an early camp at Ledges. We were forced to go on. Knowing the Last Chance camps were taken, we had no choice but to camp on the steep ledges at Sinyala.

It's not really a camp at high water and, in keeping with our luck, the river rose about fifteen feet that night. We had to scramble to move our kitchen and several passengers to safety. We were lucky we didn't lose any rafts. To make matters worse, Hal lost some of his gear and went into another murderous rage. It took three of us to subdue him. It was a bad night.

Havasu was great, in spite of the crowds. Our disaster had made us the center of attention, and somehow sharing our experience with so many strangers seemed to help us put the bad days behind. The rest of the trip actually went quite well, except for Wild Man Josh's swim in Lava.

We'd come to rely on the little paddleboat to relieve the crowding on the snout boats, but had decided not to let anyone take it through Lava Falls. It would flip for sure, and I didn't want to take any more risks than necessary. Unfortunately, earlier in the trip I had told Josh that I had taken the paddleboat through Lava before and it wasn't a bad swim. After all, the rapid only lasts about twenty seconds, and even in cold water most people can hold their breath that long.

Since we planned to use the paddleboat after Lava, we decided that Marilyn would tow it out and cut it loose when it was her turn to run the rapid. I arranged for Moley to hold onto Josh to keep him from jumping into the paddleboat after she cut it loose. I went first, had a good run and caught the eddy on the right below the rapid. There's a lava boulder out in the eddy, and I was standing on the boulder holding my stern line when Marilyn entered the rapid.

As planned, while Moley held Josh she cut the paddleboat loose. When she entered Lava, Moley let go. Josh immediately jumped into the river. He must have forgotten to grab a good breath and hold it, because he looked pretty miserable when he swam up to the rock I was standing on. I was secretly proud of him, but felt that it was necessary to step on his fingers as he tried to climb on the rock. The river had humbled him, now it was my turn. My passengers applauded me, and Josh was a good boy after that.

Hal eventually sued ARTA for his trip fare and lost equipment. I told them to pay cash—don't give him a free trip! Everyone else left Diamond with mostly good feelings about the trip, and even about Randy. In retrospect, I too am glad I was on the trip, but I'm thankful I've never been on another one like it.

I've always wondered what would have happened if Louise had been able to make the trip…

YO MAMA'S A MULE DEER

Brad Dimock

I couldn't have been more than twenty-five feet from the bighorn sheep when the trouble began. He was quietly eating bushes and minding his own business; I was tiptoeing towards him, barefoot through the boulders, trying to see just how close I could get. I had read somewhere that if you walked straight towards an animal, freezing whenever it looked up, it could not perceive your advances. So far it was working quite well.

Vince was back puttering about at the boats. He and I had the day off and were moving the boats from Tapeats Creek to Deer Creek while the folks hiked over Surprise Valley. We had made a stop at Owl Eyes Camp and I had walked upstream to get a good look at the bighorn we had seen from the river.

The ram finally realized how close I was and jumped up onto a rock to assess me. He was a fine specimen: strong and solid, with a good three-quarter curl to his horns. I was thrilled to be able to observe him at such close range. He bore little resemblance to the domestic sheep I had grown up next door to back east, the ones my childhood friends and I used to spend hours baahing at. Nevertheless, it occurred to me to say something to this fellow.

"Bahaahaaa," I said. The ram tilted his head, giving me a quizzical look. "Bahaahaaa," I said again in my best ovine baritone. This time something registered. Flaring his nostrils, he lowered his head and charged.

I didn't even have time to say "Oh shit!" I was already sprinting towards the river across the boulders, knowing full well that bighorn rams run across boulders much faster than gangly barefoot boatmen do. I have witnessed the appalling violence with which bighorns bash each other's skulls, and I knew that at any moment now he was going to connect with the small of my back with a sickening crunch and I would land several yards away in a crippled, crumpled heap.

But as I glanced back, I saw that although he had gotten VERY close, he had stopped. A few bounds later I too stopped and turned back to look at him. He was standing on a rock, once again regarding me quizzically.

Now here is where my sanity gets called to question. Some part of my mind just had to know if it was what I *said* that upset him. And without another thought I blurted out "Bahaahaaa!"

Yep, that's what did it all right. *Idiot, idiot! Dumb, stupid idiot!* I was thinking as I sprinted for the river. Again, I was expecting well-deserved total destruction; yet again he stopped just short of me. But this time I didn't stop. I ran all the way back to the beach and over the dune to where Vince was standing, still puttering.

Heart pounding, chest burning and hands trembling, I blurted out my story. He didn't believe a word. "Right, Brad," he said. "Sure."

"No, *really!*"

"Right."

Then, looking back I saw, staring down at us from the dune, my proof. He had followed me. "Watch this," I said, elbowing Vince. "BAHAAHAAA!" As I bolted for deep water, I could hear several feet thundering behind me, and Vince hissing unprintable expletives.

SWEET REUNION

Ghia Camille

I divided my clothes into three piles. There was the "not going" pile, the "maybe going" pile and the "for sure going" pile. For a second, I considered putting all the clothes into the "not going" pile and canceling the whole trip. *You're crazy*, I thought. *But I guess it would be just as crazy not to go. Who in their right mind would pass up a chance to row the Grand Canyon?*

It had been over eight years since I had worked for a commercial river company in the canyon. My biggest concern was whether I still had the stamina to survive the trip. A boatman's day starts at the crack of dawn and doesn't end until after sundown. I had to cook, clean, carry, row, bail and entertain, all in sweltering heat while my hands, feet and lips began to dry and crack. Plus, this time I was working the trip with my teenaged daughter, my ex, John and his beautiful, long-legged, blond girlfriend Alice, who I had just met for the first time.

Now that I think about it, I don't know any boatmen that I would consider completely right in the head. I may as well include myself in the ranks. The reality was that I would do whatever it took to get back in the Grand Canyon again. Tired of the debate I threw one more pair of shorts into the "for sure going" pile and called it good.

Packing light, in my book, has always been a desirable characteristic in a boatman. Still worried about the shorts, I asked Alice before leaving the warehouse, "Does six shorts for eighteen days sound about right?"

"Are you kidding? I have two different outfits for each day. One for on the boat and another for dinner." My jaw dropped and I couldn't say a thing. Where did John find this one? I later learned that she had developed a masterful way of rolling each pair of shorts with a matching bikini top and T-shirt and stuffing all thirty-six rolls into one dry bag—quite impressive.

Rivers changed my life. I started working on the rivers in southern Utah when I was twenty. Almost overnight I went from a glamorous co-ed with perfectly curled hair and plenty of black mascara, to a long-haired hippie girl who didn't wear make-up or shave her legs, much to the horror of my mother.

While on the river I learned that my body, so terrible at conventional sports like soccer or basketball, was strong and useful in the outdoors. I could row a boat through monstrous rapids, hike steep canyons to water-falls, and carry heavy buckets of water. I could drive huge trucks loaded with gear. I could sleep on soft sand or hard rock and I could live outdoors in weather from freezing snows to scorching heat. And I was good at it.

I loved the Utah rivers, but late at night after the passengers were in their tents and the boatmen were gathered on the rafts, I heard stories about the Grand Canyon—eighteen-day trips without having to de-rig the boats, rapids that rivaled those I was familiar with in Cataract Canyon and the beauty of a canyon that exposed rock two billion years old.

During these stories, I would close my eyes and wonder if I would ever get to row the Grand Canyon. From what I could ascertain it was almost impossible to get a job. Every boatman from Idaho to Colorado and beyond wanted to work there.

I waited, content to stay in Utah for the time being. I got married and had my baby girl, Parley. To make a living we moved every six months between Park City and Moab depending on whether it was ski season or river season.

Then one day the company John and I had been working for in Moab invited us to join their Grand Canyon operation. They were selling their Moab interests. Parley was shipped off to Grandma's house for the sum-mers and I got to work in the canyon for a few seasons. At that time, our company only ran the occasional row trip, preferring to run the more lucrative thirty-foot motor rigs that could hold fifteen passengers. I was never as comfortable with a motor as I was on the oars, so I had to be con-tent working as a swamper, and never got my own boat.

The canyon was everything I had ever imagined it would be. The rapids were huge and the side canyons were amazing. I worked until I thought I would drop and then I worked some more, but it never stopped me from wanting to go back.

Then my life changed. Almost as quickly as I had gotten married, I found myself divorced. I got the kid and the dog and moved back to Southern California—a place I had sworn I would never live again, but I needed to be close to my parents. John got the truck, all our climbing gear and the Grand Canyon job.

At the age of ten Parley began taking river trips with John during summer vacations. By now he had gone through several women but seemed to have settled on Alice. Parley liked her. I tried not to be jealous. With mixed emotions I packed her up and sent her off.

Parley always came back golden brown, hair bleached out and full of stories. She had played football in Redwall Cavern and swum in the brilliant blue waters of the Little Colorado.

"…But there is this place called Elves Chasm that was my favorite," Parley related to me, running all her sentences together. "There's moss and ferns growing everywhere, and at the end there's a waterfall and you can climb behind the waterfall if you're really careful on the slippery rocks and then you can jump off!"

"Then I swam around with my goggles on looking for stuff passengers have lost in the pool. I found a watch and it was still working."

And she was off again, so excited to tell me all her adventures she barely took a breath. She told me about the passengers too, the ones she sat up all night and talked with, the ones that complained the whole trip and the ones that upon departure pulled her aside and gave her her own individual tip.

"Twenty bucks, Mom. Dad said I could keep it."

I listened to her stories and longed to be with her, to be back in the canyon.

Then my big day arrived. A few more row trips had been added to the company schedule. Parley was going to join her dad on her first row trip.

"Any chance you could use a baggage boatman?" I casually asked John, when we were making arrangements for Parley's summer airfare. A baggage boatman doesn't have to have a Grand Canyon license and doesn't carry any passengers, only extra baggage. To my surprise he said he would check into it and to my utter amazement there was room for me. I was going to row my first Grand Canyon trip! Never mind that I had hardly touched a pair of oars in eight years and never mind that I would have to live and work in close contact with my ex and his girlfriend. I was going back to the canyon.

———

I was tired on day four, by day twelve I was living on pure inertia, but I was exactly where I wanted to be.

Every commercial boatman knows that on any given trip there is always some little pain in the body to cause annoyance, some little cut on the finger from a can lid, some little scrape on the toe by a poorly placed foot, some little strain in the elbow from helping someone back into the boat. Today, unfortunately, I was suffering from more than a little something. My fingers ached from pulling on the oars, the top of my feet had been rubbed raw where sand had gotten under my sandal strap and subsequently burned, my shoulder had been strained while pulling myself back into the boat after a swim. Over all, I was beat. I wouldn't say I was out of shape; I was just out of shape for the rigors of a boatman's life.

It was day fourteen and we were hiking up Havasu Canyon to Beaver Falls. My senses were on overload. I had been hiking with a group of passengers, but slowly the group had spread out until I found myself alone. I enjoyed the time to myself and began adjusting my speed to stay between the group in front of me and the group behind me.

I'm just a baggage boatman on this trip, I reasoned. *I don't have any real obligation to the passengers.* The solitude gave me time to reflect on the trip.

I had managed thus far, to keep my boat upright. I had been scared to death at House Rock Rapid, the first sizable rapid on the river. During the half hour scout I had to pee twice. And, to top it off, I knew that I was the only reason John, as trip leader, had called for the scout. All the other boatmen were seasoned veterans who knew the river like the back of their hands.

While scouting my run, I had stood transfixed, staring at the unnaturally clear, green water crashing in the monstrous hole in the middle of the river. I closed my eyes and imagined my run. *I'll break through the lateral wave at the top, but not too hard because I don't want to hit the rocks on the right shore. Then I will slide past the hole. Piece of cake,* I tried to encourage myself. Then I peed again.

"That was a great run you had in House Rock," Greta, one of the boatmen (who happened to be Alice's best friend) told me in camp that night. I was relieved. I could still row a boat and now John, Alice and all the other boatmen knew it, but most importantly I knew it.

I made good friends with the crew; river trips have a way of accelerating relationships. I also had a couple of enlightening conversations with Alice. "So, tell me this: John's not exactly a ladies' man, how did he catch two such outstanding women?" Alice asked as we hiked down from the top of Deer Creek Falls. "He isn't afraid of beautiful women the way lots of men are," I grinned in reply. I didn't usually refer to myself as beautiful. "Well, you've got a point there. Despite his faults he does have good taste in women," Alice laughed. *I like this lady,* I thought.

Upon reaching Beaver Falls I jumped into the turquoise pool at its base and swam to the far side. I sat and watched as a group of boys jumped off a fifteen-foot cliff into the pool. In the past, I never would have resisted the urge to jump off the cliffs with those boys, not because I love to jump off cliffs, but to prove who I was—a tough, brave, adventuresome girl.

Now, as I sat and watched, I thought with relief, *I don't have to prove myself any more. I'm older now, more mature, more sure of myself. The wrinkles around my eyes don't just show up when I laugh; they're permanent. The boys aren't going to wonder who the cool girl is; they're going to wonder why the old lady won't get out of the way.*

It's fun just to watch, I told myself and I actually believed it. I sat quietly and massaged my swollen finger joints.

Slowly, the passengers left the falls and started down the trail, back to the waiting boats and food. *I'll just hang out by the pool for a little longer,* I thought, wanting to enjoy every last minute. *If I have to, I'll jog down the trail to make up time.*

Solitude settled over the pool. It was quiet except for the sound of the waterfall. Unexpectedly, I heard footsteps on the rocks across the pool. I looked up to see BJ climbing another ten feet above the ledge the boys had been jumping off. He ran and took a flying leap off the cliff and landed in the water.

Before his ripples had subsided I made up my mind and swam back across the pool. As I stood on the bank, I smiled to myself. Instead of turning toward the trail, I climbed up the cliff to BJ's ledge and without more than a moment's hesitation, I ran off the cliff letting out a yell as I went. I threw my arms up in the air and kicked my legs out behind me like I was doing a "Daffy" on skis. I straightened out just before hitting the water, sliding through the blue surface into the underworld beneath.

When I popped out of the water I was exhilarated. Life, work, divorce, wrinkles, teenagers, car payments, dental bills—all washed away in one exhilarating free-fall, one plunge into the amazing blue water.

It would all be back, but today I was free. Today I could do anything. Today I was beautiful beyond reason. Today I was in the Grand Canyon.

84

Matkatamiba V
Elizabeth Black
2000

BOATING BY BRAILLE

Brad Dimock

L et me preface this by saying I was younger then. A lot younger. I had a lot more energy and many more lessons to learn. I've still got many more lessons to learn, but back then—wow. I still thought you could launch a river trip midway through day one, hike everywhere, do it all, and camp within sight of Pearce Ferry on night six, two hundred and eighty miles down the road. Of course I was a motor boatman then, but that's still a tall order.

My trainers had taught me the routine: a few minutes at Redwall, a few minutes at Elves, half an hour at Deer Creek and, what the hell, a whole hour at Havasu if you were on schedule.

I might have been too inquisitive. Now and then I'd find out about a new place down there, something new to see, somewhere cool to hike. And I'd think, *If we got up a little earlier, we could go there too.* And we would. And it'd be great. And then I'd feel like we had to go there every trip. Then I'd hear about *another* place...

I'd been motoring for about five years and was "Lead Pilot" for the company. I had a pretty scary routine by then. Up at the crack of dark, jam out breakfast for forty over an open fire, hurl everything on the boat and haul ass. Hike up Saddle Canyon, back to the boat, full throttle to Nankoweap, send the folks to the ruins while we made lunch, buzz on down to the Little Colorado and on to Unkar for camp. Sleep when you're dead.

Then I found out about Mooney Falls. Pretty much a full day hike. But god dammit, you were cheating folks if you didn't do it. Swindling them. So we'd get down to Deer Creek by night three. One boat would jet to camp while the other took most everybody up above the falls. Thank god I didn't know about roping folks down into the narrows.

After dinner I'd get the folks together and tell them about the morning. "Tomorrow morning you're going to hate me," I'd say. "By lunch you'll love me. And by dinner you'll despise me. Here's the plan." And I'd run around, wave my arms and rave about how incredible Mooney Falls was and how it was a brutal hike but worth it and how anybody could do it if they really

wanted to and how this might be the only chance they'd ever get and…
Late one night after such a spiel one fellow told me, "You could sell shit to
a cow."

About 4:00 A.M. on this particular morning I started shrieking, banging
pans and pounding the table. WooOOOF went the firepan as I chucked a
match into the gas-soaked heap of wood, and we were off and running. I'd
managed to convince about half the group to go on the mad dash with me.
The others would go with Bruce, pull into Matkatamiba Canyon for a
while, then hike to Beaver Falls and go on down to camp at National and
start dinner. By six-thirty we were all loaded and motoring down river,
waking the occasional sane group as we roared by.

This was a good group. We hit the shore running and were at Mooney
for lunch. It was everything I had promised, liquid crystal blue and the
grapevine jungle was head high. As promised, they loved me.

"Well, I reckon we'd better mosey," I said, herding them back on the
trail. "It's always twice as far home." That's for sure. We hadn't gone more
than a few feet when Glen, a strong, stout fellow in his twenties, stepped
into an overgrown pit and landed hard on his ankle, sideways. I heard the
snap. So did the fellow right behind him who immediately jumped down
to his side. "I'm an orthopedic surgeon," he announced. *Great*, I thought.
#@%#&·# great.*

But an orthopedic surgeon he was and, after a survey announced, "I
don't think you broke the bone. You snapped a bunch of soft stuff, but I
think you can walk on it if you can stand the pain."

"Or we can fly you out," I said.

Glen grimaced for a while and said, "I've broken my femur before. This
isn't so bad. I'll try to walk on it." We started down the trail, one of us
under each shoulder. He was one tough hombre, but it was soon apparent
that we wouldn't be back to the boats any time soon. "Doc," I said. "Would
codeine help?"

"Hell, yes," he said.

"I've got some but it's at the boat." I picked out one fellow who seemed
faster than the rest and told him to run to the river, stop Bruce's boat if he
could, get the codeine out of the first aid kit, tell the other folks to hunker
in for a while and get back up here ASAP.

"Doc," I said. "Um, what's your name?" Here we were all the way to
Havasu and I didn't even know his name. But it was only day four and he'd
been riding on Bruce's boat.

"Bob," he said.

We were creeping back across the high trail above Beaver when my runner got back (I never did get his name). He had the codeine, but had missed Bruce. They'd already left for National. Bob prescribed a handful of pills and before too long Glen's condition began to improve. By the time we got close to the boats he was whistling and downright jolly. The only problem was it was pitch black out and the moon wasn't due to rise till about 3:00 A.M. As promised, everyone despised me.

"I want everyone's lifejacket on tight," I said. "Sit in the middle of the boat and don't say a word." I drank my thermos of coffee and fired up the Merc.

Somehow the human mind knows it's in training for something. It picks up information subconsciously and stores it away for times like this. It helped, too, that I'd been running back-to-back trips all summer. I pulled out into the blackness using the black skylines against the nearly black sky for guidance. When I thought I was far enough out I pulled the engine and drifted through the rapid. No problem. I'd motor a while, then drift and listen. Motor and drift. Riffles sound like rapids in the dark. But I'd line up for whatever it was and drift on through. I recognized 164 Mile Rapid, putted on through and started to relax. Only two more flat miles to camp.

By the time he finished dinner Bruce was concerned. So were his folks. Most of their camping gear was on my boat and vice versa. Oops. Scenarios started running through his head. *I didn't tie his boat up right. It got loose and is in an eddy and they're at Havasu... He's stuck on a rock at 164 Mile... They're lost at Beaver Falls... Someone's had a heart attack... I can't motor back up there with this stupid boat...* It got darker, people got colder and Bruce got worrieder.

Then he heard, or thought he heard, my motor. He jumped up. Then heard nothing. Then again, definitely a motor! *What if he doesn't see us?* he thought. *He'll motor right by!* Quickly he threw the rest of his firewood on the fire. But it wouldn't catch fire in time! *Dammit! The gas!* He grabbed the can of Coleman fuel, poured a ladleful and tossed it on. A great billow of flame leapt up, illuminating the cliffs. *Perfect!* He poured another ladleful, but this time the whole can caught fire! He threw it. Spewing flame, it landed near some dry bushes. *Shit!* He kicked it away from the bushes and it tumbled wildly across the beach, emptying itself, leaving a holocaust in its wake. The entire beach was in flames.

Out in the eddy my relief turned to confusion, then horror. *What the....? What's going...?* It only took a few seconds for the main conflagration to subside enough to where I decided I could land. Full throttle, we hit the beach. We met halfway down the boat, both laughing and shouting.

⁓

Glen's ankle wasn't broken but he didn't walk, smile or whistle much for the rest of the trip. A month later I turned in my motor handle and earplugs for a pair of oars. A year later, Bruce fell off the falls at Fern Glen and broke both his ankles. After a few weeks in the hospital, he married his nurse.

This is true. Every word of it. I swear.

HAVASU

Lew Steiger

August 6, 1988. Tim Whitney and Richard Quartaroli are running an Arizona River Runners trip. They're coming down from Deer Creek to Havasu and it's cloudy. It dumps on them pretty good there at Last Chance; they float a minute, the rain passes and the sky begins to clear. They go on to Havasu and tie up at the motor rig place down below the rapid. Richard is leading this trip. He says it doesn't look like a good day to be on the other side of the creek and instead they'll just go up to the first crossing and take a few pictures. About ten people stay behind with Whitney.

Richard gets everybody up to the first crossing and says, "OK everybody, there it is. We'll be here ten minutes or so." Then he turns around and trots down to the mouth, where two Western boats and two Wilderness River Adventures boats are tied. Carl and Mike are running for WRA, a guy named Darrel is there for Western. Richard says, "Hi. Where you camping?"

Boom, right there the creek starts to rise.

Richard takes off up the trail, back to where his people are. As soon as he's gone, a two-, maybe three-foot wall of water hits the mouth: red and thinly disguised as water. Filled with sticks, tree limbs, logs—a person. A face in the water.

The face comes roaring through the creek mouth and spills out into the river.

Carl is down on his boat and he throws a lifejacket in the face's direction and just that quick they're gone—jacket and swimmer both.

Meanwhile, back at the ARR trip, people are starting to return from the hike already, trickling in by twos and threes. Whitney is on the ledges meeting them when he looks up and sees the flood. Then he sees both Western boats get blown out of the mouth. They're tied together bow to stern and they are totally out of control, pin-balling down the rapid.

"Get ready!" Whitney yells to his people. "They're gonna try to come in here! Get back! Stay out of the way!"

Whitney runs down to the water. They've had a policy at ARR for years that whenever you're tied at this particular spot everybody wears a lifejacket at all times on the boats. So Whitney puts his on and runs out across his boat to do whatever he can if the Western boats somehow manage to get into the eddy. Darrel's got one motor started by now and he's screaming at the swamper, a guy named Garvin, to start the other one. Garvin's having trouble, though, and it looks to Whitney like it'll be a miracle if they ever make it. Whitney looks down into the muddy red water and sees an empty lifejacket. *My God*, he thinks. *It's already washing stuff off the boats up there.*

Then he sees the face. No hair, no hands, no neck and shoulders. Just two eyes, a nose and a mouth that is open in a neat round circle, gasping for air.

He's got about one second to figure out what to do.

He jumps in, too. He grabs the body that belongs to the face. It's a woman, but Whitney doesn't know this yet. Immediately, she's all over him, trying to claw her way up out of the water. "Take it easy," he says. "Just relax, just breathe easy. I've got you now, it's all over, you're gonna make it." One jacket isn't great, but it's floating them at least. Their heads float just above the water.

We could go to Tuckup if we had to, Whitney thinks. *We'll just swim down here along the wall and grab onto the first good thing we find and get the hell out of here.* "Piece of cake," he says out loud. "No problem. We've got it made."

Then the Western boats manage to get into the eddy after all. They hit the cliff downstream bent double, in V-formation, with the upstream boat pointed out into the current and the Johnson 35 on the other boat absolutely screaming its noble, loud, American-made head off. They're just happy to be here, man. They survived a hell of a flood is what they've just done, and they have no idea there's anybody in the water just upstream of them.

Whitney looks downstream and thinks, *Uh-oh, now we've got a problem.*

And yep, whammo! He and the face hit the upstream side of the Western boat. *One chance*, Whitney thinks. He grabs for the lifeline and snags it, grits his teeth, sees a couple of passengers up there, then—bloop—the current takes them under, just that fast. *God*, Whitney thinks. *Two Western boats. How long is THIS going to take?*

His eyes are wide open and he can't see a thing. It's black. The water is totally dark around him and the swimmer has him hard by the neck and he can feel himself bumping against the tubes of the boat as they're being swept along. He pries her hands off his neck and whoosh—the current rips her away.

Oh man, Whitney thinks. *That's it. She's gone.*

Just hold on, he thinks to himself. *Just hold your breath. You gotta hang on…you're in the current, you're gonna come out.* So he holds on and holds on and holds on, and finally pops up and gets a breath. Comes out of the red water into light brown water, gets a huge OhThankGod kind of breath.

Well, that was it, he thinks. *That was the one chance you had, Bucko. You're never going to see HER again.*

But no. She pops up a few strokes away, tries to catch a breath, goes under. Whitney swims over. She's going down but he can still see the blur and he dives for her. He grabs her by the hair. He pulls her up and gets another handle on her, a cross-body carry. He looks around. They're between the boats and the wall now.

At this point, Whitney starts to lose it a little.

Now we're gonna get squashed, he thinks. *We'll have to swim under the damn boats just to get away.* So he starts to squall at Darrel. "Don't run me over!" he yells. And Darrel sees him finally, and somehow Whitney and the woman end up alongside the boat. A couple of passengers reach out to grab her, but one of those guys starts to fall in, too. He catches himself on the lifeline and he's yelling for somebody to grab his feet. A thirteen-year-old kid appears, finally, and even though he's utterly goggle-eyed at what's happening, he grabs the woman and manages to pull her up.

Whitney sees the stern of the other boat and swims to that. He pulls himself up through the motor well. Garvin is still trying to get the motor in the water; he can't figure out the latch. Whitney puts it in the water and gets it started. The handle's broken but it runs anyway.

They pull in at the first little beach downstream on the right below the rapid. The woman sprints off the boat and jumps on that land like she's gonna kiss it.

She was a marathon runner, it turned out—a New Yorker, of all things, from Whitney's own trip, in her late forties, early fifties. Weighed about 110. She got swept away right there at the first crossing, went over that first fall, down the narrows and out through the mouth. Clear through the rapid without a lifejacket. The whole thing was over in less than five minutes.

You have to really press Whitney to get him to tell the story, and even then, after you try to say what a good job he did, he'll manage to come up with a bunch of baloney like, "Oh, come on. This is the Grand Canyon, right? That kind of thing happens every day down here. Some little move made real fast that prevents an accident, you know? We see those every trip and they're just part of the job. I mean, hey, I lost her under the boat, man. That's the part that keeps coming back to me."

Whitney will say a line or two of hogwash like that and he'll dig his toe into the dirt and watching him do it, you'll think, *All right. It couldn't have happened to a nicer guy.* A life was in the balance and Whitney had about two seconds to scope the thing out. He jumped in without hesitation and now he has that forever, nobody can take it away from him. It's all his own. He saved that woman's life for sure, and even though he's more the kind of guy who'll forever say, "I lost her under the boat, though..." the fact remains that he jumped when he had to, smack at the head of one hellacious flood. And how many of the rest of us will ever know for sure that we'd have done the same and not tried to go after her with a boat instead? Or screwed around too long with the #@!*% *throw* rope?

Why is it we do this job anyway, and what exactly are we after if it isn't what happened to Whitney or at least something similar; one of a thousand little intangibles that are forever cropping up, which have nothing to do with fame or fortune, but rather just living your life well in a beautiful place that'll keep you honest all the same, that will make you have your act together from time to time?

Anyway, way to go Arizona River Runners, for having that lifejacket policy in the first place—one of those pain in the ass procedures that finally paid off. And yahoo Whitney, most of all. Good job, amigo. It couldn't have happened to a nicer guy.

ON BIG BOATS WITHOUT WATER

Shane Murphy

As a professional river pilot, I have found it wise to be wary of stories about boats and fast water. They have the aura of mystic heroism about them. It is well, also, to avoid stories about boats and slow water. Or even, stories about boats entirely without water! Laugh at such tales, shun them as freak occurrences that could never happen to your boat, the boat you pilot, and you—and your boat—will be the next bit. Your number is up, your bolt shot. You, friend, will crap out. Soon.

For example, I once had the captain of the nuclear aircraft carrier *Enterprise* under my charge for four days in Grand Canyon, this outing being between Bright Angel Creek and Diamond Creek. On day two, during a swim stop at Havasu Creek, I got to talking about big boats stranded on beaches. This phenomenon is due to water releases from Glen Canyon Dam, a hydro-electric generating facility near Page, Arizona. Because power demands and legal requirements typically dictate river level, the Colorado can exhibit creep-ing tidal "bores" (more at: severe gradations in river level) which often vary ten feet or more during any given twenty-four-hour period.

I explained to the captain and his family why these fluctuations force pilots of big boats to maintain a nightly vigil about their boats. In the morning pilots wish their boats to still be floating in deep water since, without water beneath it, the boat serves no purpose whatsoever. I told him that each and every night the boat must be parked with great care, in the deepest pool known, against the steepest shoreline, that when the water "goes out" the lines must be loosened and the boat pushed farther into the river. Otherwise the boat is stranded. Big boats, stuck on like-sized boul-ders are, under most circumstances, impossible to budge. They are parked for sure, buried to the gunnels.

Should the river rise, as it sometimes will, the boat must be drawn up. In any event, the boat will be, at all times during any encampment, at right angles to the shoreline, perpendicular to the current, with only its snout touching the shore. If more than one boat is parked for the evening all must be tethered together in strict contract, as if to form a huge inflated playing field magically afloat, wanting only a stadium filled with cheering spectators.

Let the games begin! Say it is Tuesday night, river mile 118, Grand Canyon, Arizona. The water, the river itself, will drop. As a river pilot you know this. At no cost do you want to rise in the morning to find yourself stranded, your boat far from the river, the water still dropping. Such circumstance paints the pilot and crew in unpleasant caricature. It is one of those small professional faux pas unforgivable in the eyes of those who know of such things: the other boatmen will laugh at you. I told my man that I sleep on the boat, up front, and drink gallons of water, which causes me to pee frequently. This is how I monitor river level, and I said so. I will rise half a dozen times during the night, checking my boat each time. After that I do what I need to do. After that I crawl back into my sleeping bag.

I discoursed freely on this topic for one complete hour. I told the captain stories of boats I had seen, boats so contorted over rocks so huge that nothing could be done except wait for twelve hours for the water to come. Really, I rattled on, a fine grin pasted to my face, such things rarely happened. Said occurrences had never—and most probably would never—happen to me. At any rate, there was slim chance it would happen on this trip. I told him that, too. Besides, I thundered in grand summation, it was Wednesday! If the river did anything, it would rise!

The next morning, at first light, it was "snake eyes" staring me straight in the face. Sure as I am one inch tall, my boat—a genuine, living and breathing thirty-seven-foot, six-ton leviathan of the Colorado—was fifty feet from the river, resting peacefully on a very flat, generously wide, sandbar. When waking I had the immediate sensation of dreaming. Certainly this was not real. My next bright idea was to shove the beast back into the water before anyone found out. It was not long before I got to calling this quaint notion One Damned Stupid Idea. I woke my co-pilot. I told him. In an instant he was off the boat, standing beside me on the moist sand. We were both naked as jaybirds.

We got dressed. Very quickly. We started to unbuckle the two outriggers, the outside tubes. I sent my other crewperson off to roust the passengers. The captain came down. He took a look, a walk around. He did not say much, except to express satisfaction that it was my boat and not his own. He asked what he could do to help. I said we needed everyone in the outfit on the beach right now, ready to help. He hurried off immediately.

While most of us pumped air and shoved equipment and lugged gear and hauled water and pushed and pulled and got the boat back onto the river, one of our lady passengers oversaw a small auxiliary operation that served fresh omelets and hot toast, and washed every dish. We were gone in ninety minutes, airborne, floating our way freely downriver. It was great good fortune. Not another boat had gone by. No one would ever know.

After we were underway the captain told me a story, a fine story about how he had once run the *Enterprise* sideways beneath the Golden Gate Bridge. This particular maneuver was entirely unscheduled, completely unrehearsed. Somehow the great ship had ended up athwart the current and had to be got under the bridge just like that—sideways—between two massive pylons fully one-half mile separate. There was little room to spare. It was a real-life, big-time, nuclear squeaker. If he had smacked one of those bridge abutments he said, he would, today, be digging potatoes in Kansas someplace. I told him that I understood, that I would probably be standing right next to him in the same field, that we would most likely be foraging the very same tuber. He laughed loud. He asked what the water would do tonight, Thursday. I said it wouldn't do anything and was correct.

Boatman Working II
Mary Williams
1993

SLITHERING COMPANY
Teresa Yates Matheson

This trip had been as meaningful for my mother as it is for most passengers who experience for the first time what the river can do for their soul. She never dreamed her only daughter would become a Grand Canyon river guide, so at my first opportunity I swept her away on a trip with Georgie Clark. She had never left for ten days straight in her many years being married to my father.

Georgie liked to pull in early a ways into the trip to give everyone some time in camp. After dinner, the passengers gathered for the evening's conversation. This soon turned into the array of familiar jokes a river guide hears on trips. Realizing the need to catch up with my mother I suggested we go to camp to set up and lay down on our bags. The only thing Georgie supplied at the time to sleep on was a sleeping bag. No tarp, no pillow, and no sheet. My mother was trained by now in the art of setting up camp.

When she showed me where camp was, it was already laid out and set up. Sleeping bags out, river bags in their appropriate places and the ammo cans close by. The passengers had tired of setting up camp in the dark. We sat on top of our sleeping bags for about forty-five minutes until the heat came out of the rocks. We were taking advantage of the time together without the rest of the group, and I listened to her describe the trip from her perspective.

Sliding into my sleeping bag, I felt what seemed like a rope coiled up in the corner down by my feet. But a rope with movement. It was then I realized I had company. Thoughts were passing through my mind in record time, and all the while my mom was talking and carrying on about something. I don't remember where the conversation had gone. I just acknowledged with short responses, a little less talkative than before I knew about my uninvited guest.

Should I let my mother know there is a snake in my bag? No, she would panic and it would bring the group. Do I want the group of drunken joke-spewing passengers to come help? No, I think I will let them continue to entertain themselves. I don't want to move and make my guest feel unwanted, let alone angry with rejection. The only safe option in my mind was to be patient and allow my guest to let itself out.

You know the feeling sometimes when things seem to be happening in slow motion and every moment is vivid? Time was moving with absolute turtle speed as my mom just kept on talking away. My contributions to the conversation were words like "really?," "oh," and possibly a few others. To me it seemed like a half an hour, but I am sure it was only minutes when the snake decided to make his move.

It began by unraveling itself at my feet, finding its way up over my left leg into the space between my legs, moving along the inner thigh of my right leg towards my shorts. *I hope that it makes it all the way out and doesn't delay somewhere along his path.* It continued up to the top of my abdomen to the base of my neck. At this point I wasn't contributing to my mother's dialog at all. I am sure my breathing was altered by attempting to remain still and calm. From my perspective, the snake still had a way to go before completely emerging from my bag. I could feel its entire length on my body; its head was approaching my neck and its tail had not yet stopped touching my thigh.

It did peek its head out into the night air after a hesitation to view its escape route. Thoughts of the loud group, my mom's talking, and the people in the camp next to us made me wonder if the snake would have preferred to remain where it was. Why leave a perfectly comfortable hiding place? But it did propel its slithering size out of the bag little by little with a hesitation here and there along the way. It was getting too steamy in the sleeping bag at this point, I think. The scales from its body brushed against my neck and slid past my ear inch by inch.

At this point everything seemed to be exaggerated. The noise from the group was loud, my mother's voice was loud, and the people in the camp next to us started to move around, as if to distract the snake and make it retreat. *Patience, patience, it will leave.* Now almost all of it was out of the bag. My head turned to see the rattles held high in the open air—the last to exit.

It ventured towards another camp where people were sleeping, probably looking for another resting place. I yelled to wake them up but they stirred only when I said, "Snake coming your way." Once they moved, the snake made a U-turn back my direction and found a safe place under my river bag. Soon we had the whole camp involved in its removal to an upstream area. Seems I made a good choice not to get anyone else involved while it was still in my bag.

As we bagged the snake and moved it upstream, the group became restless and concerned. Each person had set up camp early in the evening and their bags were out. We made our rounds to discover all was well around camp and everyone decided to call it a night. Upon returning to my own camp I found my mom had changed the direction of her sleeping bag. Apparently, this experience had taught her that snakes only travel in one direction. I asked her, "Do you think they only travel from downstream to upstream?" She laughed and said, "I just had to do *something!*"

LEAVING EDEN

Christa Sadler

"In their hearts they turned to each other's hearts for refuge…"
-Jackson Browne, *Before the Deluge*

For a long time now, I have been under the impression that there was one place in my life, in our lives, into which the outside world could not really intrude. A personal and professional Eden, a paradise where lost childhood could be regained, and all social and political distinctions become completely unnecessary. In Grand Canyon, we joke that "World War Three could be happening and we'd never know it." At first uncomfortable with the lack of daily communications from the usual information sources, our guests slowly adjust, and in the end become oddly proud of their lack of knowledge, and how unimportant all that knowledge really seems to be. Truly, we all find Eden in this canyon for a short time, happy in our innocence.

On September 12, 2001, we were given the apple and forced to eat it. All that day, traveling through the narrow limestone walls of the Muav Gorge, we had noticed the lack of planes—both the big jetliners that usually cross the canyon from L.A. to points east and back again, but also the smaller planes that fly over that part of the canyon on their way from Las Vegas. We noticed this, but it didn't really sink in, so intent were we on our thirty-mile destination; so delightedly were we watching bighorn sheep families picking their way delicately over cliff faces and talus slopes.

That night in camp the outside world crashed our party. While we were cooking dinner, the crew from another trip told our guides what had happened to New York and Washington, D.C. the morning before. They had heard from hikers down from the rim at Havasu. The boatmen stood in tight knots talking as dinner cooked. We were still smiling and laughing but we were anxious, not really believing what we had heard, and yet knowing the truth of it in our hearts. The taste of that apple hadn't really sunk in yet.

Then I remembered the planes. The sky above looked deceptively calm and peaceful. And I looked around at our group, happily celebrating

Marilyn's anniversary. Marilyn, who to all of us had been a stranger just twelve days ago, was now surrounded by her clan, celebrating the day she and her absent husband had joined in marriage. Marilyn, whose son Otis—whom we all felt like we knew as a friend by this time—had just moved to New York City to teach bilingual elementary school. And then I understood. I was going to have to tell these people that their world had forever changed, that loved ones and friends had died. I was going to have to be the one to take them by the hand and lead them out of Eden.

We forced smiles around the circle that evening, listening to Marilyn's poetry, and laughing about the sweet pictures she handed around of her husband and son. I anxiously declined a request to tell stories, hoping that everyone would retire to bed and leave me and the other guides alone with our fears and uncertainties. I spent a lot of the evening on the satellite phone gathering as much as information as I could, finding out which among our group had been affected. I learned that Mark's family and Marilyn's son were fine, but that Carol's brother was missing from the World Trade Center, and that her husband was trying to contact her. They were happily in bed, sleeping to the mutter of the river and the brilliance of the stars. I lay awake most of the night, thinking about the role we would play in the morning. We are the guides in this paradise, showing people the way down the river, up the cliffs, and back into themselves and their bodies—happy places. And now we were going to have to guide them through sadness and fear and loss.

In the morning we moved slowly, watching the glorious, gilt-edged clouds build over National Canyon. Peach and cobalt, silver and violet let loose in a pounding fifteen-minute storm. Lightning shattered the sky and a rainbow stitched it all back together at the end. It was time to talk to the group. I talked individually with the people most affected by the events, and then I asked everyone to gather in a circle. I could tell that they were curious at the unusual request, and my uncharacteristically stern expression. I told them in the simplest way I could, and as I talked I watched their faces crumble and their bodies sag against one another for support. I wanted to take it all back, swallow the words and move backwards a few hours in time, anything to be able to erase those expressions and give them back their canyon. Afterwards people wandered the beach for solitude. Some sat by the river and watched it swirl by. Others sat with loved ones on the rocks and held each other, sadness and confusion and disbelief in their faces and their bodies.

It wasn't until later that morning, while resting in the silver-gray womb of Fern Glen, that I lost it. I watched a swallowtail butterfly with tattered wings float by, pure fragility holding up against the ravages of its life, and I began to cry, thinking of all we do to hurt and destroy, and how resilient our spirits are in the end.

Our group stayed in the canyon, in all ways. All of us, even Carol, played fiercely that day: wiffle ball and tag and mudfights. We laughed and we cried and we splashed and bathed and gloried in the mid-September sun. And by the end of the day, the separate little knots of people had broken up and rejoined to become one again. Our tribe had survived its exit from Eden, even though that knowledge stayed with us, and we knew things would never be quite so innocent again.

———～———

Now, when what I hear on the radio is the rhetoric and political analysis of terrorism, fanaticism, weaponry and hatred, I am left with a bitter knowledge that I know I always had, but hoped I didn't have to believe. The canyon is not apart and separate from the world. Whatever happens outside will reach us there. But the canyon and places like it must shelter our souls and our spirits so that we can survive what happens elsewhere. We must have the world of nature's making to nourish and support our humanity when the world of our own making seems senseless and inhuman. With the sorrow of taking people away from paradise comes a sense of wonder at what I observed in the process. In the early days of our trip, I had watched a group of strangers become friends. Through these events, I watched these friends become part of a family—the family of man.

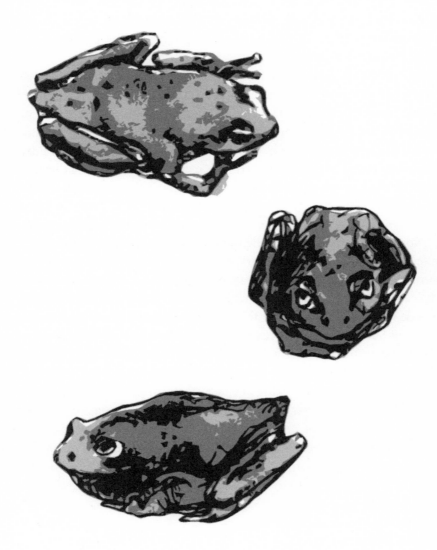

Still Life With Frogs
Mary Williams
2000

A RIVER TALE
Kent Erskine

In the late summer of 1971 I was invited to come down from my favorite mountain rivers and train as a guide, rowing for ARTA in the Grand Canyon. I was, needless to say, feeling blessed. And I was a little daunted by the reputations and very gruff demeanors of the guides who would be my trainers. It was the end of the season you see, and everyone was a bit short on social frills and etiquette.

The whole trip is probably worthy of an entire night's tales by the fire. I was in heaven; challenged and supported—pushed to the limits of my being. And despite my river experience, I found myself going along obediently with some rather outrageous decisions.

As I now realize is common, throughout the trip we talked more and more of Lava Falls, which loomed like a specter downstream. Its reputation had recently been solidified by the *Life Magazine* photograph of the motor rig flipping in the bottom wave. We all knew the guides involved and could feel the agony of their slow rollover.

On the beach at camp on the morning of our run through the rapid, we spoke of how, in order to make up for being behind schedule, we would all stop to scout it, and then run together through the rapid, proceeding on to make miles. This made photography of the rafts in the rapid impossible for the passengers. There was a bit of grumbling, so we concocted an alternative plan. Two boats would depart immediately from camp, leaving cleanup to the other three, who would come along as soon as possible. The first two would run Lava Falls without scouting, and stop to allow photographers to shoot the other three as they came through. This was considered somewhat risky for a first year boatman in the canyon.

Alan and John were to take off immediately, and I hopped in John's boat. He had me row the miles to Lava, while he lounged around like a Greek god on the stern, shoes off and lifejacket draped over a spare oar (no, not on his person).

As we passed Vulcan's Anvil, we could hear a horrific roar from downstream, and I turned to check on John—when would he take over the oars?

He looked calmly at me and continued to relax. As we got closer and closer I began to feel a bit frantic. I could see the top of what was obviously a big drop, and could see nothing below on the river—a bad sign. And the noise: I hadn't heard anything like that in my river career.

My face must have said it all, because John finally sat up and said, "OK, I'll take over now." Picking up his shoes in one hand and lifejacket in the other, he casually stepped over the oar, stubbed his toe on the thole pin, and fell off the boat into the river. Looking down I saw his lifejacket and *nothing else*. My terror for him was surpassed only by my terror for myself and for the passengers.

In probably the longest second of my life, John came to the surface. His relaxed expression was totally gone, replaced by the biggest-eyed look of shock I have ever seen. He abandoned his shoes, slipped the lifejacket over one arm, started swimming toward the boat and yelled "Get the boat straight!" as he scrambled up the side. I put in a few frantic strokes on the right oar and rolled off the seat as John took the oars.

We were staring down into the big hole at the top of Lava Falls. I grabbed a rope and was underwater, deluged by waves of muddy river. In an interminable fifteen seconds, we slowly rose up from the first hole, all intact and present, went into the big wave at the bottom, and came out into quiet water below: upright, alive, ecstatic!

There sat John, clenching the oars, with his lifejacket still slung loosely around one arm. He said not a word as we floated by the other boat offloading photographers. It was a long time before he turned to me and asked meekly, "Do you think you could row for a bit?"

THE STORY

Tim Cooper

It's time for bed again. The Boy will need to hear another story. Preferably a long one; ideally one that doesn't end. Lucky for me I have this vast treasure of a tale that I've stored on the leaky floppy disk of my cortex; a story of Remote Glacier and the River Kleena Kleen, of Granite Mountain, Copper Canyon and The Maze. It's a tale all true, richly embellished, misty and more heroic in the soft focus of time, with a cast drawn from that pantheon of characters who were and are my friends: larger than life, bright and timeless as the stars, strong and wise and funny. All handsome men and lovely women who could perform the impossible with a wink and a laugh.

This is a story drawn from the most Golden of Ages, the best and worst of times. It is filled with crisp images of desert mornings and snowy mountain moonlight, of wet rope and rotten handholds, of longings deeper than the sea, of moments when there was no time for terror, of aching love and hate and beauty. These things are in my story. I think it best to introduce the Boy to it while he still thinks it natural for bears to talk.

More often than not, the stage is set in that most sublime of earth's scenic spectacles, the Grand Canyon, where the actions of men easily take on the grandeur of their surroundings, where there was, once upon a time…

"…a trip where your daddy was rowing the old *Roaring Springs*. She had a little bit of magic in her, that boat. I think it must have been in the left side hatch, 'cause rocks never got anywhere close to that, while the right front footwell, on the other hand—"

"Tell me the one about the 'Too-Cool Doctors in the Matching Gold Chains,' Daddy."

"You just heard that one. Anyway we had made it down to Lava Falls, which some people call Vulcan, after the God of the Forge—"

"How about 'Andre's Big Water Run,' Daddy? Could you really have thrown a cat through the hole in the boat?"

"A little one, but this is a better story. See there we were, and we'd been there for a long time. Everyone was getting jittery and it was late in the day, but it was a nasty water level."

"*Way* to the Ugly?"

"Yeah. But RD wanted to go. He needed to go. His markers had told him that the water wasn't coming up until the next full moon—"

"Did he brush the sacred cornmeal with an eagle feather?"

"No, that was another guy. But maybe we should have blessed a little Bisquick for him that day, for all the good his calculations did. Kenton said it was the same water level as when he got hurt going over the dome rock upside down. It had squeezed him pretty good, and conked him on the noggin."

"Did it bust Kenton's head, Daddy?"

"I don't think anything could do that. But Kenton didn't want to be punished again thataway, so he elected to watch a run. The rest of us were hoping the dam would give us enough water to run the left side."

"Those sonsabitches?"

"Yeah, but don't say that, OK? Anyway, we sat up on the rock while RD and the raft went through. Regan always has the two biggest, strongest guys on his boat through Lava. For luck, I guess. But when Vulcan saw those big bruisers sliding down the tongue he must have thought it was three fatted calves. He flipped them over like this—plop—no up and down or spectacular sideways action. Just—flop—like a pig on a spit. Then they went over the dome rock upside-down with nary a lifejacket showing above the surface. That scared the devil out of everyone. We found out later that one guy got a little scraped up and the boat had a gouge on the deck from one side to the other; but it looked like they all three could have been pinched in half, like you might do to a red ant that bit you for no reason. The raft made it somehow but he went right over the domer too. We all thought that would wreck a dory."

"What did you do, Daddy?"

"Well, we all sat there with our jaws on our chests for a while. Then Kenton said he was going to run the Slot."

"But wasn't that closed, Daddy?"

"It was closed, liquidated, gone, pao, completamente finito. But Kenton saw it there. I stood on my head and crossed my eyes and couldn't see anything but a solid wall of water seventy-five feet high. Kenton said, 'There's a little tongue feeding through right....THERE! Did you see that?' Well, maybe there was a bucketful of water that wasn't falling back on itself but I think it was just evaporating in the terrible wind that hole was making.

"Kenton was going to try it anyway. Said he'd rather flip in deep water than go over that rock again, which made a certain amount of sense, I guess. Anyway, he told this one guy who wanted to go with him what to do, and they went out there. He lined up on the bubbles just like there was a run there, pushed twice into the throat of that thing, and while they were falling, he jumped onto the shoulders of the guy in the front seat—"

"What happened?"

"Well, conviction is a marvelous tool, buddy. Kenton manufactured a slot in that wave that was just big enough for the *Emerald Mile* to climb out of the bottom of the trough. When he got almost to the top, the wave exploded underneath him. The boat came clear out of the water and did two complete backflips, maybe three—it was hard to tell from where I was standing. But it landed right side up. Nobody could believe it."

"I don't believe it either, Daddy."

"Well, that's what happened. And the rest of us were still up there wondering what to do. It was Andre, Ren and me and we weren't going to try either of those runs we'd seen. But we had to try something. It was getting dark, so we went back to the boats and saw that the water was coming up. We decided to go across to the left side and check out the run from there.

"I had this woman on my boat whose name was Lydia. She had been down the canyon once before, but the last time she had walked around Lava Falls. It had been eating at her ever since. She really wanted to go but she was scared to death. When she saw RD flip, she had just caved in on herself, like a wounded swan. For some reason she had singled me out as the boatman with the qualities she required. She knew if she came across the river with us she would have to run the rapid 'cause we couldn't pick her up below on that side. The worry was wearing her down. She only weighed about forty pounds by the time she got on my boat. She sat down, and said in a voice about this big, 'Can I go with you, Coop?' Well, I had a lot on my mind and was pretty much convinced that I wasn't going to survive the afternoon anyway, so I said sure. And we went across.

"Ren had put together in his mind this run that only he could have thought up. It involved four complete three-sixties, and oar vaulting over one rock that was three feet out of the water. He wasn't as good then as he later became. Later he got this kind of ruthless concentration to him, like a gunfighter, and he was really good. But that day he was spooked. He didn't want anyone in the boat with him 'cause he was going to do all those pivots and that leapfrog stuff without going any further than eighteen inches from the left bank. Thought the added weight might slow him down. He had a wild look in his eye, like a cornered weasel, and he went down along the shore to check out his run by himself.

"Andre and I went high to look at the regular left run, but mainly to let the water come up. It was almost dark, and Lydia was down to about twenty-five pounds. RD had flipped three hours before, and the rest of the group probably figured we had decided to hike out Prospect Canyon.

"Andre and I finally got up the gumption to run when Ren burst out of the brush like a flushed pheasant. 'Snake!' he yells. Ren hates snakes. He's running to the boat waving his arms like this: 'Snake!' It was hanging in the trees, and he had come face to face with it. 'Snake!' he keeps yelling like it's after him. He didn't even see the rapid. Since he doesn't have a knife he had to stop and untie the boat. Gone are all thoughts of pivots and twists; he's getting the *hell* out of there.

"Then it occurs to him that he needs weight in the boat and someone to bail. 'Lydia!' he screams. 'Get IN the boat!' I don't have the chance to explain to him that she is, by now, without mass. They are pulling backward down the tongue. Ren somehow gets the bow around and the last thing I see is the *Hidden Passage* on the face of the biggest hole on earth with Lydia plastered on the bowhatch like decoupage."

"What happened, Daddy?"

"Well, frenzy works too sometimes, son, and they made it. Went right through the bottom hole too, but we didn't get to see that because we were in the rapid by then."

"Did you make it?"

"Piece of cake. We had the water. Didn't even have to bail."

"Wow, Daddy. You must have been the best."

"Well, for a while there, I guess we all were."

"Tell me another story."

"Sure, buddy. I really only know this one story, and it doesn't really end. We'll pick it up tomorrow after you've had a good sleep."

"Can I go down the river someday too?"

"Hey, I'm making your boat right now and I'm going to put a little bit of magic in every hatch. I'll even put some in the footwells, too. Now good-night."

THE TRUTH OR TOMATOES?
A Loose Story About a Loose Boat

Bob Melville

T he first story I ever heard about running the Colorado River through the Grand Canyon remains my favorite, but I don't remember where I heard it, or who told it to me.

"Crazy" Allen Wilson was running a single motorboat trip during his spring break from college. While fixing dinner at Ledges Camp, Crazy went out on the boat to get a tomato. He had to pull up a fresh case, which he then left out on top of the hatch. Crazy meant to go back down to the boat and loosen the tie-up ropes after the dinner clean up, but one of the passengers began to give him a back rub. Unable to muster the energy to take care of any more of his nightly duties, he succumbed to relaxation, hoping his swamper would take care of the boat.

When Crazy heard the snap of the rope, he knew his hopes were unfulfilled, and his worst nightmare was beginning. He sat up in time to see, by the dim night light, the boat sliding down the ledges, out into the river, and downstream. Crazy would have preferred to keep this event quiet until morning, since there wasn't really anything they could do, but his swamper also heard the rope snap. The swamper sat bolt upright and watched the boat slide into the river, at which point he screamed, "THE BOAT!"

Now everybody was awake and while not everybody realized what the problem was, they knew there was a problem. Several folks ran down to the end of the camp, and confirmed that the boat had indeed floated off downstream, and was not waiting obediently in some nearby eddy. It was a long time before Crazy could get everybody to go back to bed. And needless to say, the folks were up pretty early. There wasn't much to do, since all their food was on the boat, so they packed their bags and sat on the rocks waiting for another boat. Crazy assured them that one would come along, he just wasn't sure when, or if there would be enough room on said boat for his folks.

Eventually, a boatman named Henry showed up with an empty boat.

The charter he was supposed to pick up at Phantom had cancelled while he was on the water, so he was running out without passengers. Since he was deadheading, he knew who was upstream. There were enough boats scheduled to come past them that Crazy decided they would catch a ride with Henry only as far as Havasu, where he was confident he could catch a slower ride out for his folks. According to plan, a Western rig picked them up at Havasu and fed them that night.

The next day Crazy found his boat tied up below Lava. Upon inspection he found everything as he had left it, except that the case of tomatoes was gone.

That's a happy ending to an interesting story, but it isn't the end.

A year or two later, Crazy went to Big Bend to run the Rio Grande. Apparently there is a spot at the put-in where people congregate and share their stories, imbibements and whatever else is up for sharing. Over a bottle of Southern Comfort (or some such honey fur-wrapped poison), someone started telling "the damnedest thing I ever saw…" stories. One fellow owned up to being a motor boatman in the Grand Canyon, and the damnedest thing he had ever seen occurred when he was running a single boat trip. There weren't any other trips around when he got to Lava, so he couldn't leave anyone on shore to shoot pictures of their run, which disappointed a bunch of his folks. After he ran the rapid, some of them wanted to climb back up the rapid along the shore and get one last look or picture. When they reached the viewpoint, they yelled back that there was another boat coming, and the rest of the folks got off the boat and ran up to watch.

When the boatman joined them he could see right off something was strange about this boat, and then he realized there were no people on it! The empty boat drifted down and executed a perfect run down the right side (not quite straight for the big wave at the bottom, but how many of us are?). He gathered all his folks back on his boat and motored downstream, retrieved the loose boat and tied it to shore. There was a case of tomatoes sitting out on the deck, so he took them, figuring that was fair payment for tying up someone's loose boat. "Damnedest thing I ever saw…"

After a short silence, Crazy said, "So you're the son of a bitch that stole my tomatoes!"

⌁

Later I got to work a little bit with Crazy, rowing snout rigs for ARTA Southwest. I loved telling that story so much I never told it to Crazy for fear it wasn't true. More recently I realized it didn't matter if it was true or not; the distinction didn't affect my telling any of my other stories. So one year at the Guides Training Seminar I told my version to Crazy and asked if there was any truth in it.

When I finished the story he looked at me incredulously and said, "No. It was a case of oranges."

A HERO STORY

Creek Hanauer

Every kayaker has a hero story—some for great derring-do with intent: hero runs in Crystal or Upset, some for great derring-do in spite of themselves: running the Ledge Hole in Lava twice, thinking to improve that first mistaken line. It was in 209 Mile Rapid one year that a kayaker named Elliot made his hero story, under the latter circumstances.

We found ourselves lunching at Granite Park, river left at the top of the rapid. 205 Mile Rapid had issued a small post-Lava wake-up call to the kayakers, so lunch above 209 seemed a dandy idea.

As we set up for lunch we noticed the *whomp* of the big wave crashing in the middle of the rapid below. A couple of moments later we noticed it again. Soon we realized that we could feel the concussion of water and air with each *whomp*. That was enough to make folks wander down to look this beast over.

The rapid is created by a huge rock bar deposited by the discharge from 209 Mile Canyon. Standing on river left, looking out across the bar to the rapid on the right side, we could see the wave that was periodically shaking the ground. It's in the center of the rapid, just below the entry. It builds, then subsides to gather more energy, builds again, multiple times, until its concentrated mass is so great that it abruptly crashes, causing the top-heavy wave face to collapse straight down into the hole it has created, with a river-shaking *whomp*. God bless the inattentive soul who strays in there at the wrong time!

The wave is there at every flow. It's always impressive—an obvious place to avoid, accomplished by an equally obvious move to the left at the top of the rapid. Most kayakers enter at the center of the tongue, move smartly left above the hole and skirt the edge of the monster wave, staring into it in admiration and relief as they paddle past.

Elliot was an easy guy to like: quiet, unassuming and fit, a gamer who had celebrated his sixty-second birthday on the trip. He'd arrived on this day having run most of the rapids above, but he had exercised good judgment and ridden the raft for a day here and there throughout the trip.

That day he was back in his boat and apparently going to be the last kayaker down the rapid. We had eighteen kayakers that trip. I'd set up as safety boater, hanging in the roiling excuse for an eddy on river left, just beside the *whomping* wave. I watched people run, and counted as they went by so I wouldn't space out a client. That's harder for a safety boater to do than you might imagine, because we often need our toes to count over ten, and what with feet in the boat, and booties and spray skirts in between, it can become pretty stressful. Well anyway, here came our last boat and it's Elliot; I hadn't missed anyone after all.

Elliot entered a little right on the tongue, but he was pointed left and paddling left, so we were both pretty relaxed at that point. Elliot's kayak began to gain the speed of the rapid as he dropped in, and though he'd gotten the correct angle, I feared he was staring at the wave, which was in six- to eight-foot form that day. Still pointed left, he paddled with greater intensity, but he looked at nothing but that big ole wave. We've got a saying in kayaking: "Look where you want to go, not at what you fear most!" Elliot's eyes were fixed on the ever-building might of the wave he had no desire to engage. I sat to the left of the wave with growing alarm. I started whistling and thrusting my paddle in the air, indicating the urgent need to get left, but Elliot had eyes only for the giant maw directly below him—and then he was in it. Faster than he could have consciously registered he was stopped cold and by god, he was facing me, side surfing! He was bloody side surfing the monster. He was holding onto a high brace, being bounced around the bottom of the hole like a basketball being dribbled by an NBA point guard. Elliot's eyes were now on me with that deer-in-the-headlights look. I could only stare in wonder.

He must have been able to feel the wave growing above him. He must have known the enormous mass of water would soon crash down on him. The wave finally reached critical mass and crashed. The mountain of water came down on him, with its trademark *whomp*—but he wasn't there! Elliot had shot out of the imminent carnage on a horizontal geyser of water, like a human projectile. At mach one, he headed straight across the eddy and onto my front deck, up on my spray-skirt—still in a high brace position. His eyes were as big and round as saucers; his mouth formed a perfect O as his boat came to rest on top of my cockpit. We just silently stared at each other, both of our mouths open wide enough to catch flies; his in shock, mine in awe. His boat slowly slid off my deck, back into the water while I stared in amazement at Elliot, the living proof of good karma and the benevolence of the River Gods.

Elliot gave me a disarming smile as our boats rested, side by side. We silently high-fived, then went to join the others, waiting below.

WET ANKLES

Mathieu Brown

Many first timers, particularly women, can find the indoctrination into the art of peeing on the river strange and awkward. Most self-respecting river guides can comfortably carry on a conversation while nonchalantly relieving themselves. Obviously the river is not a setting for modesty, and this behavior, in accompaniment with ample food and drink, sparse clothing, and loose language only adds weight to the theory that river runners are primarily hedonists with no sense of social etiquette, but you should make up your own mind on that matter.

When I deliver the orientation for a Grand Canyon river trip I always emphasize the part about peeing. First of all it is important to pee in the water, and all the way in the water. For most of us this is counterintuitive, but the environmental consequence of peeing on the beach is that our campsites smell like cat boxes. Furthermore, if we are too relaxed with our riverside aim and pee on the shoreline then those green spots of algae show up. They make the river feel less like a desert paradise and more like the warm shallow end at the public pool. Second I tell people not to be ashamed of their pee. I do all of this because it puts a kink in things when people walk over a quarter mile up or down the beach to hide behind a distant rock so they can attempt privacy. On occasion, I will even go so far as to have a female guide demonstrate how to pee with a few pointers: 1) face your danger, don't face the river and stick your buns in the air for everyone to see; 2) use nearby objects such as the side of a parked raft to help shelter yourself; 3) lastly, do not say, "Don't watch me, I'm peeing," because nothing draws attention to yourself faster.

In the late 1990s the water levels in Lake Mead started to drop, exposing shorelines of fresh sediment. All of the sand that had been washing downstream had settled out in this upstream part of the lake and was now making mud banks of the highest quality. Our river trip got a new group of passengers at the Whitmore helipad. We were going three days to the lake, and everyone received the standard orientation. But with such a brief trip it is nearly impossible to get everyone trained in the nuances of river running before it comes to an end, and sometimes we guides are not as good at telling people all the details they should know. For instance, we did not give any pointers on the art of peeing. With this in mind, imagine a lunch stop at Lava Cliff, mile 246.

We pulled in at the long beach and one of the guides took some of the sturdier patrons through the tamarisk maze to look at the Buzz Holmstrom, Amos Burg and Willis Johnson inscription. Upon returning, the lunch table was out and people scattered up and down the beach like ants looking for nooks of privacy so they could pee.

We were enjoying a nice deli lunch spread when we heard screaming coming from the far downstream end of the beach. "Has anyone seen Cindy?" someone asked. At the sound of the cries two guides dashed downstream, triggering an all-out passenger stampede to the far end of the beach. Upon arrival we found Cindy with shorts around ankles and butt straight up in the air. She was laughing hysterically in a pretzel position with both her hands and feet stuck in the mud. Luckily Cindy was not too embarrassed and was doing a good job making fun of her predicament. Despite the temptation to stand around and soak up every moment of the situation, one of the guides stepped forward to help. He got about three feet from the shore when his flip-flop was swallowed by the wet goop. He struggled to help get Cindy's shorts back up before aborting the mission, barely escaping to regroup for a more thoughtful approach. "Get the spine board!" someone yelled.

While we waited for the extraction equipment, Cindy relayed her story. She had been in this position for about ten minutes before she started hollering. Making sure to pee in the wet sand she had waded out a few feet into ankle deep water to do her business. She ignored the mud that lapped at her feet, but while squatting and peeing she had quickly sunk inch by inch up to the point of no return. When she went to stand up, she lost her balance and had to put her hand down, sinking it into the mud. She then tried to pull her shorts up with her one free hand when she lost her balance again and sank that hand in the mud. The more she struggled the deeper she sank and the more she laughed. She waited in crab position thinking of what to do, all the while slowly sinking deeper.

Within seconds of Cindy telling her story we had the spine board on one side of her and a folded table on the other. We performed a well-executed rescue and pulled Cindy from the mud.

After thinking back on the event I half wondered if Cindy called for help because she figured we just had to see the absurdity of her situation. I am sure she could have wiggled out without all the hoopla, but sometimes all our modesty is worth pushing aside for a good laugh. The following day Cindy's adventure inspired us to celebrate sympathetic Pee-Like-a-Girl Day, during which all the men crouched in the water up to their ankles when peeing. After that experience I think I finally understand why women always go to the bathroom in pairs.

Rock Squirrel
Larry Stevens
1983

MY FAVORITE RIVER HAT

Pete Winn

I was really attached to my river hat. It was part of my identity. I needed it. That is, until I met Helen.

She was one of those unforgettable characters you get to meet in the canyon. Everyone loved her. On our oar trips in the early 1970s, we used to encourage our passengers to switch boats every day. After a few days, people would wait to see which boat Helen got on, and then rush to join her.

Helen was a great storyteller. She could also read palms and tea leaves. Before we had even floated through the Paria Riffle, she asked me if I was a Scorpio, then told me it was really OK if I was.

She really liked my hat. I don't know why, it was just a dirty old cowboy hat that had long ago lost its shape and looked more like a Huck Finn hat. She was always stealing it so she could wear it. As long as she rode on my boat that was OK with me.

I tried to teach her how to row, but the oars were just too heavy and the eddy fence currents always dragged her off the rowing seat. But she loved to help out in camp. I recall she made the coffee almost every morning.

Back in those days, the Diamond Creek road wasn't maintained, and there wasn't a boat ramp at Pearce, so we always had dinner at Bridge Canyon or Separation Canyon, floated all night to Emery Falls, and a motor boat towed us from there to South Cove. We had a wild party on the boats that night, and Helen was the star.

The next day, we'd said good-byes with tears in our eyes, and no one was really ready to face the world we'd completely forgotten about. The passenger bus was about to leave us behind when I impulsively hailed the driver. I jumped aboard, ran back to Helen's seat, gave her a big kiss, put my cherished old river hat on her head and rushed off the bus.

I later went to visit her at her home in San Francisco. My hat was hanging on the wall above her fireplace, surrounded by pictures of her canyon friends. Did I mention that Helen was a seventy-five-year-old retired fortuneteller, with several grandkids my age?

ALL THE WAY
Lees Ferry to Diamond Creek or Lake Mead

IT'S ONE OF THE GREAT experiences of a lifetime: a river trip all the way through the Grand Canyon. You're going to climb into a boat and float, motor, paddle or row all the way down: two hundred and twenty-five or two hundred and eighty miles. You might be taking six days on a motor rig; you might do it in twenty-two on a dory. During this time you will come to know your fellow voyagers and your environment better than you ever expected, and you become comfortable sleeping on sand and rocky ledges. The routine of loading and unloading the boats is simple and welcome. You begin to believe the old superstition about river karma and start helping with the dishes. After all, "clean dishes, clean runs," right?

Something happens to one's sense of time on a full-canyon trip. The length of days begins to melt into the walls of the canyon and the rushing water. People who stay to see the whole canyon sink into the rhythm of the place. The light feels more natural than any they have experienced since they were children. They wake up with the dawn and go to bed with the dark, learn stars never seen at home. Someone might fall in love.

People who are together for a whole trip often become fast friends. Sometimes events conspire to create a situation in which everyone, guides and passengers alike, learn something. Guides help guests stretch their limits. Guests help guides continue to appreciate the canyon. No one who has been down the entire river can fail to be changed somehow. The length of time you are on the river matters some, but what is more important is seeing a canyon begin, deepen and wind its way across the land until it reaches its end. It is a powerful experience to watch a landscape be shaped, and you come to understand something of the span of years this place has been under construction. That depth of time makes one feel at once insignificant and infinite.

You may only see the canyon once, and those images will remain imprinted in your mind as images of an unchanging place. We all take these images home with us. We'll be reminded how it felt to wake in the early light to the sound of the canyon wrens. We think of how good that cold drink of water tasted after the hike we thought would never end, how that little waterfall seemed like heaven on earth after the burning heat. And we remember how surprised and proud we were to be using our bodies, pushing our boundaries, recalling skills long unused. These memories won't change, yet the canyon will ever change: day to day, season to season, year to year. Boatmen and women who have done fifty or a hundred trips are not bored; they keep coming back to a different world every time they arrive. There are as many reasons for returning as there are travelers, yet the ultimate reason remains the same: the river and her canyon keep calling us back…

GLORY DAYS
A Boatman's Story

Lew Steiger

It was 1972, a three-boat trip. Bill Gloeckler was the trip leader. He was twenty-three at the time and this was maybe his tenth trip. The other boatmen, way junior in experience, were Bruce Winter and Bart Henderson. Bart was freelancing that year and had just met the others. This is his story. He told it to a bunch of us at Vermilion Cliffs years ago and we laughed so hard we cried.

They had a tight schedule, but overall the mission seemed simple enough: run in empty to Phantom on the first day, then pick up forty-five passengers on the morning of the second day. Deposit everyone at Diamond Creek early on day five and drive the boats back around to the ferry that same night, rig the next morning, and start another trip.

They got to the warehouse at the crack of dawn on day one and to their surprise the food wasn't packed. That set them back an hour or two. They finished rigging at the ferry about noon, still only a couple of hours behind schedule, but then none of the motors would start. None of 'em. They carried three per boat, but all of those were mismatched. They'd been given three different sizes: thirties, thirty-fives, forties.

Gloeckler grinned and said a few swear words. He tinkered around, they cannibalized what they had, and finally left the ferry late in the afternoon with one working motor for each boat.

They ran the Twenties in the pitch dark and tied up in the rocks below 25 Mile Rapid, pretty scared. Gloeckler rubbed his hands together and drew a big breath. "Well, we've had a hard day boys, but I think the worst of this trip's behind us," he said. "Let's cook some steaks."

They lit a Coleman lantern and rustled up some wood, got a little fire going in the rocks. Then they had to have some steak sauce too, so Bruce took the lantern and went down to find it. He crossed 'em up on the rocks, though, and fell, just as he got to the river. The lantern exploded.

A huge ball of flame erupted next to the upstream boat, and then everything went black. Up on shore their eyes were all adjusted to the light and after the fireball nobody saw anything but spots. "Bruce!" Gloeckler yelled in the darkness. "Are you okay?!"

No answer but the hiss of the shattered lantern. That and the swift rush of current sweeping along the shoreline and stacking into the boats, running under a half acre of rubber. They groped their way down to the upstream side of the boats. Really, it was too dark to move. "Uh-oh," Gloeckler said. "He's under the boats."

"He's dead," the swamper moaned. "He's history." The swamper's name was Joe and this was his second trip ever.

Thirty yards downstream they heard choking and spluttering, then a cry. "I'm okay!" Bruce yelled.

"Whew," Gloeckler said. "Thank God."

For a moment there was silence. Everybody breathed a huge sigh of relief.

"No I'm not!" Bruce yelled. "I'm NOT okay!"

They got a flashlight and checked him out. He had a twelve-inch gash from knee to ankle and the blood was pumping forth in great spurts. Gloeckler sucked a little air through his teeth and squinted at Bart. "We'll have to sew him up," he said. "Better get some whiskey."

They didn't have any sutures in the first aid kit, so Bart got some cotton thread and a straight needle out of the patch kit instead, and Joe brought the whiskey. Bruce's dad was a surgeon so they figured maybe that qualified Gloeckler to do the job. Bruce didn't want any whiskey though, so Gloeckler drank some and then Bart had some too; then Gloeckler poured a healthy shot on Bruce's leg and stitched it up.

Next day they promoted Joe to boatman and moved Bruce up to coach. Joe did pretty good until they got to Hance, but he dinged his motor there, so they had to stop and cannibalize a couple more of the dead spares. They arrived at Phantom Ranch around four in the afternoon.

The people weren't there. They went to the ranger station and summoned a chopper to evacuate Bruce; then Gloeckler called Henry, the owner of the company.

"You boys just sit tight," Henry said. "Hear? Don't you leave without 'em."

So they begged the ranger to let them stay the night at Phantom, and finally he acquiesced. Bruce got evacuated, and the others went to bed. Just before he went to sleep, Bart had a thought. "Maybe they won't come," he said out loud. "Please God, don't let them come."

The people came down the trail that night, as luck would have it, all forty-five of them in the darkness. So next morning there was nothing to do but go. They had a hundred and fifty miles to make in a little over two days, and as long as they didn't hike anything or let the people have too many pit stops, Bart figured, they might just make it.

Gloeckler took a good boat and the second-best motor, which was kind of a clunker. He gave Joe the worst boat and the worst motor, and he told Joe to stay right close and just follow him. To Bart he gave a good boat and the fastest motor of all. "Okay, buddy," Gloeckler told Bart, "you just hang back and pick up the pieces."

So off they went, rrrrrr, balls to the wall. Somehow they made it through intact until they got to Crystal. Naturally they didn't stop to look, there was really no time for that, but then again there was Joe, never run the river before and uh-oh, there he went, straight-off-Adolph into the big hole: Caraaaash! Forty-five degrees. The boat contorted wildly, people tumbled every which way, and then it plowed straight over the rock island with Joe crouched in the cockpit maintaining a death grip on the throttle, still motoring away…rrrrBAM! rrrrrrrrBOOM! rrrrrrCRUNCH! Bart could see the motor jump every time it hit. The boat hung here, spun there, finally it floated off somehow and Bart caught them down below, just drifting.

Well, that motor was destroyed and about four sections of the boat were completely flat, hanging dead underneath the frame. The thing about Henry's boats and those aircraft carrier decks, though, was you could lose a few sections anyway and still keep going.

Gloeckler came over and studied the situation. "No problem," he said. "We'll patch her tonight. We've just gotta make another engine work now and we're doin' fine." So Gloeckler got in there; they took a lower unit off the one, stole a carburetor from that one and finally they made one work.

They camped somewhere not all that far down, and cooked dinner in the dark. It started to rain.

It rained all night.

They took off the next morning. It was still raining. The river became a chocolate brown swirl and water streamed off the cliff faces. They ran all day long and the rain never let up for a second. The people were in shock by then; they were starting to look and act like prisoners of war.

The boatmen went full throttle all the way. The only thing they were thinking of by that time was escape. They made it down to just above Lava and here came a plane, circling. It was Henry himself. "Diamond Creek's washed out boys," he said. "You're gonna haveta make it on down there to Pearce Ferry with these people." Henry was sweating bullets over his next trip, was the deal. He had to have Gloeckler there to lead it and at least one of those same boats.

They forged on. But somewhere around Parashant Wash, Joe dinged another engine. And this time it wasn't quite so simple to get a new one going. Plus, that boat of his was losing air all over the place. In fact, it was sinking. But there they were, and it was getting late. They had to reach Lake Mead that night before it got too dark to see. Once they hit the lake they could just motor all night and get to Pearce by morning, easy. Heh.

"Damn," Gloeckler said. "I sure do hate to do this Bart, but I'm gonna have to take your engine (the fast one) and break for the lake empty. I hate like hell to do it to you buddy, but you're gonna have to take Joe and lead him out of here with these people. It's the only way."

Bart squinted at Gloeckler and kept his real thoughts to himself. "Okay, Bill," he said. "You're the trip leader. I'll give 'er my best shot."

So they loaded about thirty-five folks onto Bart's boat, maybe ten on Joe. Gloeckler got the good engine and Bart took Gloeckler's old clunker. Rrrrrrr… Gloeckler escaped in a cloud of exhaust. The last thing, Bart remembers, Gloeckler turned and looked back at him with an all-knowing little shrug and just the briefest wave imaginable—he was genuinely apologetic. Then he was gone, vanished into the sunset.

So Bart and Joe forged on, too. They were chugging along and then they got to a simple place, just a split around an island, but the water was really low, and rrrrCRASH! Joe's motor bit the dust for good.

Well, they tied Joe alongside; it was nearly dark by then. Bart had forty-five people and two boats on one old clunker motor and no more spares. All he wanted then was a camp, any camp at all would do.

He got hung up once, then again. He couldn't miss the islands because full throttle at that point was just barely faster than drifting. By that time, of course, the people had turned to drink. They'd ceased to care. They were standing up and yelling obscenities at the rain, swaying to a beat all their own. Bart couldn't even see over the top of them anymore.

Bart rounded a corner and there was Gloeckler tied up in an eddy. Bart caught the eddy, barely, and eased the flotilla over to him.

"I couldn't do it," Gloeckler groaned. He was shaking his head. "I wanted to, dammit. I tried to. I just couldn't make myself do it."

The next day their double-rig became two singles in 205 Mile Rapid, with the motorless boat getting stuck in the little eddy on the right, minus a boatman and only carrying a few passengers. Bart had to go back up the left eddy and ferry across to save them. And it kept raining of course. They left Joe's boat at Diamond Creek and Henry had to make a new plan for his other trip and finally they got to the lake, just one day late. Then Pearce was washed out too and they had to go on to South Cove and finally it was the end. Everybody lived happily ever after.

It's hard to say why we laughed so hard when Bart told this story at Vermilion or why it made us feel so good. Most likely it was thinking about Gloeckler making his getaway, and then that he couldn't do it, couldn't leave old Bart. Or maybe it was remembering that particular time overall and how wild and fun it all was back then, or just thinking how tough and resilient you are at that age, even if you are dumb, too.

Now Where Did I Put That?
Mary Williams
2000

PIRATES OF THE GRANITE GORGE

Creek Hanauer

Ravens fascinate me. My daughter's middle name is Raven. Around my home at the mouth of Knownothing Creek on the South Fork of the Salmon River in northern California, ravens are loud, bold marauders, soaring on the late afternoon air currents above the mouth of the creek, raiding nests and generally making sure every other living thing in range of their abrasive, coughing voices is aware these plunderers are in the hood.

But by far the most audacious of the ravens make their homes along the Colorado River through the Grand Canyon: the pirates of the Granite Gorge. At the beginning of Grand Canyon river trips we remind each other to secure our camp gear against the intrusion of a host of potential nefarious pests: mice, fire ants, scorpions, ringtail cats and rattlesnakes, to name a few. And ravens. River rangers have been known to warn private groups, "You will be assigned two ravens..." Folks tend to scoff, "Come on man, it's a *bird...!*"

...We arrived at Carbon Creek too early for lunch, but with plenty of time for a hike up the creek. It was a warm, sunny day, no ravens in evidence, so it was pretty easy to overlook their probable presence. Thinking ahead, our food organizer decided to get a jump on dinner and pulled the partially frozen halibut steaks from the cooler to defrost them on the raft tubes while we hiked up the canyon. Bad move number one. Everyone went on the hike. Bad move number two. I remember glancing at the bags of halibut steaks, thawing in the sun and having the fleeting shadow of a discomforting thought cross my mind before I turned up the canyon and immediately forgot anything but the adventure ahead. When we returned a couple hours later the warmth of the summer sun coaxed us back to the river, very pleased with the day. Pleased, that is, until someone finally woke up to the fact that every one of our bags full of halibut was missing—dinner gone before lunch.

To the ravens sitting in the rock crannies above we must have looked a lot like a colony of ants that had just lost its queen. We jumped around the boats cursing as we scrambled to look in the bilges, under ropes, straps and duffel, all to no avail. Probably too stuffed to move, the ravens politely refrained from rubbing it in with their infamous laughter.

…122 Mile Camp is a big one at lower flows and folks like to camp far and wide. On this trip a young fella had spread his sleeping kit out on the upper reaches of the sandbar. After he had bathed in the river and spruced up he went off to the kitchen to grab a brewski and snag some munchies before dinner. He had stuffed some of his gear back in his dry bag, but hadn't secured it (not much of a challenge either way as ravens have been seen unzipping closed tent flaps). Feet crossed and laying back up in camp, he was startled by a cry from the sandbar and looked up to see another boater pointing to a raven with a baggie of stuff in its beak, struggling to fly off with its ill gotten gains.

"That's my wallet! My ID!" he shouted as he sprang from his beach chair and took off across the sandbar after the fleeing thief. The raven was laboring mightily, dragging the cache across the sand, never quite able to lift its treasure off the ground, but unwilling to quit trying, so our young man was closing on the tenacious buccaneer. Another thought had crossed his mind and it caused him to greatly accelerate his pace with the cry, "Shit! That's my stash!" With this realization our young hero—with a Herculean burst of speed—overtook the scoundrel at river's edge, but the raven fled the clutches of its pursuer at the last second by dropping the weighty booty in the river, luckily just within reach of our desperate dupe. Up in camp, not a dry eye to be found, we rolled around holding our sides with laughter.

…The morning our group would be hiking to Thunder River our camp activity raised the bar far above the normal levels of chaos. We prepared for the river while putting together sandwiches, fruit and cookies for a sack lunch. With the camp scene in such a tizzy, two ravens sitting across the river made their move. They flew into camp together. Cawing loudly to announce their arrival one raven made a feint toward the gear piling up by the boats at the river's edge, distracting the easily distracted resident humans from noticing that the other raven had made a beeline to the lunch table and snatched a package of cookies in its beak, quickly swinging out over the river and back to the other side. Their taunting cries of victory followed us down river as we departed camp that morning.

This was a blow to the trip. We were running dangerously low on cookies too early in the trip for comfort. Then, a couple days later at Havasu, we were saved! A guide from a motor trip said their group had plenty of cookies and he could let us have a couple of packages. Since they'd be pulling out before our folks were back from hiking, their guide said he'd stash them in a shirt and stuff them in one of the nooks in the riverside rock shelf. What were we thinking? As the first hikers returned to the mouth of Havasu that afternoon they witnessed two ravens pull the tee shirt-wrapped cookie packages from the rock shelf. The dismayed hikers looked on in open-mouthed horror as the cookies tumbled down the rock, free of the shirt. Quicker than thought the ravens had both packages snatched up; once again our cookies disappeared in plain sight across the river.

⌒

Grand Canyon river guides are more than a little superstitious about the Colorado River's ravens. We all curse the stealthy devils when appropriate but—secretly—we all admire the freebooters' brazenness.

River guides and ravens. It must be the pirate thing.

SMOKED BOOGERS, EGGS AND SUDDEN DISCOMFORT—
Kayaking the Canyon in January

Ebb Exranger

E bb is not my real name, and this story isn't just about smoked boogers, eggs and sudden discomfort. It's really about an ex-pig (the human variety). I think it started with the Free Speech Movement in Berkeley, in the late '60s. Someone demanded the right to call policemen "pigs." Of course, the policemen objected, so the name stuck. Well, park service rangers are kind of quasi "pigs," so when I got a job as river ranger for Grand Canyon National Park, my old river guide buddies started calling me Piglet. The name grew on me, so I named my kayak *Piglet Too*. Made me think of Tigger, Eyore and Winnie the Pooh. I regarded the name as a term of endearment and didn't mind being identified that way.

Being Piglet was great during the river season. I got to run the canyon, literally and figuratively. For example, on one of my patrol trips, near Nankoweap I caught an old friend, who was lead guide for Willy World, without his lifejacket on. I could have given him a twenty-five dollar fine and a slap on the wrist, but he'd just be more careful not to get caught again. So instead I pushed him into the river and wouldn't let him out until he understood why it was a good idea to wear a lifejacket. There was no way he could file a complaint about Piglet brutality.

All The President's Men (Nixon's cronies) came on one of my official patrol trips. They were great party boys and fantastic liars. We realized we were going to run out of beer by the time we reached Phantom, so I radioed out for a dozen cases of whole blood (our code word, since we weren't supposed to drink in uniform). The message got to the wrong secretary, and political panic overcame the powers that be. After that, the park superintendent ordered us to change our code word.

I was a GS-5, bottom of the totem pole. Of course, Nixon's men were all GS-15s and were constantly telling me what to do. One at a time, I convinced them to take the oars and proceeded to direct them into a bad spot.

After a few good scares, they decided they could get their own beer.

The biggest problem, however, came at the end of the river season. I was a full-time river ranger with no reason to continue patrolling the river. What was I to do? I started going on backpack patrols so I wouldn't get stuck in Peyton Place (the rim). My supervisor tried to justify this to his supervisor, but the chief ranger didn't buy it. He was short on law enforcement rangers who could pass for a hotel employee, and I was selected to infiltrate the dorms of those dirty hippies. It wasn't my fault I was the only ranger with a beard, long hair, sandals and a necklace.

Well, I liked those hippies more than I liked being Piglet, so I quit. There was no way I was going to bust those guys for doing the same thing I used to do. And for sure I wasn't going to go off to twelve weeks of cop school and learn to shoot Hell's Angels.

After going through all that crap, I needed a great escape. The park service wouldn't let me take *Piglet Too* on a patrol trip, so I decided to do a trip without their permission. I wasn't too worried about being caught; I knew their only river ranger had just quit.

Kayaks don't hold much food or gear, so I made a couple of bust-ass trips to stash food along the river. I got a bad case of tendonitis from hiking Desert View to Tanner and back in one day, so I took two days to hike to the mouth of Havasu via Beaver Creek for my second stash.

So how do eggs, smoked boogers and sudden discomfort figure in? Well, I was proud to be a survivor of Black Beard's Death, which means you really have to like eggs. You had to put a whole raw egg in your mouth, stand on your head in a three-foot pit in the sand, break the shell with your teeth and swallow the entire egg raw, shell and all, without letting any of that nauseating mix dribble out your nose. If you did, you'd probably lose your Oreos and for sure lose your only chance to join the Survivors. But that didn't have anything to do with why I stashed eggs for my kayak trip.

I got the idea from a book called *Diet for a Small Planet.* I figured I needed a high protein, high energy diet that consumed the minimum amount of volume in my kayak. Eggs are the most complete source of protein, there are lots of calories in the yolk, plus they keep really well. So at each cache I stashed twenty-seven jumbo hard-boiled eggs, nine for each of three days.

Eggs are boring, even with Tabasco, so I needed to bring a luxury item to compensate. My favorite food was smoked boogers. Not the human variety, those are better raw. These are canned. (One of my biggest frustrations as a river guide was to fail to convince a pretty female passenger to stop wearing makeup on the river. When I finally accepted the fact that I'd failed, I would wait until she was almost done with her lunch, then I'd palm a big ugly smoked oyster, dripping with oil, sit down next to her, make a big show of picking my nose, show her the oyster and then gobble it up.) So I packed a tin of smoked oysters for each meal, full of laughs and greasy energy.

The sudden discomfort was actually a bad habit that I had no intention of kicking. I packed a bottle of it in each stash for general medicinal purposes. (Most of you have seen it called Southern Comfort, but it has nearly killed a few of my friends. At first it really warms your tummy, but it often leaves suddenly, and can cause severe discomfort.)

The final preparation for my trip involved a paint job. I chose canyon colors and did a good job of camouflaging my kayak, helmet, lifejacket and paddle. Just as I finished, the phone rang. It was Henry, an old river guide friend. He'd heard I quit my job and wanted to know if they'd hired a replacement. I told him no, he could probably have the job if he wanted it.

He didn't want it. He wanted to know if he was going to get caught if he did an illegal solo kayak trip that winter. Turns out he'd stashed food at two locations on his last commercial trip that fall and had just finished camouflaging his kayak. After some discussion, we decided we'd break the law together.

He drove out to Flagstaff, and we headed for the ferry on January 1. We both knew the Lees Ferry ranger and didn't want to upset him, so we arrived after dark and put in below the Paria Riffle. In the dark, we paddled past Navajo Bridge to make sure no one saw us, and began what became a truly unforgettable adventure.

Kayaking at night was spooky. Even the little riffles seemed huge. We were constantly yelling to each other, hoping the other guy wasn't swimming. It occurred to both of us that by going together, we had added an unexpected degree of responsibility to the trip.

I won't bore you with the day-to-day details of our adventure. Only a few memories really stick out. First, we were really surprised by how easy it is to kayak the canyon. It was the second time for each of us, and we didn't feel threatened at all. I swam House Rock, Lava Falls, 219 (the whirlpools got me) and 232. The swims weren't bad, but putting my sprayskirt back on with frozen fingers was a real hassle. Henry rolled in Soap Creek and Crystal. He lost his helmet in Soap, but had a wetsuit hood to keep his head warm. We spent several days kayaking solo, not knowing where the other guy was.

For the first few days, I had eaten my eggs with the shell on. I hated peeling them and figured the calcium wouldn't hurt me. I was wrong. It took three days for the shells to find their way out, and when they did they were rough. After that I started peeling the eggs.

By the time we got to Hance, it was apparent that my diet wasn't giving me enough energy. So we hatched a plan to buy a box of candy bars at Phantom Ranch. Since the hippies down there knew me, Henry hiked up and bought thirty Paydays, full of nuts and caramel. He told the cashier it was his friend's birthday, and he was giving everyone in the camp a candy bar since he'd forgotten to bring a birthday cake. I really doubt she believed him.

We kayaked past Phantom in the dark to avoid being seen. Those few miles were probably the scariest of the whole trip, especially near all those whirlpools under the silver bridge. The next day, we ran all the biggies without a hitch.

Henry made a couple of mistakes when he cached his food. First, he had too much to drink, and we couldn't find where we buried it. We had to break out the Southern Comfort to help jog his memory. Then, after we found the stash, he popped the cork on a bottle of wine to celebrate. He learned the hard way that a little wine on top of Southern Comfort makes for sudden discomfort. He also stashed a backpack stove with his food, and white gas had leaked out and been soaked up by his granola. White gas farts and belches not only stink, they're flammable.

There were some backpackers camped at Lower Bass. We tried to sneak past without being seen, but one of them yelled out. He announced that he was a National Park Service backcountry ranger, and that we were busted. Curiosity got the best of me, so I paddled over to see who he was. He certainly wasn't anyone I knew, so I told him I was an NPS river ranger and asked to see his backcountry permit. Turns out neither party had permits.

After a good laugh, we headed on downriver. We were full of Grand Canyon energy. We ran over the top of Rancid Tuna Fish Sandwich Rock, down the little channel on the left side of what was later to be called Randy's Rock, through the narrow shoot on the left at Bedrock, and into and around Helicopter Eddy above Granite Narrows. We laughed all day.

From Lees Ferry to somewhere around Deer Creek, the air temperature in the shade never got above freezing. We both had ice in our beards and our lifejacket buckles were frozen from spray in the rapids. It seemed like our hands were permanently wrapped around our paddles. During long flat stretches, we'd pry them loose and stick them in the river to warm them up. Other than cold hands, we were hot, both literally and figuratively. It was the best place in the world to be.

Ten days after we started, we cruised into Pearce Ferry. It was time to think about ice cream and beer. Our shuttle driver wasn't there, so we walked the ten miles to Meadview, catching the store just before it closed. On our way back through town we disturbed a dog that just happened to belong to the Lake Mead ranger.

The ranger caught us about a mile down the road and offered us a ride to the lake. We knew each other, and he knew I'd just quit working for the park service. Word travels fast in Peyton Place. I did my best to convince him we'd put in at Diamond Creek. I'm sure he didn't believe me, but all he did was drop us off by our kayaks on the beach.

The next morning our shuttle driver showed up. She claimed she was really a day early, and we were the ones who were lost in time. We had no choice but to agree with her.

JUMPING WITH MICE

Shane Murphy

Not everybody can just go get on a raft and paddle away. Some folks don't have arms or legs. Sometimes when they have arms and legs their arms and legs don't work like they're supposed to work. Maybe all the parts work but the person using them has the mental ability of a three-year-old. Some people are blind or have polio or have been affected by cerebral palsy. Some have been hit by more than one of these physical challenges.

So what? These people play horseshoes, ride horses, drive cars, ski or even pitch baseballs. You name it and they can do it.

They go raftin' too, on no less than the Colorado River through Grand Canyon, with an organization known as Jumping Mouse Camp. Jumping Mouse was founded by Jeffe (HEF-ay) Aronson, a Grand Canyon guide and cancer patient in remission. While fighting cancer, Aronson discovered a universe of crippling disabilities compounded by hospital life, impersonalization and depression. He figured nothing could change an attitude for the better like a Grand Canyon river trip.

The first trip launched in September of 1991, a twelve-day motor trip led by Cam Staveley at Arizona Raft Adventures. It carried cancer patients. A row and paddle trip for physical disabilities went out later that month. They all came back. They're still comin' back.

For the last few years Jumping Mouse has, with substantial help from Grand Canyon outfitters, orchestrated spring and fall trips for persons with severe disabilities. One trip goes with oars, the other with motors. Both trips take thirteen days to travel from Lees Ferry to Diamond Creek, two hundred and twenty-five miles.

I got stuck with the paperwork. As trip leader for a Jumping Mouse motor run of the Colorado, my manifest showed twelve persons with disabilities, an attendant for each of them, a doctor, two nurses, physical therapists, a television crew, a crew for the two baloney boats I was leading, a group leader for the disabled and the boat company's owners. Thirty-eight people; a fair-sized load under normal conditions, which these weren't. Right. It was nuts—and one of the best trips ever.

At the first lunch, eight miles from the put-in, our cancer patient, a lady terminally ill and not expected to live three months, required ministering by the doctor. He turned out to be a New Age physician who held her arm and touched her ribs, sending positive vibrations via this method. We set up umbrellas for everybody, especially those in wheelchairs, after unstrapping the chairs from the boats and erecting the accessible toilet under a tent. Most of our special population wasn't able to get off the boats by themselves; nearly everyone required help. The beach was narrow, long and rocky. Everybody staggered and crawled all over everybody else while offloading and later, when headed to the toilet or the lunch table. The wheelchairs didn't work in the sand. Those folks had to be carried to the john. Only thirteen more days and two hundred and seventeen miles left to go.

Camp that night was on a beach smaller than our lunch stop, if that was possible. The duffel pile, a minimum of forty-five overstuffed waterproof bags, *lived* in the middle of our kitchen. Boat snouts massaged our backs while we cooked the spuds, made salad and stirred cobbler mix. Dinner was around two Coleman lanterns, with a tight bunching of hungry faces nestled uncomfortably around them. People had to wade in the river to wash dishes because the hot water buckets went in the only place they would fit, along a few thin inches of precious shoreline between the huddled masses and the river. You couldn't miss the toilet tent—it was everywhere. You should have been around for breakfast, when the water came up and the beach shrank!

Camp the following night was an equal disaster but for different reasons. Too much room, and at forty-five degrees to the river's horizon line. Nobody hardly budged. The TENT was in the middle of this vast, open space; it took hours to move the folks to and fro through incredibly thick and heavy sand. It was dead quiet. The river didn't even whisper. There was an overhang that threw off a tremendous echo. Everybody could hear everything at all times, day and night. Just pouring coffee water the next morning I woke everybody up, and they were sleeping at least fifty yards away. Man, was I glad to get out of there! After, that is....uh...well, some of us pushed the big boats off the beach.

And worse: the VideoCam. Curse the VideoCam. The VideoCam was mounted twelve inches in front of my nose, on a tripod. I had approximately thirty-seven feet by fourteen feet by six tons of rubber and people and waterproof bags in front of me and a VideoCam the size of Kansas stuck in my face. I saw *nothing*—except my own reflection in the camera's lens. I ran most rapids, from Bright Angel through Lava Falls, looking at myself in a mirror. How is a guy supposed to drive like that?

But it got better. Not because the camps improved (they did), or because everybody learned how to walk or talk or whatever (they did not), or because we became more comfortable with the VideoCam always stuck in our faces (how to get used to that?). It got better because it was a big job. It was love, devotion, respect for good people with original humor and a job well done. Looking after those folks demanded everybody's full, complete attention all day long. Through the heat and sun and rain and lightning and a thousand trips to the tent we were at it always, every second, day and night.

Our routine helped. By the third day we got camp logistics whittled down to an ongoing but very fuzzy kind of systematic mayhem, a healthy perspective not uncommon to most river runners. In the mornings we started early, before first light, with a coffee call. While breakfast was cooked the doctor and nurses made their rounds. Somebody would drag the handwashing cart through the sand so people unable to walk could wash their hands before eating. Others took food orders, after the breakfast menu was shouted out:

"Good morning, campers! It's a lovely day here in Grand Canyon. To delight your culinary palate, we have prepared, especially for your enjoyment, the following taste-tempting food items: scrambled eggs with Swiss cheese and chunked ham, toasted English muffins with butter—toasted to absolute perfection. We have large, very succulent and delicious sausage patties in the big steamer tray and, as always, an inviting and delicious assortment of hand-sliced fresh fruit. Honey is available, as are ketchup, salsa, salt, pepper and a wide variety of other condiments. At the present time there is no coffee; we are brewing more, even as I tell you these things. Sorry for the delay on that one. Chow's on, folks. Let's eat…"

Then the attendants would come and get the trays and fill them with the requested items and everybody would eat. Afterwards the dishes would be washed, usually by the nurses who just about demanded the work. After that came further portages to the tent, if people weren't busy packing their bags or dressing, tasks most were unable to accomplish by themselves. The group would get a Grand Canyon geology or history lesson while the crew packed the boats. There were twenty lawn chairs, three wheelchairs, several sling assemblies, litters, umbrellas and various specialty items, like the handwash system, that had to get tied in. It took forever.

Even something as simple as getting people onto the boats might take hours. First came the wheelchair-bound. This required a dozen support per-sonnel with pads, pillows and seat cushions placed as needed, like a bucket brigade, but with a wet, slick, round rubber surface for footing. Comes the first customer, who is passed up and over the boat's snout and down the line to the back near the motor compartment. She needs her daypack, camera and cup, which have been left on the beach; they're out there among the gathered horde. This news travels back down the line and, eventually, the requested items appear.

The halt, infirm and blind then do their best to scramble aboard. There is mass confusion everywhere; the fellow with the crutches is in the way (who, I ask, is *not* in the way just now?). In the middle of this, the lady to come on first discovers she's gotten on the wrong boat; she wants to go next door and ride with her friend. Back down the line, which has long since disintegrated, she goes, followed by her wheelchair, camera, daypack and cup.

The last thing aboard, every time, is the tent, which takes up about six acres in the back of the boat and is impossible to tie down completely. Meanwhile the group leader—not the trip leader, who is me—sits resting in the nearby shade determining the progress of his twelve charges.

We did a hike at Unkar Delta, to the closest Indian ruin we could find, seventy-five yards away from the river. We all went. It took four hours to get everyone up the trail, talked to with demonstrations of Indian ways and farming habits and building styles and whatnot, and back down the trail. After that we ate lunch all crammed together in deep bushes smothered by flies, seeming miles from the boat, which was a total of thirty feet away. It was chicken salad that day, with potato chips and pickles and peanut butter and jelly. There were bagels too, with cream cheese, cookies and dried fruit.

After two more camps the cancer lady asked if it would be okay with me if she died in this camp. I told her yes. I told her that it was her trip and that she could pretty much do whatever she wanted, that if she wanted to die right there it would be okay with me. Some of the other women helped her wash her hair and braid it and dressed her up before dinner, which we all ate together seated in a broad circle. She said her thanks and good-byes and went to bed. She came to breakfast the next morning, and every morn-ing after that.

Last camp. Dinner was a stir-fry creation of my own invention: all the leftovers. There was loads of food, and nobody ate any of it, except for some bread and peanut butter. Oh, well. There is only so much that can be done with old vegetables smothered in green slime. We had Dagwoods coming into Diamond Creek in the morning, anyway.

Then came the awards ceremony and, as always, everybody got an old piece of burnt steak or a tennis ball or a pair of suspenders, something significant and individualized. There was a lot of chatter and fun and laughter and singing. Then it grew quiet and somebody—I believe it was the fellow from Oklahoma City who'd been in a car wreck—cleared his throat. He said he didn't know if it was proper but that it was time to say a few things. He started and everybody else followed. When his turn came the severely retarded man grunted, and cried; he understood. The young black man with incredibly short, floppy legs said his life had changed. Forever. And the blind woman: she had *seen* Deer Creek Falls, had seen *rainbows* there. There was no mystery to it. The testimonies came. I've no other word for them. They were as emotionally packed and weighted as any I've ever encountered in Grand Canyon. We carried on like children, babies, all of us, for hours.

That happens at certain times in life, sometimes on river trips with special people. Like I said, it was one of the best ever.

Editor's Note: While Jumping Mouse is no longer in existence, many of the river companies in Grand Canyon encourage and welcome people with disabilities or illness, and often run special trips for such groups.

Crowding in the Canyon

Ellen Tibbetts

1995

HIGH WATER

Christa Sadler and Dave Edwards

Editor's Note: This story was first told by Don Briggs, Martha Clark and Dave Edwards at the 1993 Guides Training Seminar. That telling was videotaped and transcribed by Don, who graciously supplied those transcripts, from which this story was written.

This story should really be called "The Last Time That Don Was Ever the Head Boatman, and The Last Time Don Will Ever *Be* the Head Boatman." It was 1983; an Arizona Raft Adventures launch on HIGH water, and the trip was about two days behind everyone else on the river. In fact, there may not have been any trips that left after this one at all. They were going to run a lower half oar-powered trip with a guy from California who was sort of a New Age guru; we'll call him Rodney (not his real name). Don had met this guy on the Tuolumne River in California, and they'd had a pretty good time. Rodney had asked about other trips, and Don talked him into coming down the Grand Canyon. This was back in— well, who knows when, but long before the dam had developed this problem and the water had gotten so high.

They scheduled an eight-day lower half, and Rodney was going to hike his folks down; that was supposed to be part of their enlightenment. They were all set to go.

But then Glen Canyon Dam started spilling water. In the morning someone would call up the Bureau of Reclamation and ask how much water was coming over. Then they'd call up the park service and ask, "Can we go or can't we?" The park response would be, "Well, we have to talk to the Bureau of Reclamation." The water was rising higher and higher behind the dam, and Don was calling Rodney on the phone in California because he didn't know if the trip was going to happen or not. The park service would say, "Yes, you can." Then, "No, you can't." Back and forth. Then they decided, "We're just going to leave it up to the outfitters. It'll be self-regulating." AZRA was going to run paddleboats originally. But that didn't seem like such a good idea without being able to try it first. There was a big meeting, with no consensus. Some said it wasn't safe, and others said it was safe, but only with small boats. And *no* paddleboats. There was some question about snout rigs. In a snout rig at high water you'd put in at the ferry and be down at Lake Mead before you could blink. And there would be no stopping anywhere.

In the meantime, Don was getting calls from Rodney, who wanted to know if the trip was happening or not. Everyone talked. Somewhere along the line Don got the idea that, because it was so fast out there, they could run the entire canyon in the eight days they had planned for the lower half. So he called up Rodney and convinced him that this was a good deal. "Not everybody's gonna get to do this, Rodney. You're maybe the only guy that ever gets to. So come on ahead, we're gonna try it." (See, they figured they might not be *able* to stop at Phantom to pick anyone up who hiked in.) So the group showed up at the ferry…

Now Rodney had once been a doctor, a surgeon. He had been in the operating room and had some inspiration that he shouldn't be cutting people up. Instead he should lay his hands on them and enlighten them. So he took people and worked at group energy healing, group meditations and those sorts of things. He had a little following around the country that he had taken on different trips all over the place, but he had never done a trip like this on a river with one of his groups.

He was into this thing he called Transformation, and the people who were coming on this trip were going to a Transformation conference first. Then they were going down the Grand Canyon. When the guides asked, Rodney could never really explain what Transformation meant to him. But he was about to find out. They were all about to find out.

Lees Ferry. The boatmen had no idea what the river would look like. When they got up to the ferry they were told that the water was going to be sixty-two thousand cfs around the clock. It was huge. Scary. But there was a trip to run—what else could they do? As they were pulling away from Lees Ferry, the NPS ranger came running down to the ramp and shouted, "It's going to seventy-five thousand!"

The boats just *flew* downstream. They camped way down, by mile 40. Got there in about five hours, as opposed to two and a half days. The trip was going great. It was the first night on the river, and Rodney called everyone around, including the crew.

Now, part of the deal was that the guides had to be part of the group. They couldn't get off by themselves; they had to blend in. It wasn't like they could just *be* with the folks, get to know them, talk to them. They were going to be *part* of the Transformation. They were supposed to hold hands in the circle and all that. And there was no alcohol. That was another part of the deal—very important.

So the group got together that night and everyone sat around, chanting and humming, trying to create a little circle of energy. Well, Don was pretty nervous as head boatman, and he found that all his energy went towards just thinking about how all these people were going to stay alive on that big, fast, HIGH river out there. So while everyone else was chanting their special sounds, Don was humming to himself, *Ohhhh, be gooood to meeee, be goooood to meeeee river.* He wasn't sure what everyone else was thinking, but that's where *his* thoughts were.

The next day the trip floated down to the Little Colorado. They got down there by two in the afternoon. The flooding Colorado was acting like a dam, holding back the Little Colorado River, which was unbelievable: about fifteen feet deep and turquoise blue—gorgeous.

The boatmen had found a river bag in the willows above the Little Colorado and hauled it aboard. The name Ken was marked on the bag, the same name as one of the passenger's husband, who had drowned on the Green River the year before. She was hysterical with grief. The situation was tense.

A motor rig came towards them from out of sight around the corner coming *down* the Little Colorado. It had gone up there so far because the water was so high, which was surreal enough. But at that moment a helicopter flew over and a guy with goggles threw a bag out of the chopper. Bob and Don ran up the hill to get the bag. Bob got there first and brought the bag down. Inside was a note weighted down with gravel. They both read it. Don said, "We're gonna read it in front of the entire group. That's what this is all about: a group experience." They both chuckled.

They went down to join the group by the peaceful blue water. Don sat up above them, and they all looked up at him. He was enjoying the moment. He said, "We just got this note and I figured you want to know what it says." He proceeded to read:

All trips must stop at Phantom Ranch and check in with the ranger. You must leave a copy of your pass, and manifest, including names, with the ranger. Below Phantom Ranch, notice: as set in 36 CFR.6A, Closures and Public Use Limits: The superintendent may close to public use all or any portion or part of an area when necessary for the protection of the area or for the safety or welfare of persons or property by posting of the appropriate signs indicating the extent and the scope of the closure. All persons shall observe and abide by officially posted signs designated closed areas and visiting areas. Rangers and notices will replace signs. The superintendent has closed Crystal Rapid to all passengers of both private and commercial trips. Passengers must walk around Crystal with only boatmen and swampers to run Crystal.

Don looked down at his people. They were getting a little concerned; they clearly weren't ready for this.

This closure is due to the extreme hazard of Crystal Rapids. Four motor rigs and numerous oar boats have flipped. Ninety people were in the water. There have been one fatality and fifteen injuries. This closure is in effect until further notice. Water levels are expected—*that's the key word here*—to remain at seventy-five thousand, with possible increases.

Don looked down at his people again in the lovely blue water. He could see what they were thinking: *I'm gonna die tomorrow.* He began to wonder if it was such a good idea to read the notice to them. *What the hell,* he thought. *It's a Transformational experience.*

On the way downstream the group passed two Sanderson motor rigs on a beach; they had their stuff spread out all over camp. Don's group waved, but the Sanderson crew was just walking around and everything seemed very solemn. Don figured, *Hell, they're probably scared to death, too.*

They camped at Carbon Creek, which was so tiny that the group had to sit up in the rocks to do their circle that night. The next morning there was a constant stream of helicopters going back and forth. One right after another, all the time from first light. They were cleaning up camp when the Sanderson rigs pulled up. They were pretty somber. It turned out that one of them had decided to run a long lateral wave at Nankoweap. It was the only significant whitewater he'd seen in sixty miles; everything else was washed out. He'd flipped his motor rig. They were trying to dry their stuff out and everybody was really concerned, so they called the trip off. They decided to fly their people out. The boatman who flipped his boat was in a state of shock and the other boatman proceeded to tell everyone about the flip.

That didn't do a lot for the confidence of the group. They saw those two huge motor rigs. They looked at their little tiny rafts. Don tried to calm his group down. "Hey, everything is going fine, you know? Things are going just fine." *Uh-huh.* They finished doing breakfast. The people worked their tails off so that the crew would be able to come to the Transformation, and couldn't use breaking down camp as an excuse not to join in. They sat down in a big circle, holding hands. It was a huge trip, around thirty-four people. Rodney finished his monologue and then proceeded: "Well, we have these guides on the boats, and they know how to run the boats, and they know about the geology and the natural history and they're great cooks, but we don't have anyone on the boats to make sure the energy is moving in a good direction. Now, we're not even sure the rangers are going to let us through at Phantom, but if they do, we're about to run the whole gorge, down to the top of Crystal, a place where ninety people have just swum. One fatality. Fifteen people injured. So what I'd like to do today is have an energy monitor on each boat, to make sure the energy is going in the right direction."

So amongst themselves they appointed energy monitors for each boat. To the crew it felt more like informants. It was kind of ironic, really, because any boatman's job just naturally involves being an "energy monitor." But with Rodney's energy monitors, you *had* to be happy. You couldn't be nervous: bad energy. The boats headed downstream. At Hance, they all got out to scout. Every boatman's heart was way down deep in his gut, looking at Hance at seventy-five thousand cfs. It was ugly out there: holes the size of condominiums and water moving really fast. As they coiled up the lines before casting off, the energy monitors came up to each boat and tried to get the boatmen to hold hands while they sang a song. *Right* before going into Hance. The song felt more like a dirge. "The river is flowing, flowing and growing. The river is flowing, down to the sea." Over and over again. They had energy monitors for the rest of the trip.

Boating-wise, they did pretty well through the gorge. Everything was going so fast they hardly noticed what they were doing. Or they were so scared they forgot. The trip stopped at Phantom to get permission to go on down. That night, camp was at mile 96, Schist Camp. Just two miles above Crystal.

In the morning at Schist Camp all the crew wanted to do was go downstream and run Crystal. But there were holes in the bottom of three of their boats. The water was so high, and there was such a surf that the boats were all pushed up on sharp rocks that weren't water-worn. So they patched the floors, which took two or three hours. There was no shade and it was really hot out there in those black rocks. The guides were nervous and uptight and were beginning to lose it with Rodney. They were thinking, *We're not going to have to Transform today? Rodney's not going to sit everyone down in this hundred and ten-degree heat above Crystal and make us all Transform is he?*

Sure enough, they sat down and held hands in the hundred and ten-degree heat above Crystal. After fifteen or twenty minutes of silence, Rodney said, "You know yesterday was a great day. We ran all those rapids and we had our energy monitors. But you know how we got to the bottom of these rapids and everybody would yell and cheer because we had good runs, and we were really excited to be down at the bottom and safe? Well, what I'd like us to do today is to try and save that energy."

And he started to talk about these far-eastern Tantric sexual practices. He equated this new idea of boating to a practice where the men don't ejaculate. When they get excited they save it and come "within." The guides were thinking, *This is right above **Crystal**, for godsakes. We're supposed to run this rapid at seventy-five thousand. We're supposed to get down below Crystal and crack a **tomato juice**? In **silence**?*

All the passengers walked around Crystal. The guides ran each boat with two boatmen, one to row and one to paddle assist and bail, one boat at a time. Crystal had been demolishing motor rigs. The hole was about eighteen feet deep, the wave behind it thirty feet high and about two hundred feet long. The rafts had to run through flooded willows and tamarisk trees. If one hit a tree the boat would spin in the current and there would be no recovery—the small rafts would go straight for the hole.

They made it and at the bottom they cheered loud and drank beer.

The next morning there was a big circle in camp. The trip was starting to become fractionalized between Rodney's hard-core followers and the people who were beginning to realize where they were and that what was happening was really special. They were clueing in to the fact that running the river at this water level in such small boats was extraordinary. They wanted to experience the place, let the canyon do its work. So the group discussion started getting a little wild.

Rodney said, "There's something I want to say. I've been noticing that the focus on the trip is not where I want it to be. The focus is on the guides and what is happening on the river." The guides were thinking,

We don't even know what's around the next bend. We don't even know if we're all gonna live through this, when Rodney continued. "People paid to come on this trip with *me* and they are focusing more attention on the guides, and I'm really upset that this is the case. This is something I would like to correct."

Martha lost it. "Rodney," she said, "you told everybody to get involved in this trip, and I've never seen you in the kitchen. I've never seen you lift a hand to do anything." "Thank you for sharing," Rodney said.

On the trip went down to Olo, where they had to pull in and see what it looked like. The boats pulled right in to the wall, right up to the lip of the first pool, usually a twenty-foot vertical climb. Don started thinking that the trip should just camp there. It would be a great place to have a circle, above the pools in the amphitheater.

When Don told the group, Rodney started to get worried. He looked up at the pool and the rope you had to climb to get to the upper amphitheater, and he couldn't quite figure how they were going to get everyone up there, plus all the equipment. The guides didn't think it was such a good idea. Rodney didn't think it was such a good idea. Don could see mutiny about to happen, and he finally just said, "I want to camp here. You'll thank me later."

Everybody clambered up the rope into the bowl. The crew cooked something simple, like gazpacho, for dinner down in the boats and passed it up so they didn't have to cook up there and could keep the place clean. Everyone was all set to camp, when Rodney decided to do some chanting at night, instead of the next morning, like he usually did. The moonlight was really bright, and the frogs were just going nuts. It was outrageous in there, and Rodney asked them all to close their eyes and chant. They couldn't see the moonlight on the walls, or hear the sounds of the canyon.

Martha was thinking, *This is one of the most amazing places in the canyon. All these people have to do is shut up and open their eyes and they would be Transformed.* Martha and Louise were punchy. They felt like they were drunk. They *wished* they were drunk. So they just got up and took off. They took their black bags down to the rope and just heaved them into the bottom pool above the boats. Laughing hysterically, they jumped off into the pool and climbed down to sleep on the boats. And there was Dave, sitting on his boat with a forbidden bottle of Glenlivett scotch. The girls were overjoyed. They passed the bottle quietly and watched the river roar by. In the background there was faint chanting.

Their last night on the river, everyone was supposed to sit around and tell their favorite part of the trip, or something special that had happened to them. Rodney broke out and passed around three bottles of expensive sherry, for thirty-four people. Time to lighten up finally. Everyone was saying this and that, only Don wasn't saying much of anything because he was thinking about the take-out. He was thinking about how they were all going to stop at Diamond Creek, if there even *was* a Diamond Creek. Maybe the water was too high.

It was hard for the boatmen to talk because they felt on the spot. When your turn came with the bottle, you had to say something. The bottle had gone around about two-thirds of the circle, and then it was Dave's turn.

Now at some point in the trip, every guide had lost it with Rodney and the whole situation, publicly. But Dave had been in control. Oh, he had lost it privately, with the guides, on the boats. But never out loud. But finally the bottle got to Dave, and he sort of sat there with it. He looked at it like Dave does. He looked up, and he said, "Well, first of all Rodney, you're just about the biggest asshole I've ever met in my life." He continued talking on, calmly, for a few minutes. And when he finished he said, "And furthermore, Rodney, I will come *every* time!"

⌒

Well, the river won out in the long run, because two years later Don heard that Rodney had contacted AZRA and wanted to do the trip again, but only under the strict stipulation that none of the guides who were on the first trip would go with him. He came down the river yet again in 1992, on a family trip with his kids and wife. Dave was somehow on that trip, and he said Rodney was an okay guy. Dave figured the river really had worked on him back in '83; just took him ten years to be Transformed.

Confluence of the Little Colorado River, Mile 61 1/2
Elizabeth Black
1990

Kayaker Running Travertine Dams in the Little Colorado River

Dugald Bremner

1992

Emily at the Little Colorado

Tom Hansen

2004

Raven at 75 Mile

Matt Fahey

2005

Anne Cassidy and Lester Bleifuss
Raechel M. Running
2006

View Upstream from Bass Cable Crossing
Sam Jones
2003

Elves Chasm

Nathan Jones

1986

Elena Kirschner and Passengers
Raechel M. Running
2006

Expect the Unexpected
Charly Heavenrich
1993

Zoom Upset

Geoff Gourley

2001

Breakfast at the Upset Hotel
Elizabeth Black
1992

Bighorn Silhouette
Jeff Behan
2005

Drops of Life

Marieke Taney

2003

Havasu, the Fairytale
Ote Dale
2004

Gretchen Younghans
Kyle George
2005

Wade Takes it in Lava Falls
Jeff Behan
2005

SPEED

Lew Steiger

June 26, 1983. It began in the dark, an hour before midnight. They were two days off the full moon and this was a clear, still night weather-wise, but everything else was wound up tighter than blue blazes. Everything and everybody. The water rolled by in a great rush past the launch ramp at Lees Ferry; you felt it in the groin more than heard it. The river had covered the ramp by then, it was practically up to the parking lot.

They slipped into the ferry in Rudi's van with the *Emerald Mile* on the trailer. They were trying to be considerate of course—didn't want to be rude and wake the ranger or anything—but to their surprise they ran into a few night-owls down by the ramp anyway; boatmen from other companies engaged in a little ritual pre-trip partying. A dirty job, but somebody had to do it. (These were troubled times, after all. What if tomorrow the dam actually broke and washed everyone away? Wouldn't be proper not to eat, drink and be merry tonight.)

Bruce Helin saw them and ambled over to help. Did the others even notice as they backed down to the river and slid the dory off and got in? Hard to say. It happened fast. Cliff Taylor, who would drive around to get them at the bottom, gave a quick countdown and punched the stopwatch and they left—whoosh—just like that.

In the dark somebody yelled something, but they barely heard it. They were already gone.

Kenton had the oars. He pulled out of there with long, hard strokes. *Really* hard strokes. The *Emerald Mile* was so light that almost instantly she began to trail a wake and on shore you could've heard her hiss through the water in quick spurts, maybe, or heard the oar blades cut the surface a time or two before she disappeared into the darkness. Then there was just the river again, ripping by and on through the night in a huge gathering mass, like a silent, pent-up howl.

Did you see that? What was that? Was that a boat out there?

The water rolled on.

*It was 1983, and the West that year had **had** a winter. High in the Rockies it started to snow and never quit. The snow fell and fell… It just kept falling, a clean, white blanket flung clear across the region, double thick.*

Twenty years earlier, in 1963, the Bureau of Reclamation had closed the gates on Glen Canyon Dam and stopped the Colorado River, started to raise up Lake Powell. In 1980, they'd finally filled that lake to the brim.

Politically and economically, the full lake was considered ideal. Money in the bank for upper basin water users; maximum efficiency for power production.

What about all that snow up there? "Not a problem," said Reclamation. They'd adjust as the situation demanded.

Badger, the first rapid, had enormous waves. The sound was tangible now—a force with incredible mass and density, it hit them in the bones every time the boat rose and fell on the dark glistening water. Soap Creek was smaller, a straight shot. Big waves but clean, and all Kenton had to do was keep it straight and let Rudi and Ren do the rest: lean just the right way at just the right time with just the right force. Match the river curve for curve, swell for swell. They began to digest the difference in size, how much bigger and faster it was tonight than they had ever seen before, the fact that this was real; they were really out here on the spine of this beast. No turning back.

They were on a quest, of course: World's Fastest Trip Through the Grand Canyon. Kenton Grua, Rudi Petschek and Steve Reynolds were the boatmen. The boat was a seventeen-foot dory that had sides made of quarter-inch plywood. It was fast and spry, but kinda tippy if you weren't straight for everything. Actually, it was tippier than hell. And the river, it's safe to say, was just about out of control.

"What the hell is going on?" "Well sir, it looks like we've got a situation here." In June of '83, Reclamation was sweating bullets. They'd seen a cool April and only light runoff. The mountains were far away and scattered, or something… Somehow it just didn't sink in how much snow was really up there. In May it snowed even more. Then the rain came hard and melted the snow. Then it got hot. And all that water headed for the sea…

House Rock, at lower stages the worst, was completely smooth. The rocks were gone; they passed through in a heartbeat. They were flying. The moonlight shattered off the current lines in the channel before them, catching every eddy, every wave, every ripple. Other times it splayed the cliffs above and left them in shadow; came to them translucent.

They braced for the Twenties: a narrow limestone gorge and a chain of quick-turn rapids rife now with boils and whirlpools that were—at seventy thousand cfs—unspeakably gnarly. They'd decided to leave at night and run this stretch in the dark because, as Rudi says, "You multiplied hours of darkness by average speed and it came to about seventy-two miles." He laughs. "Of course there is no such length in the canyon that is without risk." They wanted to tackle the dark portion while they were still fresh. They wanted to hit the Inner Gorge and the *really* big rapids in broad daylight, the following morning.

"We didn't use the lights so much," Rudi says. "You could usually see at least one or two waves ahead, and that's all you needed because we knew the river well enough to judge where we wanted to be. Our anxiety was not so much being unable to see at night, but to have an incident and be forced to deal with a rescue operation in the dark. That was our greatest concern. There was no relaxing. Not for anybody at any time. A few minutes' catnap now and then, but aside from that it was so fast between one rapid and the next. You know in that water, in a small boat, you're always dealing with the turbulence. The passengers had to be shifting their weight, making adjustments all the time."

All three boatmen worked for Martin Litton's Grand Canyon Dories, a company that prided itself on running not the fastest trips but the longest, most leisurely trips around. They weren't on a company trip now, though, or even in a company boat.

The truth is, they didn't have a permit, either.

In fact, the park service had expressly forbidden this particular trip. But Martin Litton had hung it out there for them at the last possible second and opened up what they saw as an infinitesimal crack in the door, just big enough to let them through. Were they aware the park might not see it that way? Well, they'd adjust to that situation when they had to.

*At the dam that night, they were making adjustments. And pretty soon, they would **really** have to make adjustments.*

April on the river had seen a constant twenty-eight thousand cfs. In May the water had started coming up in large increments. Thirty-five. Next week forty; then fifty. In mid June, they'd opened the spillways in earnest for the first time ever and gradually increased the water bypassing the turbines. They were cranking out a little over seventy thousand cfs when the speed run left. Finally, two days after the speed run was over, they would raise the bet to ninety.

Suddenly, with thirty-two thousand cfs blasting through the east spillway alone, the roaring plume at that outlet would change from white to reddish orange—the same color as the Navajo Sandstone bordering the dam.

Tom Gamble, the operations manager of the dam, would lean over the edge to take a look at the calico-colored plume. It would not be pretty down there. Boulders the size of Volkswagons would be spewing out into the river.

North Canyon wasn't even a rapid. *This is cake,* Kenton started thinking. "Then we hit 21 Mile and that had some pretty big whirlpools and wild stuff, hydraulics. Boy, there were some big rides—24 1/2 Mile was nuts! We didn't cut too far, otherwise we would have caught those big eddies, but whew…" He shakes his head. "We were staring right at the wall and it was just coming at us, we kind of veered to the left… Nobody said much at those times, but in between we were loving it. It was an incredible rush."

A few days later, on the ninety thousand, the next dory trip behind them would call for motor support after flipping two boats in boils and eddy lines through that same stretch. Suddenly it would seem imprudent to be there on a commercial venture in such sensitive little boats. The water was too unpredictable; it wasn't as though you could play to the dories' strength and just anticipate trouble; then finesse your way around it. You couldn't catch a swimmer ahead of you was the main thing. The current took them too fast.

After seeing the spillway vomit its load of rusty red rocks, Tom Gamble would order it shut down immediately—a precautionary measure. The damage couldn't be that bad, could it? Next morning he'd send a crew down to check it out.

They'd be dumfounded by what they saw.

Meanwhile the lake would still be rising fast, coming in at twice the rate they were able to release it.

Thirty-Six Mile scared the Wheaties out of them. The river blazed straight into the wall and under a big overhang on the right. "We could see it as we came in," Kenton says. "We all thought, *Jesus, that looks terrible!* So

I just started really booking it for the left shore and cut across those laterals. It wasn't a hard run, but oh man, the consequences…"

They kept going. The boat had nothing in it; it was a little sports car. They got corked around a lot, but they were so pumped and moving so fast all the time that whenever anything really tried to suck on them, they were able to power out of it.

"We never did get truly terrified…we kind of just slid through, all night long…" Kenton says. His voice trails off wistfully as he thinks of it, marveling at how the river let them go.

On the river below, not everybody had been skating by. In the month of June, big motor rigs had started turning over. One in Nankoweap, of all places; another at President Harding. The week of the speed run, down in the Inner Gorge, life got wild. In the previous two days, at one place in particular, it had been beyond wild. The wrecks were downright historic in scale.

The night the speed run left—unbeknownst to Kenton, Rudi and Ren—the superintendent was awake in his bed, wondering if he should close the whole river.

At dawn they were to Nankoweap, passing trips on their second, third, even fourth days out. They traded off at the oars, each guy rowing as hard as he could for fifteen or twenty minutes. "By the end you'd pry your hand off the oar. It wouldn't work; you'd have to bend your fingers out one by one before they'd finally start working again," Kenton says.

The first bolt of sunlight hit the *Emerald Mile* at the head of Lava Canyon. They were feeling pretty good. They weren't going as fast as they'd anticipated, but still they were on a record pace. Leaving that cool unforgettable night behind was something, and looking at the bright warm sky overhead, feeling that sun hit, they could already tell that the tempo of this thing was only going to escalate. It was fixing to be a clear, hot day.

The river in Furnace Flats was big and wide and moving on. The shoreline everywhere was a whole new ballgame; the old one they'd grown up with in the 1970s was history. Most of the tamarisk trees were gone or half under. The water was full of stuff: trees, logs, tires, old fifty-five gallon drums.

Down below the Inner Gorge that day you found another kind of flotsam: ammo cans, broken boxes, lifejackets, upside down motor rigs ghost boating through the canyon. Side tubes out joyriding all by themselves, with nobody else and no other thing around. At seventy thousand cfs, Crystal Rapid had changed. A monster would live there for five days, then be washed away forever by the ninety thousand yet to come.

It was there right now, though: a fire-breathing dragon, absolutely huge. And anybody coming along who didn't know how to make a hard cut or do a turnaround run in a motor rig was in big trouble.

There was a center run in Hance and then a gigantic ride down the left side of the wave train. They were flying high. Holding their breath, they sailed over the tops of absolutely mountainous waves and kept going.

The jagged cliffs rose ominously to greet them. They were at the bottom now; a mile deep, and already the river had carried them through eons worth of rock—limestone, shale, sandstone—more time than you could shake a stick at; primordial stuff, blacker than hell down there in the bowels of the earth until it got laid bare by a river just like this one, a howling beast that didn't stop for anyone or anything.

They began to pass other trips on the water, rowboats on their fifth and sixth days out, motor trips on day three or four. People didn't know what to make of them—didn't care, really.

"Everybody was wound up," Kenton says. "Oar boats especially…you didn't see anybody smiling in a little boat." In the gorge the currents were too strong for anyone in charge of other people's safety to be ecstatically enjoying the program. The eddy fences were stupendous.

"Okay, go." Kenton gave the oars to Rudi and jumped to the stern. Ren shifted to the bow. *So far so good*, Kenton figured. Everything was shaking out pretty much according to plan.

Down at Crystal that morning, NPS ranger John Thomas was already in place on the beach with his tools of the hour: badge, radio, clipboard. His new mission that day was to stop all traffic and make sure nobody but boatmen went through the rapid.

Officially, Crystal was "closed."

Well actually, there *was* one little flaw in their plan.

It had to do with the intransigence of your average bureaucracy—the difficulty of explaining to an entirely different mindset what a boon these big flows were; how extraordinary it was to actually see the river unleashed again, and how important it was, for everyone really, to rise above the petty concerns of liability and official propriety (in the face of utter impending chaos) in order to foster a little joy by demonstrating just how powerful the natural river actually *was*—with the graphically poetic gesture of getting a dory down through there in the least amount of time possible. Or something like that.

Okay the real truth is, it was just important to them personally. It wasn't about having the record and getting their name in the history books. It wasn't about conquering a dadburn thing except their own horizons. It was about having the *experience*. Them and the place. Them *with* the Grand Canyon, doing this one little thing on this one little day. Strictly personal.

The trouble was, they already *had* the record. They'd set that a couple years earlier on test flows of thirty-seven thousand. Rudi and Kenton's names were already in the book, along with Wally Rist, who'd thought of the idea in the first place and inspired them to knock half a day off the existing mark set by the Rigg brothers in '51. And this spring, when they'd felt the real flood coming and asked for permission to "test evacuation procedures" one more time, the park service had waffled on them a while, then turned them down flat.

They'd had to beseech Martin Litton to get it wormed around to where they could maybe kind of just go anyway. But unbeknownst to Martin, or them either at the time, the feces had already hit the fan, before Martin even got into it.

The old Crystal had what was arguably the biggest hole in the river. Maybe not the very biggest, but certainly the biggest one you had to work hard to stay out of. There was a lot of other stuff too in that rapid; you had to work hard all the way down, couldn't just grease the entry and then it was over. But the hole stuck in your mind.

As the water came up, the hole got bigger. Anyone who saw it at fifty thousand, however, would have sworn it would wash out with a little more water. It was big but it had a soft shoulder to it on the right side. Looked like a fun ride, maybe, if you did get over there.

The day before the speed run started, Jon Stoner was on an ARR trip just above the gorge, and the water went to seventy thousand. The trip leader on that trip was the cautious sort, but he didn't think Crystal was going to be any big deal, wasn't even planning to stop. He asked Stoner if he wanted to do anything special that day and Stoner said, "Yeah. Look at Crystal."

They got there and announced this would be a boatman only scout, because they were in a hurry. Tied the boats and started up the hill. The TL glanced back over his shoulder and couldn't stand it. He turned around and ran back down, tied another line from the boat to shore. His bowline had been sawing tight against a sharp ridge of rock and all those people were just sitting there happily ignorant on the boat, trusting, and it just felt wrong to have all those lives hanging by one slender thread chafing on the rock. The current along shore there was that strong.

They got to the top of the hill and what they saw just punched them square in the gut. "Holy shit," the TL said. He actually grabbed his stomach. Stoner nodded in agreement. "Anybody goes in there, they're dead," the TL said. "Dead meat."

The hole had moved upstream somehow. It stood straight up, about three stories tall—definitely taller than a motor rig. It broke hard clear across, exactly perpendicular to the current, and the corners had serious suck on both ends. It was all recirculating; there wasn't any water going out of there on top. They had about twenty-five feet of room over on the right side, between the hole and the half-buried trees.

While they stood there, a helicopter blazed by heading fast downstream.

They made the run. To do it just right you had to come in hard behind the lone tamarisk flapping in the current at the top and keep going. Don't quit for anything.

If you did it right, it was an easy turnaround run.

They got to the bottom; somebody was screaming for help in an eddy halfway down toward Tuna Creek. It was a Georgie thrill boat that had pan-caked and was stuck up against the cliff. They started to pull in, then realized it was too tight and too fast—they'd wipe out the whole wad trying to get into an eddy that small.

"Our big boat flipped!" somebody screamed. "Save our big boat!"

A Cross Tours motor rig was parked in the eddy on the left above Tuna, and the whole crew of that boat looked completely wigged. Eyes bigger than grapefruits.

"What's this about a Georgie flip?"

"Yeah! Oh yeah. It flipped all right."

"How long ago?"

"Twenty, thirty minutes."

"Is anybody after them? Who else is down there?"

"I don't know," the Cross boatman said. "Don't care."

"Has anybody else run since then?"

"Nope. You're the first ones."

"Well, what are you doing here?"

The Cross boatman shook his head. He was having a hard morning. "I got two more boats coming and I'm waiting right here till they get through."

"Terrific."

The ARR boys took off after the lost Georgie boat and found the first people on the cliffs below Tuna. Babbling. Totally shell-shocked. The TL got impatient waiting for them to climb down. He could see another lady at the next bend. "Stoner, you better get these guys. I'll see you again when I see you. I'll just keep going till I hit that boat or know they're all accounted for."

Stoner nodded. He got the first two people on his boat and turned around. Out in the current a mass of fresh debris was on its way down, new casualties from Crystal. Blue box lids. Ammo cans. Duffel. Pretty soon another motor rig. He couldn't tell if it was right side up or upside down.

Stoner stopped the crippled boat. It was right side up but it might have been better off the other way around. The frame was in pieces. Nothing usable was left on it.

The other two Cross boats came limping down. It looked like a war zone. People were bleeding, crying, fractured, in shock. Stoner talked to the boatmen. They were shell-shocked too.

He looked around for a place to land a chopper. Couldn't see one so he did a little triage and gathered up the worst victims. Before he could leave, the Georgie thrill boat showed up too. "Please. Please take us with you. Don't leave us here alone." He took them aboard. He had about twenty-eight on his boat now.

He laid one lady across his motor box on the way down. He'd offered a hand to comfort her and then she wouldn't let go of it. "What's your name?" she wanted to know. "Jon," he told her.

"John," she said, squeezing his hand for all she was worth. "John the Baptist."

They rendezvoused at Lower Bass and helicoptered everybody out there. It was the first place you could really land a chopper. Over eighty people evacuated, and it took all day.

A Georgie thirty-three had flipped in Crystal and kept going until it washed ashore on the point down by 110 Mile. A Dories trip camped at Bass had helped with that rescue. The Georgie thrill boat pancaked in the trees. The first of three Cross boats hit the hole and surfed in there about six times, then got spit out straight backwards. Parked above Tuna. The second one *through was surfing in the hole too when the third one came in right over the top of it. Wiped the second boat out completely. Pretty much trashed the third one in the bargain.*

The NPS, in the midst of its peak season anyway, had been forced to mobilize an all-out effort to clean up the mess and in the middle of that effort they'd gotten a call from Martin Litton about a special trip three of his boatmen wanted to make…

Martin Litton was silver-haired and imposing. He was a man who knew a thing or two about grand gestures, himself. He had been a Sierra Club director in its heyday, eloquent and principled enough to be credited by David Brower as the one man, more than anyone else, who was the conscience of the club. It was Litton who had inspired the club to take up the Marble Canyon Dam fight, among others. With characteristic flair, after he started his company, he named his boats after places already lost. "Environmental sins," he called them. "Places we ought to be remembering."

On the morning of the same day that the Georgie and Cross boats were mixing it up with Crystal, Kenton had called Martin on the phone. Martin was home in California at the time.

"You've gotta help us," Kenton said.

Martin sat back in his chair. Wearily he closed his eyes and pinched the bridge of his nose. "What on earth for?" he said. He shook his head and sighed, then asked a question he already knew the answer to. "Why go again?"

Kenton set his jaw and transmitted an imploring silence out over the wires. Martin groaned. The truth is, there was a lot of history between them. Those two went back a ways, and so did Martin and Rudi.

Kenton Grua, a.k.a. "the Factor."

Years ago, his pals had affectionately nicknamed him that because that's what he was: this additional element you always had to factor in whenever you were on a river trip with him.

"Help me out over here," the Factor would tell you in the warehouse at 7:00 P.M. "This will only take ten minutes." Hours later, covered with splinters and sawdust, you'd finally finish ripping the entire floor off an upside down dory Kenton had suddenly decided to fix right this time.

A popular book called The Man Who Walked Through Time *was written by a guy who walked alone through the middle reaches of the canyon from*

Havasu to Nankoweap—a distance of about a hundred miles. Kenton read it and liked it, so a couple of winters later he marched all the way through, from Lees Ferry to the Grand Wash Cliffs. It was over three hundred miles by foot, and the Factor did it in thirty-six days. Never called a press conference; didn't publish a single word about it. He'd just kept thinking of it and decided that would be how to do it right, if you wanted to get nitpicky about things.

He started out first in moccasins but ended up canceling that effort after about thirty miles.

He spent the whole next summer plotting, before he did it for real. A certain stretch was giving him fits because he couldn't see a route until finally, in the fall, he watched two fat bighorn rams—an old one and a younger partner—traverse a narrow lip of rock in the Muav Limestone across the river from the ledge camp below Upset. Kenton climbed higher to see where they went and the sheep showed him the way.

He'd gotten a job running motor rigs for the Hatch brothers in 1969, at the age of nineteen, the same year he saw Martin for the first time. Litton was on a trip honoring the Powell Centennial and when Kenton passed him, Martin was out there hamming it up in the hot sun dressed in a suit coat with one arm tucked into the jacket, the sleeve just dangling loose, while behind him two of the boats were upside down on the beach drying out so they could be repaired after taking rock hits in the Inner Gorge.

The Factor wasn't brave enough to stop. Litton had a thing about motors even then and Kenton was in a hurry. They were funky dories, Kenton says. "They were flat ended. None of them had much rake." Still, the first look got to him. "You know," he says "if you're a river person all you have to do is see one…"

One of the first boats Martin ever had was the Emerald Mile. *Built by Jerry Briggs of Grant's Pass, Oregon, this boat became the grandmother of all the really good dories in the canyon, as dozens of her clones, taken from the original jig, joined the fleet.*

The real Emerald Mile was a mile-long stretch of redwood trees along a creek in northwestern California. Some of the trees were the tallest in the world, and four hundred- to four hundred-fifty-foot redwoods had already been logged there when the Sierra Club began to lobby for a park instead. "Truly something to cry about," Litton says.

Kenton went to work for Martin in 1973. He got the Emerald Mile *in '77, after an oarsman down from Idaho missed the Slot in Lava Falls and was blasted into a vicious little eddy on the right side called the Corner Pocket, which basically made toothpicks out of her. Litton chuckles describing the run from there to the end of the trip. "It was quite convenient for the people sitting in the front seat," he says. "They could dangle their feet in the river as they went along."*

The rest of them were going to give up and simply call the boat firewood after the trip, but the Factor stepped in and said no, he'd fix her himself and take her for his own. He made her a double-ender and put false floors in the passenger footwells so that she was completely self-bailing.

At the Dories, Kenton was the resident mad scientist. For years he'd been driving Martin and everybody else in the company crazy with his visions— half of which were out there—but the other half were inspired, and made a difference. It was Kenton who'd thought of righting flipped boats in mid- stream, and having people high-side vigorously when a boat was out of kilter in the big waves. Kenton came up with the best way to fix damaged boats, both on the river and off, and a host of other ideas big and small that had advanced the operation significantly over the years.

And Rudi? Rudi had come with Martin as a passenger on the Emerald Mile's *maiden voyage; they'd known each other almost twenty years now.*

The Factor and Rudi had both felt this winter hit and watched the spring unfold and seen this flood coming a mile away. A meticulous and gifted crafts- man, Rudi never missed a trick where the water was concerned, and this flood… this ride, he could feel in his bones long before it happened. And Kenton could too. Together, with Ren, they had reached terminal lift-off mode about the ultimate speed run. They were like fifteen-year olds poised to lose their virginity. They were as ready as you could ever get.

Martin sighed again and glared down at the phone. "All right. I'll see what I can do." He called the superintendent but didn't get him. Too busy. At the end of the day, when the superintendent still hadn't returned his call, Martin tried him at home and caught him at a cocktail party.

The super had already been through a rough day as it was and frankly he didn't want to talk now about the river or the high water or any of it. Yeah, something had happened at Crystal, but he wasn't interested in giv- ing out details. Kenton imagines the glasses clinking in the background. He guesses that all the guy really wanted to do was have a drink or two and eat his dinner and enjoy his visitors right then. Here was a fellow who never had connected with the river itself or its people, and never would actually, and now he just wanted to forget about those things. And Martin, cunning old master that he was, kept him on the phone for an hour and then some, rambling on about the human spirit and the meaning of life, the legacy of the Grand Canyon and the value to all mankind of certain symbolic actions… whatever other general nonsense he could think of before he put the question to him, so that finally the super would have said almost anything just to get off the phone and be left alone. And what Martin got out of him was: Okay, he'd sit down with his rangers the next day and talk about the speed trip, and if the answer was still no, then he'd call Martin back that same day and tell him the reason why.

Martin shrugged as he relayed the message. "He says if the answer is *no*, he'll phone tomorrow. Now if he doesn't call me again, what do you suppose that will mean?" Kenton grinned.

Dave Stratton was down there on a trip the next day. A guy named Darrel was leading that trip and on Darrel's boat was a kid named Wayne. This turned out to be Darrel's last trip. Dave Stratton would see him on a golf course ten years later and Darrel would come over and give him the eye. "You doing it?" Dave would nod proudly. "Still doing it." Darrel would shake his head sadly, as though they'd been talking about an incurable disease Stratton had.

They got to Crystal and looked her over. Suzanne Jordan was there too, leading an AZRA oar trip. The thing was, Wayne wasn't a boatman yet, but he was scheduled to get his own boat next trip, so this time he was supposed to run everything.

"We got up there," says Dave, "looked at the hole and said, 'Okay, you see the tammies that are in the water, you gotta be running right over those. Don't worry about the motor. Just stay out of the middle of the river. There's no hitting the hole today. You get in there and it's over. If you get in where it's rocky and you have to lift, lift. But if you're there, you'll be to the right, you'll be where you want to be.' And they took off and ran it and I guess Darrel, you know he'd been there the week before and ran it and made it… I don't know, for some reason they just ended up in the middle of the river heading right for it…and the results weren't good at all."

Dave didn't see the wreck. He was untying from shore when Suzanne came storming down off the hill. "She came running down and said 'You just had a boat flip.' And immediately my heart was going about a million miles an hour. So we got everybody off except my two helpers and two volunteers. Two guys on my boat wanted to help out; one was a paramedic. 'You know we may end up flipping too,' I said. 'Possibly. No guarantees there.' They wanted to go for it, though. So I said, 'Okay, let's go.'"

This was D-Day, the day they were supposed to get the superintendent's call. Kenton, Rudi and Ren held their breath all day long. They put the boat on the trailer and packed a cooler full of sandwiches and good beer in case of emergency. In the side hatches they put two twelve-volt batteries to run hand-held floodlights if they needed them. Rudi gave Ren and the Factor a mini Maglite each to put around their necks in case they fell out during the night. They squirmed around until 5:00 P.M. on the dot. The call never came.

Stoner and the ARR trip, it turned out, had stayed at Lower Bass until almost the end of the first big day of Crystal wrecks. They couldn't find a camp that night until the ledges at the bottom of Conquistador Aisle; the rest of them were taken or underwater.

They camped below Deer Creek the next day and while they were cooking dinner a brand new batch of flotsam went rolling by. A familiar sign of disaster: ammo cans, drink coolers, box lids. "Uh oh," Stoner said. "The park's going to close this thing down if we're not careful."

That night, while Stoner and crew slept, the speed run started.

Next morning Stoner's trip got out early and headed for Havasu. Down below Kanab they found a lone motor rig side tube, floating in an eddy all by itself. They tied it to shore. At Havasu, with their people already up the canyon, they stood on their own boats alone and watched the rest of the rig, minus that one tube float by upside down in eerie silence. "Boy, I hope nobody's under it," the swamper said.

Stoner shook his head. "If they are, we're not going to do them any good now."

The *Emerald Mile* got to Hermit and Rudi was rowing. Jimmy Hendrick was there leading a Wilderness World trip on day six or seven, just pulling out from the scout. They passed the rest of them but Jimmy wouldn't pull over. He and Rudi ran the rapid together with Jimmy screaming colorful obscenities the whole time. "$%#!@ Dories. Who the &%#@! do they think they are?" Stuff like that.

It was pretty exciting. The waves were huge.

By the time they got through the rapid, Jimmy had figured out what was going on and that made him even madder, if anything. That he had to be working while these bozos were having all the fun going through on a speed trip.

"I got into the Jewels," says Stratton, "and the first person I came to…I immediately had a bad feeling. And the closer I got to him the more and more I felt that this guy wasn't alive. So we took our little ring buoy and tied it onto the end of the bowline and my helper jumped in and hung onto him while the others pulled him in. They checked him out, but they couldn't get anything. The one guy, the EMT, says 'I just don't think this guy is going to make it. I don't think we can get him back around.'" The EMT was right, of course, and that death led to the closing of Crystal.

The *Emerald Mile* rounded the turn above Crystal at about 9:00 A.M. the day after the fatality. "We were very confident," Rudi says. "We'd just done a commercial trip in the fifty to sixty thousand water range and we figured how different can it be?"

Tied to shore on the right side was a sea of rubber. There were motor rigs galore and about twenty rowboats and maybe a hundred and fifty people all wearing their lifejackets on dry land, people swarming around like ants on a gumball. It could've been Coney Island. Yellow, orange, red and blue. Black stone, white sand, a grey-green river. Bright sun. Blue sky. The smell of water, of twenty-year-old trees dying in the flood.

The commercial passengers were being force-marched around the rapid and the boatmen were running through empty. There was one little eddy— Thank God Eddy—tucked into the cliffs below on the right side and afterwards you had about thirty seconds until the next big rapid, Tuna Creek, and it was long and nasty too.

The Factor thought Ren should row because he was the strongest, he could move the boat significantly faster than the others, but Ren said nah, it was Kenton's boat so he might as well do the honors for this one. "What do we do," Kenton said, "if they wave us in?"

"Wave back," Rudi said.

"We fantasized that it might be okay," Kenton says now. "Not getting the call and everything. But we kinda knew the truth, too." He laughs. "We knew we had God on our side, though…"

John Thomas was pretty cool, actually; he was a boatman himself. He was out there standing on someone's motor rig when they rounded the turn, and for a long time he just looked upstream at the *Emerald Mile* as it came, glistening down through the heat waves, one little dory all by itself, painted beryl green with a bright red stripe on its gunwales, carrying three maniacs bound for glory. Thomas watched them come and shook his head.

"He didn't even wave," Kenton says. "Before we could even get close he turned and walked off the motor rig, started heading up the hillside to watch us run. 'Cause he knew we weren't pulling in. And after he turned around he never looked over again. He was just looking down at his clipboard and walking, talking on his radio, reporting that we were coming by, I think."

So down they went, bravely around the turn and into the rapid in front of God and all those people.

And then they saw God's Own Hole.

"Yeah, we knew there'd be a big one down there," Kenton says. "But basically we were totally unprepared for what we saw."

It's always been a deceptive entry. The river is wide and smooth there, pinched into a broad turn at the very last second. You look at it from shore and you think it's one thing but then you get out there in a boat and you *realize.* What's never clear until you're out in it is the speed of it. How fast it is, how big it is, how little time you really have.

Kenton says, "We're just thinking, *Oh man, we've gotta get through this thing.* And I said, 'Hey, I want you guys as we're coming in to say how close I can go.' So we're dropping in and I'm getting over as far as I think I can and we look down, we see where we've gotta go—you can see where that lateral starts and you know you've gotta be in above that lateral or you're dead meat. But there were rocks there, really shallow rocks. There was a little tamarisk tree out there waving in the current and behind it looked like a pour-over and I just thought out loud, 'God, can I go over that?' And everybody said, 'God…uh…no!' So I came in just as close to it as I thought I could and it went uhn-UHHHhhh…"

"We were just talking about running it the same way we did two or three weeks earlier on the last commercial trip," Rudi says. "We felt that it would be washed out and that it wouldn't be any big deal and there was a lot of room. But as we approached we saw that *huge f—ing wave.*" (He lowers his voice for this.) "We were totally blown away by finding that…barrier there. And I remember Kenton saying, 'Should I try to go right of it?' But of course it was much too late to even think about that."

"We were coming up on it and Kenton asked if any of us wanted to row," says Ren (one of the best dorymen alive). "But it didn't bother me that he rowed, 'cause his boat was made for him. There were all those trips lined up on the side there, on the right side as we were going down. We saw the ranger. I looked at him but I tried to be a little nonchalant about looking over there 'cause I didn't want him to see us staring at him... So we went in there thinking, *Okay we got this one, it's just another rapid.* And then I looked at it and thought, *Oh God, what is this thing?*"

"I hit that lateral and we just went whoooooooosh," Kenton says. "Got the big surf right out to the very center of the hole and so I just lined it up and got it straight…"

"I wish I could have watched us," Rudi says. "I never saw where the run *should* have been, really. I suppose we didn't see the hole for more than about two seconds. I was in the back and Ren was in the front…Kenton had positioned the boat and we were just floating in. I remember looking downstream over the front of the boat, and there it was: a wall of water, absolutely vertical, that extended almost clear across the river. Between two and three stories high, I think. Just a white wall of boiling water. I remember it occurred to me that we were going to need an awful lot of luck to make it and then of course we hit it…"

"I was in the bow," Ren says. "I turned around and looked at those guys. There was nothing else we could do at that point, just go for it. I jumped on the front hatch and tried to hold on, and that was the biggest wave I've ever seen. And we hit it perfect. I don't think we could have hit it any better."

"The flip was instantaneous," says Rudi. "There was nothing rhythmic or graceful or easy about it at all. It was just—boom—we were over."

Kenton says, "I just pushed hard and stood up and went forward with Ren. Me and Ren were plastered against the bow but you could feel it before you ever got there, you know? There was no way. It just snapped us straight over. I had hold of my oars as tight as I could grip 'em. I was thinking, *I'm not letting go of these f—ing oars 'cause they're tied to the boat!* You know, you didn't want to get away from the boat at all, and, uh, I hadn't even completed the thought; they just went—bing, bing—and I was gone. I went down, down, down…felt myself coming back up, still getting tossed around and—pfoo!—cleared the water out of my eyes and two feet away was the *Emerald Mile.* I just hollered 'Yeah baby! Here we are! Don't worry, I'll get you right side up!' And I hear this gasping and I look over. About ten feet downstream is old Rudi so I stick my foot out for him…"

"Oh, I was happy to be in back," Rudi says. "Ren banged his head on something on the boat when we did the endo. And also he got sent much further away from the boat than Kenton and I did. I remember being under the water, a little bit of the Bendix effect, the washing machine effect…it wasn't that dead silence of when you go deep. I've never been real deep myself. Those who go deep say it's real quiet down there. Real dark. I just had the sense of being tumbled around in underwater turbulence for what was probably a few seconds; those few seconds that seem like an eternity but they really aren't. And then when my head popped up I could see the boat was about twenty feet from me and Kenton was right next to the boat. And Kenton motioned me to swim to the boat, which I was about to do anyway…"

"I vaguely remember," says Ren "the boat, or something, hitting my head, and then being sucked down. I felt my head under the water, because I knew something had happened, but I couldn't… I tried to look at my hand—is there blood on my fingers? Five feet under water, so there was no way to tell from there. So I thought, *Okay, just hang in there; you'll come up. That's what you're supposed to do. Your lifejacket will save you. Just wait.* I might have had my eyes closed too, and I thought, *Just wait, just wait,* and finally I was out of breath and I thought, *Well, better not wait any longer than this.* So I opened my eyes and started trying to get to the top. It was dark, black, and finally I saw some light up there. I kept swimming and swimming. I popped up and I saw the boat. Those guys were climbing up, but they were far away. I was starting to go to the boat when I got sucked back down, and that time I thought to myself, *Hey, forget that boat, you know, I've got to get myself out of this river. Whichever is easiest, whichever comes first: the bank or the boat, get somewhere,* because I was not in good shape."

Kenton says, "We all just felt…WHOAAAA… It was an intense flip, really intense experience underwater. It seemed like forever. It wasn't a regular hole. It was perfection in a hole, you know? You had about, maybe a hundredth of a percent chance of making it through. If you ran it a hundred times in a dory, you probably wouldn't make it through once. So Ren was about forty feet away right out in the middle of the river swimming along and the *Emerald Mile* was headed for the right shore. I wanted to make sure it made it into the eddy… Me and Rudi got on top of it and loosened the flip line and we were just haulin' ass down the right side and we're thinking, *Oh man. Now we're getting' close to the shore.*"

"It wasn't much of an effort for me to get to the boat," Rudi says. "Ren was way downstream. Way downstream. But Kenton and I climbed right up. It was pretty automatic: go for the flip-lines. It was a single system, straps with buckles, and the straps were kind of worn at the chines… so we went for that and loosened the buckles, leaned back, feet on the chine, and the boat started to come over and we kept leaning back and it came and came and came. And the bottom of the boat was vertical, dead vertical; our bodies were just about horizontal to the water and—boom! That's when the flip-line broke."

Kenton says, "We got it on its side and almost over, started to come over and—flunk!—the flip-line broke. Shitty old flip-line, and—MMwwhoom! It goes back down and two seconds later—crunch! We tag a pour-over. But all it did was take off the very tip of the bow and the stern posts…"

"I started swimming frantically towards shore," Ren says. "I think I surfed, actually. I got picked up by a wave and shot to the shoreline and came right into that eddy perfectly, it was great. I got pushed right into the rock and I felt like a drowned rat. I crawled up on that rock and went, *Thank you, thank you,* and sat there, not very long. I turned around and those guys were coming down the rapid. I thought, *Jesus if they go by what am I going to do?* I didn't want to get back in the water. I mean, I was worn out. And I knew I was bleeding."

Rudi says, "Ren made a supreme effort of swimming and swam himself into the very, very bottom of the eddy. He swam up to the bottom of the boat and got on too, and the three of us righted the boat. Then we got into her and we breathed a big sigh of relief, and next we looked around us and it was a crowded eddy. There were sandwiches floating all around. There was fruit floating around…where'd all this come from?" Rudi laughs. "Well it came from our front cross-hatch, which had blown open somehow."

"All of our food got wet," Kenton says, grinning. "The cooler didn't come out, but it was open. My clothes bag was open, my wallet came out of it; it's out there floating around…Ren's bleeding like a stuck pig down his face. He's got this slice right between his eyebrows. It was BAD. And we were just beat, you know? It just kicks your ass. Hanging onto the boat going over those rocks, you were just bashing rocks with your legs and stuff and hearing your boat hit and going, *Oh, Jesus… we messed up here.* But the way it turned out, you know, everything was just right. If we'd have been right side up going in there we'd have probably put holes in the bottom of the boat and been sinking. Not a good place to be sinking and trying to patch a boat.

"Then this chopper came over us, park service chopper, and we're thinking, *Uh oh, jig's up, we're finished.* So we acted like we didn't have any communication, just giving them the thumbs up and waving them off. So they just hovered there for a while. Looking at us and going, *Rrrrr, we can't get you from here, can we?* So they flew away and about that time this Western rig came bombing in there and almost plastered us against the shoreline. And the boatman said, 'Wow, I'm glad I didn't hit you, man. I'm sorry but I HAVE to make this eddy and if I was you I'd get outta here, because in about two more seconds another guy is pulling in right behind me and he isn't nearly as good at this as I am.'"

"At this point we were very demoralized," Rudi says. "I mean extremely so. We had wanted to be incognito. We didn't want to have the park service embarrassed or make a big deal out of it or anything like that. We just wanted to do it. And after Crystal we were so beat up. I remember just wanting to get out of there. To not even be there. But still, the fastest way to do that was keep going."

They kept going. In an hour they were through the stretch of rapids called the Gems. In another they were bombing down Stephen Aisle at mile 117. They passed another Dories trip below Deer Creek; it was on its tenth day. Even there they didn't stop to visit. Just kept going. Rudi laughs, "All their passengers looked like they were *not* having a good time. Can you imagine a commercial trip on that water? Regan Dale, the leader, whenever he tells the story, says the biggest challenge was to get all the boats to land at the same place. I remember thinking as we passed them that we put in last night after all those people were asleep and if the run continued to go well, we were going to be out on Lake Mead before they woke up the next morning…"

Stoner was camped at Mohawk, in the middle of cooking dinner and drinking a beer, admiring the evening sunlight when they passed him. His trip was having a hell of a nice party.

"Here come the Dories," somebody said. But there was only one boat. A solid color green one with red gunwales, three guys in her, couldn't tell exactly who. They went by fast and didn't even slow down. The one in the stern gave a quick wave and that was it. They were gone down the river. Everybody stood there and watched them go, all backlit against the glistening water for a moment. It was kinda pretty.

They ran Lava Falls at seven or so. It was huge too but they ran it on the left, wide open. Rudi at the oars, Kenton says. "A really nice run."

"God, Kenton rowed that so well," Rudi says. "Wide open. Ren was in front and I was in back…" Are you sure? he is asked. Kenton says you rowed it. "I'm positive," Rudi says. "I didn't. He did. There is no question in my mind at all about that… There were humongous tail waves, and I remember Ren saying 'Great, we made it,' or something like that, and Kenton was still working, working, he was looking at those tail waves and he said 'It ain't over yet.' It was a beautiful run. He knew the run and he knew what he wanted to do."

It was pitch black and they were using the lights by the time they got to Parashant Wash, mile 198. They went by another Dories trip there, which was on its fifteenth day.

They stopped above 205 Mile Rapid. You could see the moon on the rim, but down in the gorge it was really dark so they decided to wait a while. Took their bags out and got in them and fell asleep. Woke late. "The moon was way up," Kenton says. "I can't remember who woke up first, but we burned a good three hours right there."

205 was huge. "205'll eat you alive," Martin used to say. He'd run it before the dam. And yeah it was big, but they skinnied through. After 217 it got really dark again and in the lower gorge it was gnarly and black; they needed the lights. It stayed that way clear down to the lake, where the stars began to fade. Then Rudi rowed like a champ while Kenton and Ren slept a bit—they were too hammered to stay awake—and then they woke again twenty miles downstream. Somewhere below Evan's Heaven the Factor put another set of oarlocks on the boat and two people at a time rowed the rest of the way in.

A couple days later the water would go to ninety thousand awhile and then suddenly it would drop way down. "No cause for alarm, everything's under control."

Tom Gamble, who'd reckoned the spillway damage couldn't be too bad after they dropped the water down, was in for a surprise. The east spillway tunnel in Glen Canyon Dam sloped sixty degrees. Six hundred feet down, the tunnel hit an elbow and exited almost horizontally. The engineers went in wearing foul weather gear and hardhats and headlamps. Workers above lowered them down on a cart, using a cable.

As the cart descended, the picture got worse and worse. The spillway was a mess. Concrete gone, rebar gone, holes all over. Big ones. Red sandstone laid bare, soft as hell and full of water. The biggest hole was right at the elbow, one hundred and fifty feet long and too deep to measure.

BuRec already knew what the problem was: a recently discovered process called cavitation. They knew how to fix it too, but that wasn't going to help hold back this flood. Right here and now there was only one thing left to do. "Shut her down boys. We're going to have to wait this thing out."

The tops of the spillway gates were at thirty-seven hundred feet above sea level and Lake Powell was just a few feet below that, and rising fast. If it crested the gates, the water would rush unchecked through the spillways at about the same rate it was running through Cataract Canyon—still over ninety thousand cfs. If BuRec did nothing, the lake was definitely going to crest the gates. But at the dam somebody had an idea.

"Call the lumberyard," Tom Gamble said. "See how much plywood they've got and how long it'll take to get here."

The timers were there to meet the tired dory and its exhausted crew. They'd run two separate watches and witnessed the *Emerald Mile* disappear into the darkness at Lees Ferry and then drove straight around to pick her up the next day. Motored a little canoe up Lake Mead that night and putted along behind as she came in.

"There were our timers of course and we told them, 'Okay wait, not yet…now!' as we crossed the Grand Wash Fault," Rudi says. "And at that moment—I don't mean thirty seconds later, I mean instantly—the wind started blowing, steadily. But up until then there had been no wind at all. None. So that's another stroke of luck we had. It could easily have been another two or three hours on the lake stretch alone if conditions had been a little less favorable."

The time was thirty-six hours, thirty-eight minutes, and twenty-nine seconds. They went two hundred and seventy-seven miles, clear through the whole Grand Canyon. They quit rowing right there.

The lake rose for two more weeks after they shut the water down. Tom Gamble's crew extended the spillway gates with plywood out of Page until steel flashboards could be shipped in from elsewhere. In the middle of July, the lake crested at 3,708.4 feet above sea level—more than eight feet above the spillway danger zone.

Very slowly, the water began to recede.

They got towed in, drove to Boulder City on the way home and talked to Bill Belknap, who'd timed the Rigg brothers' first speed run back in the fifties. Told him the story. Were driven home and slept like dead men for two days. "I've never been so tired," Kenton says. "Never."

They went to court at the South Rim and were fined five hundred dollars. At first the superintendent wanted to ban them for life from the river, but someone smarter jollied him out of that. There was too much respect, grudging or otherwise, for what they'd done.

Ren disappeared soon afterwards and went off to sail the South Pacific. He sends postcards every now and then. In '87 Kenton retired the *Emerald Mile* and built a new boat, the *Bright Angel*. At the end of that same year, Martin Litton sold the company and retired himself.

The year after that, the Factor sat down with his telephone and typewriter and rounded up every commercial boater he could think of. He'd had another cockamamie vision: an organization of boatmen, banded together to take care of the canyon and themselves and the river running experience. People laughed at first, but Kenton kept pushing. It would work, by god. You could call it Grand Canyon River Guides. It would work.

Rudi speaks of retirement now, too. There are only a few dory trips anymore, a fraction of what they ran in years past. The business is getting more mainstream all the time and Rudi is beginning to think it might be best to lay out at this point, to guard the memories. He too runs a self-made dory, a beauty he built back in '81. He calls her the *Colorado*.

The best of it for Rudi, he says when asked to sum up the whole thing, was living on the boats all those years… You sleep on them, you brush your teeth in them, you go off to work in them every single day. It's been a wonderfully simple life, to live in a beautiful place, on a lovely little boat, surrounded by the best of friends.

Does he think about the speed trip? Oh, all the time. Every other day or so. And Kenton too, he knows. They dream about it often: the moonlight, the waves, the speed. The power of the water.

Would they do it again?

Well, the Factor would, of course. He's already scrunching up his face, thinking about it. He's built another dory lately, the *Grand Canyon*, but every now and then he lets his mind wander to a different boat. Twenty-four hours next time. You could build a long skinny dory with two rowing stations. Maybe thirty feet long. It'd be thin so it would track, you'd have a guy in the back to look forward and run a sweep oar, the others wouldn't even have to watch, they'd just row their guts out. Maybe you'd have to take four guys, one to rest…

It's funny to hear Kenton talk about it, to witness certain ideas coming full circle: it would be a boat not unlike John Wesley Powell's in a way.

But really. Does the Factor honestly think humans could row through there in that amount of time? "Yeah. Definitely. I guess I've got to start on that boat pretty soon," Kenton says.

"Come on."

"No. You could do it," Kenton says.

And sketching a shape with his hands in the air, he begins to describe her.

Editor's Note: Rudi did indeed retire from commercial boating in the late 1980s, although he still runs rivers with his family and friends. Ren is back from the South Pacific, and continuing with watersports as a sailing tour captain in Hawaii. Kenton was still an active boatman when he died in 2002 of an aortic aneurism while out mountain biking. His "cockamamie" vision of Grand Canyon River Guides currently has nearly two thousand members.

AFTER THE TRIP

Allen Wilson

Flagstaff, Arizona. May 1970. Monday. One-thirty in the morning and the old Ford two-ton truck, sixteen-foot trailer and eight college-aged people lumber through town and out a couple of miles past Camp Townsend to the old Burris Ranch.

Tim and Shona sack out under the truck. Mike and Richard throw their gear out in the chicken coop. I stumble into the bunkhouse. Bob and Delores come in a little later, throw their gear on the floor and we all pass out. We had been riding in the back of the truck, on the top of the boats and gear, nearly freezing in the cold mountain air. Dead tired after another take-out.

Coming back from the world of rafting the Colorado River throws us into a state of shock. Thirteen hours before we had left forty people, mostly professional couples from Los Angeles and San Francisco. The separation was sad and happy. We hated parting company with these folks. After all, we had spent nine very close days together and had bonded with them. The trip's end was a rasty breaking of that bond and we suffered from it, physically and mentally. In the back of our minds was the possibility of another great group five days from now, but this break was tough. During this emotionally charged time we were the most tired of any part of the trip. Drifting all night on the boats the night before, de-rigging in the hot sun at South Cove on Lake Mead, and the long ride back to Flagstaff had left us completely exhausted.

I wake at 6:00 A.M., shivering, hungry and in great need to take a leak. I make a dash for the door and pee on the communal bush by the porch. Purple blossoms are starting to fill the branches, but they won't last long. In two weeks the entire crew will be here and most will be using this bush.

Running from the bush to the truck in my bare feet through the red volcanic cinders is painful. The forty-degree temperature on my bare body is making it hard to keep my hands steady while I unbuckle my black river bag. I waste no time in putting on jeans, shirt, socks, tennis shoes and a jacket. Hunger is my main problem now and that can be solved in the barn. The pile of leftover canned goods from previous years and trips contains lots of Spam. A quick jerk of the pull-tab with my channel locks lets me in; one can of Spam gone within seconds.

Looking east out the barn door the sunflowers are standing tall, thousands of them beyond the bunkhouse. The sun low on the rolling cinder hills makes the landscape glow bright with reds, yellows and purples, coupled with the clear, dark blue sky—a panorama that can only come from the high plateau country. I lean against the door and gaze in a trance at the beauty of the place.

In the cold blue air my mind drifts to a broken motor handle in House Rock Rapid, a ripped tube in 25 Mile, a torn pontoon in Crystal, two motors with water pumps out, and four bad seeping leaks. Work, lots of it, and in five days we'll be on the river again. Back to reality…

FAITH IN THE DRY SEASON

Rebecca Lawton

L ate summer going into fall is when I set out to the creeks looking for clues. By autumn the streams have dried up like wrung sponges, their bare beds testimony to something lost. I must believe I can find traces in disappeared pools and past currents, because I get up and walk the bare creek bottoms.

This morning I walked to the hills before dawn, and now I'm standing in a tributary to my hometown creek. This nameless drainage winds out of the mountains, dodges under bridges, and twists past vineyards and houses, joining the mainstem creek on its north side, at the edge of some country properties. About four feet deep and three wide, this tributary channel today lies thick with everything but water—an orange carpet of fallen buckeye leaves, handfuls of wild plums. A flicker's barred feathers crown a bank of cobbles topped with deflated algal mats.

Spring floods are just a memory. In March this creek danced with standing waves, smelled of earth, and rose to within inches of its bridges. Heady days, when weather reports promised more, though the channel couldn't hold it. Glory days, but they've passed. Now here it is, the end of summer going into fall, and this dry bed won't see water again until the winter rains return.

There is water farther down and deep here. I know it's there because of the skin of dry mud that arches up from the underlying wet layers, as if pulling away from an unloved twin. If not for the telltale curling of the mud, would we know about the moisture below? Would we recall high water and have faith in the dry season? If not, the aridity of the place might overwhelm us, days without rivers stretching endlessly ahead.

Late summer going into fall speaks to others as well, especially my friends in the river guiding community. These are boatmen who ran or still run rivers commercially throughout the West. Year after year, through their twenties and thirties, and sometimes into their forties or fifties, they have matched their lives to the change of seasons. Although I left the business

Whale

Steve Bledsoe

1992

years ago, I still feel the shift in my cells: in spring, blood runs higher than water. The river calls us to get back to it, to jump in and hold on. Summers bring kinship, good food, and rapids to jar the senses with adrenaline. The weather is so easy we live on sandbars under balmy skies and stars so numerous we have no need of nightlights.

Then the summer ends in fall, a restless time. By autumn in desert river country such as the Grand Canyon, a chill lingers in the air long after dawn. Trips taper off, and boatmen find themselves more and more in town. These former bronzed gods shuttle between cars to laundromats carrying mountains of clothes that must be washed several times to come clean. Those who have no winter jobs or schools to attend hang out in coffee shops and bars, no longer surrounded by the passengers who praised their skills and worshipped their heroism. Sometimes the guides hustle to get scheduled on off-season trips, if not in the canyon, then in Costa Rica, Chile, or New Zealand. Most often, though, the boatmen simply pass through an amorphous period of transition, during which they run idle errands while making decisions about the coming winter.

An indifferent, isolated time, fall is also when we've lost many of the boatmen who have taken their own lives. Our community mourns them still, although in some cases decades have passed. A surprising number of skillful, daring men have met their end that way—enough so you could call it an occupational hazard. The death toll for guides by suicide may outstrip even the numbers dead by drowning. Sometimes they've used the bottle, sometimes more immediate, violent means, often carried out in the collapsing days and fading light of autumn.

———

Whale was a mountain of a man, soft spoken, utterly competent. I never knew him by any other name, never considered calling him anything else. He worked the Grand Canyon every season since 1970 as a commercial guide on motor-powered pontoon rigs. After nearly ten years of seeing him cruise past our oar-powered trips, I finally met him one lunchtime in 1983. He walked into our river camp from his rig parked far down the beach. Swampers, green boatmen twenty years his junior, flanked him on either side. With their sun burnt hair and mirror shades, they might have made a formidable entourage had Whale not pulled off his sunglasses and grinned.

I pumped his arm and introduced myself. "I'm the one you pulled out of Crystal last trip."

Whale smiled and nodded.

"Thanks for saving my life," I said.

He shrugged, and our conversation went no further. Wondering why he didn't speak, I peered at him, with his boyish, tumbled-blond boatman's hair and freckled, pink suntan. He just squinted and made soft little assenting sounds, as if "Ah, shucks" were lodged somewhere deep inside him. We stood staring at each other a few more moments, and I became aware of his complicated eyes—they had distance in them that seemed to reflect much more than the two hundred and twenty-four-mile stretch of Colorado River between Lees Ferry and Diamond Creek. Then he and his swampers, their curiosity about me apparently satisfied, retreated back to his rig.

To say that he'd saved my life may have been no overstatement. He'd fished me out of the river a few weeks before, after I'd flipped an eighteen-foot raft in high-water Crystal Rapid. Crystal is an unforgiving place—waves the size of ocean swells, house-sized reversals that eat boats, and a raft-ripping rock island lurking only dozens of yards downstream. In ten years of working full time as a commercial guide in the canyon, Crystal was the only place I'd even come close to witnessing a drowning. There, I saw more than a few nasty flips and more than one boater who couldn't get out of the water. A handful had drowned in the whitewater-choked gorge downstream. Crystal was one of a few rapids I never wanted to run, much less swim, no matter how many canyon trips I had under my belt.

After my own flip in Crystal's main hole, I found myself in the same speeding current that had claimed others' lives. My boat foundered somewhere upstream of me, too far away to be of help. Used to scary swims in the canyon, I told myself to stay calm and breathe between waves, but I felt panic creeping in. The river at Crystal is about fifty degrees cold, and it was numbing me. Washing through the worst of the waves and aiming desperately toward shore, I saw a few narrow eddies race by like a string of lost opportunities. The good news was that I'd been running empty—there was no one to save but myself. The bad news was I was starting to feel like I couldn't do it.

Just then I looked up and saw hope. It was Whale, standing at the stern of his thirty-three-foot pontoon rig, motoring out from shore at a perfect ferry angle to catch me. He'd been waiting in an eddy below the hole, right where I needed him to be. Although floating fast and low, I still had the sense to admire him in all his glory, coming to the rescue in full control of his boat and the situation—a supreme look of concentration on his face, his blue eyes in a focused squint, his blond hair properly tousled and wild. He looked as brave as George Washington on the storm-whipped Delaware, as alert as a predator about to pounce, as unwavering as if he were my best friend.

His crew tossed a safety line that landed squarely in my arms. "Hold on!" someone yelled. With Whale minding the helm, his crew and passengers pulled me from the river. They motored me to shore, catching and righting my raft along the way and setting me in it. None of my gear had even moved in the rigging. The rescue was over that fast—as if nothing had happened.

But Whale and I knew it had happened. He passed a bottle of whiskey to me in my washed-clean boat. To the applause of his crew and his own silent appreciation, I stood in the rowing well and threw back a few slugs. Although I felt waterlogged and cold to the bone, I'd survived it, and Whale was my hero. I raised the bottle and toasted him and high water.

———

Back in my hometown tributary, I'm separated by time and distance from Crystal Rapid. I've been retired from commercial boating for twenty years. Whale has been gone more than a decade. Near the close of the 1995 river season, with fall in the air and the cold nights upon him, he walked into the ponderosa pine forest outside Flagstaff. He stood alone among the sweet smells of tall trees with desert wind in their needles. As I imagine it, he gazed up at a sight he knew he'd never see again—blue sky above a spiral of conifer branches, wisps of white cloud passing even higher overhead. Then he ended his life with a pistol, and he left no note.

My friends called to ask how well I'd known him. Did I know he'd fought in Vietnam? In the war, he'd been a helicopter door gunner and later a crew chief, lasting a year in the job at a time when life expectancy was about three days. Did I know he'd recently broken up with his long-time girlfriend? How well had he handled that end-of-season thing? One friend said she'd seen him a few weeks earlier in line at the Flagstaff post office. He'd looked a mess, as if he'd been "sleeping in a dumpster." He probably hadn't showered in weeks, a habit perhaps carried over from the river. "But I saw him the next day and he looked fine." He'd looked fine to me, too, the last time I saw him, the first time we truly met. He'd been smiling because *he* had helped *me*.

The dry creek bed unfurls a path of secrets before me. I pause when I hear an acorn woodpecker frenetically storing nuts for the winter, and I notice that I've stopped near a low bank of gravelly spheres. Each one is tough and a few inches in diameter, a stone-thrower's dream. I break one in two, the halves parting as easily as a cloud. Inside is a center that's damp and muddy, still soft and pliable. Armored mudballs. In spring, before the wet season is truly over, high flows scoop up mud and roll it around in sand and pebbles like cookie dough in sugar. The result—small, soft spheres with tough exteriors.

Had I known how to read Whale's face as well as I've come to understand the features of this dry creek bed, perhaps I could've returned the favor he did me back in Crystal in 1983. Maybe I could've saved him somehow. But I didn't come through for Whale—none of us did. It's much easier to look inside the armor of a mudball than the skin of a man. We didn't know how to convince him that his despair would pass—if indeed it would have—as high water always comes again. Getting him to believe in the return of a better season would have taken more than a pontoon boat, a rescue line, and a boatman's cool skill.

I turn to head down the creek for home. For the first time, I notice that the sunlight looks different today—muted, thick, and angled low. Straightening up to pay attention, I hear a call from farther off and higher up, a mournful cry from the north. In a moment a single bird flies into view, wings beating furiously, neck outstretched and reaching south. It's a lone goose, calling in autumn.

DON'T LET YOUR CHILDREN GROW UP TO BE BOATMEN

Vince Welch

Every other year since 1990, we ex-canyon guides bring our bad habits, our worn out stories, and our wooden boats back to the river. Like memory-laden salmon returning to the site of their not-quite immaculate conception, we can't help ourselves. We need the life-giving oxygen of the river to pulse through our imaginations as well as our blood. And despite the underwhelming obstacles of family, jobs and mortgages, most of us, along with our spouses and lovers, attend these bi-annual floating reunions religiously.

You would think, at middle age, we would know better. To drive torturous hours on stomach churning, roadside java in order to spend time on the river with thirty or so of your closest friends taunts the imagination. Then there are the lengthy put-ins, the toilet lines, the sore backs, the toe-liosis, the hot stinking desert, and the mini-hangovers after one or two lukewarm beers. These minor inconveniences should be enough to discourage reasonable people. When your body yearns for a nap before *and* after lunch, surely it is time to put the oars aside and gracefully accept that your fifteen minutes of river fame has come to a close.

And for reasons not entirely clear, though masochistic in nature, we also bring along our children, those former gleams in our bloodshot eyes. This fruit of our loins comes in various shapes and sizes: the sodden-diapered infant, the snot-nosed toddler, the recalcitrant ten-year-old, the wannabe tweeners and the eye rolling, been-there-before teeners. All of them may also be returning to the sandy beaches of their conception.

Children on the river? River guides, of all people, ought to know better. No matter what the glossy brochures with smiling families suggest, rivers are no place for kids, certainly not large numbers of kids. They disturb the natural order established decades ago by their parent-guides.

Children of all ages require tending. Lots of it. It is easy to see why childcare is disagreeable to former canyon gods and goddesses. There are squabbles to settle, complaints to be endured, towels and lifejackets to be located. And not unlike certain commercial passengers, these children ask questions repeatedly. A surly reply or a scowl cannot subdue them. Even the help-resistant teenagers must be fed, watered, and on occasion, corralled. Warnings must be issued to them by parents who habitually ignored such warnings well into their middle years.

Nor can the negative influence boatmen unwittingly exert on the personal development of children and adolescents, usually not their own, be underestimated. Most children love foolishness, and boatmen traffic in the arcane art of silliness. Rarely will the wee sprogs hesitate when copycat behavior will get a laugh. When a trio of eight-year-old girls breaks into a rendition of Commander Cody and The Lost Planet Airmen's, "There's a whole lot of things we ain't never done, but we ain't never had too much fun," one can only shudder at the thought that one day they may be rowing for a commercial outfit. Or running the country.

Children on the river are ravenous, fun-seeking missiles. They know no boundaries; their tastes are as limitless and pagan as their unbridled imaginations. Born to play, one and all. Once they feel the warm sand beneath their reptilian toes or swim a roaring rapid like a drunken otter, your fate as a parent is sealed.

Despite all this, we drag our progeny back to the rivers of the West. They have left their watery tracks on the Green, the Snake, the Main Salmon, the Middle Fork, the Grande Ronde and naturally, Grand Canyon. Recently we embarked on yet another reunion trip with many of our mewling spawn on board.

We never learn.

⌒

On that bright, crisp summer morning, the conch shell sounds and our fleet of dories, rafts, inner tubes, and kayaks depart. It is well past eleven; the rigors of packing and partying have proved mutually exclusive. And we have yet to choose a nominal trip leader. The ex-river guides, all former trip leaders, scatter for cover. We launch leaderless. The armada circles an eddy the size of Lake Mead for a half hour. Finally, one boat pulls into the current. Another follows. We are on our merry way when a fourteen-year-old stands up in one of the boats, wringing his hands and pointing toward his lifejacket and ammo can on shore. He is speechless with desperation—his Walkman and headphones are in the ammo can.

Downriver we float, getting nowhere fast. The boats drift and circle and creep along beside one another in an extremely unmilitary-like formation. It is more parade than march. It is the floating circus, come to town.

Our offspring, born of hot river nights and cold, unemployed winters, boat hop incessantly. They yelp and bark like seals; they pester whoever is rowing for snacks. They swim beneath the oars and hang on the flip lines of our beloved wooden vessels. They attempt back flips off the stern. They care nothing about trim or quiet or boat etiquette.

The crew of the *Makaha* (with Kenly at the oars) remains composed. The boat is overloaded with females—girls and women and those in between, braiding one another's hair and painting each other's toenails and fingernails deliciously lascivious colors. They speak in whispers, chuckle at their jokes; the older women drink fresh coffee, probably laced with Kahlua, from a small, delicate thermos. All studiously ignore the floating commotion around them, dismissing any entreaty to frolic in the river with a wave of their sparkling hands.

Gwen, my own seven-year-old contribution to overpopulation, decides she wants to row my boat (which isn't my boat at all)*without my help.* Perhaps it's not such a bad idea. Already my lower back aches.

Round and round we go, oars flailing, the ultimate three hundred-sixty-degree river cruise. Mid river we bump a rock; moments later my Captain Bligh swats a kayaker in the head with an oar. The other boats keep a polite distance. I am reaching for a beer. The wooden boat dwarfs her, yet she persists. My instructions fall on stubborn ears. What will she be like at twelve? Or seventeen?

Oddly enough, ten minutes later, she is stroking the eighteen-foot, fifteen hundred pound dory downstream, albeit at the pace of a dead floating carp. She seems to know what she is doing—something in the genes perhaps. *Give me those oars back,* I think to myself.

She relinquishes the oars only when she spots Cooper in his kayak, an addled grin on his face. She wants to ride on the top of the kayak. In what can only be a moment of weakness due to last night's party, he agrees. Off my daughter goes and the empty wooden boat feels lighter in metaphysical ways I cannot articulate. Cooper smiles the grim smile of the recently conquered. *Do I have a beer to go with my offspring?* he wonders. I offer him two, just in case.

Like the children, we fritter the river morning away. We gawk and stare at the scenery; we hum to ourselves. We point to the red-tailed hawk circling high above. The sunshine falls, the river percolates, and the pretty wooden boats drift along as if they were toy boats on a make-believe river. We bask mindlessly in the indivisible sum of it all. Even in our dotage, the river enchantment never fails to take hold.

High above the river on the diving rock, a knot of gangly teenagers have gathered around an eminent grey-bearded boatman famous for his impulsive physical stunts. He is, we pray, cured of the more dangerous elements of his youthful exuberance. Surely he is explaining the safety protocols of river diving: one at a time, no messing around, and look before you leap.

Jake, my thirteen-year-old son, teeters on the edge of the rock. Even from a distance, I can see his eyes glazing over with freshly produced testosterone. His body is screaming for the opportunity to scare the shit out of itself. I avert my gaze, the memory of a decades-old incomplete flip making my stomach turn.

One by one, these fun-seekers leap out into the blue beyond. The over-forties in the audience below cringe, the memory of their own foolish descents rendering them speechless. The rest of the crowd cheers and claps. Naturally, the young performers climb back up the steep hillside and do it again. Naturally they don't know when enough is enough; perhaps it is a genetic predisposition. One river prince attempts a flip; one light-footed nymph tries a tortured swan dive. They both crash and burn. They rise to the green, sparkling surface of the river with cat-swallowed-the-canary grins. Immortality on a summer morning is wasted on the young.

This fun business only gets worse once we set foot on a sandy beach for lunch. Rock skipping commences. Moki, once a smooth stone master, has stopped counting the number of times he has separated his shoulder in his thirty-year career. After one mediocre toss, the young heathens around him have smelled blood. They crowd the shoreline, vying with one another for position and smooth stones. A new champion waits in the wings; the King of the Dancing Stone must fall.

Brad pulls out a role of black viscuine. He sets to making the longest, most dangerous, rock-infested water slide this side of the Rockies. "For the children," he mutters. Smelling danger, a crowd of glassy-eyed admirers gathers round. They recognize a kindred spirit.

We dare not take a nap after lunch, at least not on shore. The temptation to camp would be too great and we have miles to make. So merrily we row along, the young brood momentarily subdued by lunch and their own excesses. They nap, play cards, read books, pick at their scabs, and apply suntan lotion. They tell jokes, riddles, and tongue twisters.

They catch their second and third wind.

They sing *Wild Thing, You Move Me* in chant and refrain. The canyon walls ring with pop tunes. There is an impromptu rendition of Sinatra's *I've Got You Under My Skin*. Finally they segue into a chorus of Mason William's *Them Toad Suckers,* the unofficial dory anthem:

How about them toad suckers
Ain't they clods?
Sittin' there suckin'
Them green toady frogs.

Suckin them hop-toads,
Suckin' them chunkers,
Suckin' them leapy types
Suckin' them plunkers.

Look at them Toad Suckers
Ain't they snappy?
Suckin' them bog-frogs
Sure makes 'em happy.

Them huggermugger Toad Suckers
Way down south.
Stickin' them sucky toads
In they mouth.

How to be a Toad Sucker
No way to duck it
Gittchaself a toad
Rare back and suck it.

It is late afternoon when we make camp. The adults seek sanctuary from their offspring aboard one of the wooden boats. Once sacrosanct and governed by unspoken rules of etiquette, the riverside cocktail hour has been in steady decline since these reunion trips began.

The young savages swarm aboard the wooden boat, a craft built for four or five at most and now bulging with twenty. They are buzzing with excitement. The younger ones knock over drinks and devour the pre-dinner snacks. The adolescents eye their parents suspiciously, alert for behavior or language that might serve as evidence of their own superiority, while trying to cop a sip of beer. Someone is always attempting to stand on the bow and take a leak. One boatman/bar-fly suggests putting as many children as we can in the hatches and locking them in. The younger children squeal with glee; the teenagers smell danger and resist. The fall of western river civilization, we are sure, is imminent.

Nearby gentlemanly, dignified Rudi holds another informal, hands-on lesson in knot tying, both common and obscure, on the decks of the *Colorado*, his custom-made dory. Pony-tailed Greg has two miscreants rubbing white quartz (commonly known as firestones) together, sparks flying as the acrid smell of burning rubber fills their young nostrils. A hands-on geology lesson for future canyoneers.

Naturally the river banter is as cheap and free flowing as the half-gallon discount gin and the Old Milwaukee beer. Since we old boatmen traffic in embellishment, myth, hearsay and rumor, tall tale, exaggeration and outright deceit—all for the sake of a good story—it's no wonder our children are superb hyperbolists.

Mikey, wearing fake buckteeth and golf hat, is hard at work undermining years of parental authority with tales of past wicked behavior in the canyon. His youthful audience hangs on every gin-stained word. He regales them with tales of late-night eddy cruising and episodes of night crawling where certain boatmen attempt to leap over the bodies of sleeping passengers without disturbing them. The children are gleefully horrified. He yarns about magic shows and overturned boats and naked diving and underwater caverns.

As night falls on the river, the teenagers in the group establish their own camp down the beach, a kind of mini Club Med-YMCA arrangement. The younger children play night tag and rub firestones together. The eleven- to thirteen-year-olds, always sticklers for doing things right, clamor for the traditional mainstay of camping: the campfire. Though the air temperature hovers in the mid-seventies, they are not dissuaded. They collect vast amounts of driftwood as if they were planning a human sacrifice. They want matches and combustible fuel, plus a naïve adult to bless their nocturnal cravings for fire. The look in their eyes suggests that they would just as soon burn one of our dories if need be. They *will* have a campfire.

Once the fire is lit, a crowd draws around. They spin stories; fibs turn into epic tales of daring and survival. Someone heists marshmallows from the kitchen. All seems to be going well until one smart aleck asks, "Can we have a grease bomb tonight, Dad?" "They're illegal on the river," replies yawning Dad.

"What's a grease bomb?" someone else asks.

One of the little geniuses pipes up, her voice overflowing with river guide authority: "My mom says it's an environmentally unsound, potentially dangerous pyrotechnic activity that should be avoided at all costs. As the name indicates, the primary fuel is the leftover meat drippings, which are stored in a number ten can throughout a river trip, for environmental purposes of course. On the appropriate night, the 'fuel' is heated to the boiling point over an open fire. Finally, cold water is drawn from the river in a can attached to a very long stick and poured into the bubbling, distilled brew of pig and cow fat. An explosion, followed by unusually large mushroom-shaped fireball, engulfs the night sky. My mom says my dad lost most of his body hair by getting too close to one too many grease bombs. She says he's a slow learner. Rumor has it these were first developed on the Salmon River and then brought south to Grand Canyon, where they grew in popularity and refinement until the park service caught on and banned them."

There is an unruly look in the crowd's merry, dancing eyes. They hunger for an explosion, a crash, a tidal wave. River anarchy is afoot.

One of the few remaining adults to stay awake points out that the trip has only just started. Therefore, we lack an adequate supply of grease for a grease bomb. The mob's exuberance sinks under the dead weight of reason. He throws them a bone. "But we'll probably have enough grease by the end of the trip." Delayed gratification is not a bad thing to experience occasionally.

The hour grows late; the fire dwindles, despite constant infusions of driftwood. The adults have long since retired. Suddenly, one of the sand crawlers screams, "Look! Look! What is it?"

Floating midstream in the black river night is an odd shaped vessel, perhaps a foot in length. It looks like a Spanish galleon ready to explode or a Viking funeral pyre. The warm wind whips the red and yellow flames across the black water like a woman's hair. The children and even the teenagers, riveted to the nocturnal spectacle, are not sure. They scamper to the edge of the water, point, and pace up and down the shoreline. They argue over what it could be. They are thrilled and even a little unnerved. In chorus, they demand answers. They mutter among themselves, and then turn their attention toward a shadowy figure sitting alone on his dory in the dark. They smell a troublemaker.

Brad has hollowed out one of the remaining watermelons, filled it with lighter fluid, walked it upstream, lit it and launched the vessel on its final journey to Valhalla.

One by one, in pairs and trios, these creatures of the night drift off to their bedrolls, rehearsing the tale of the fiery watermelon for future river trips.

It is only day one on the river and there are a whole lot of things they haven't done.

The next morning, at a clandestine meeting fueled by caffeine, those of us over forty decide to co-opt our offspring. We will tap into their bottomless capacity for fun by officially inducting them into the Church of the Flowing Water, an organization with a murky background, no visible leadership, no dogma, no commandments, no meetings, and no dues. We will give them a secret handshake, even a code word. Once joined they will be duty-bound to share, as well as enjoy and promote, any and all activities involving positive life-affirming experiences with moving water, with their parents.

It's the least we can do for our river children.

Boatman Working III
Mary Williams
1993

Colorado River Speak

Baloney Boat - A less than complimentary name for the type of motor rig that has two outside tubes that call to mind two rolls of baloney.

Bowhatch - The hatch, or storage space in the front of a dory.

Cat - A nickname for Cataract Canyon, the last stretch of the Colorado River in southern Utah before it is drowned by the waters of Lake Powell.

CFS - An abbreviation for Cubic Feet per Second. This is a measure of how much water is flowing in the channel of the river: the number of cubic feet of water that pass any given point per second. By extrapolation, then, this number can also tell you relatively how fast the water is traveling, how long it will take you to get somewhere, and just how nervous you should be at various rapids.

Cheat - To avoid the meat, the worst (or best, depending on your preference) part of a rapid. To take a "safer" run.

Chimney - A narrow vertical crack in a rock wall that has three sides. These are climbed using offsetting pressures, i.e. jamming your body in and going up.

Chine – The bottom edge of a dory, where the side meets the bottom. One of the most common places for rocks to hit.

Commercial trip - A river trip composed of people who have paid money to take a guided river trip with one of the professional companies licensed by the National Park Service.

D-ring – A metal ring, shaped (go figure) like a D, which is glued onto the tubes of a rubber raft. These form places of attachment for the frame, safety lines, water bottles and, most importantly, your drag bag filled with beer.

Domer - A dome-shaped rock in the river, over which the water flows, making a hump of water in the middle of the river. Generally not where you want to go with your boat.

Draw - A paddle stroke in which the paddle blade is placed parallel to the side of the kayak and drawn towards the paddler. Used to try and get the boat to move sideways while still pointing downstream.

EDDY - An area of water along the banks of the river where the current has swung around to avoid an obstacle (a rock or an irregularity in the bank) and ends up coming back upstream. These calmer spots are places to stop the boats, either intentionally or not.

EDDY FENCE - The boundary between the downstream current of the river and the upstream current of the eddy. Usually this water is very swirly and filled with small whirlpools. Sometimes eddy fences are the hardest part to negotiate in getting to shore or back into the main channel.

ENDO - An end-for-end flip, most common with kayaks, most spectacular with rafts.

EXCHANGE - When you leave some passengers off at Phantom Ranch, Pipe Creek, or Whitmore Wash and pick up new ones.

FLIP - When the wrong side of your boat is up.

FOOTWELL - The place where the boatman puts his or her feet when rowing. It is lower than the rest of the surface of the frame. A good place to hide when running the V-Wave in Lava Falls.

GROOVER – Otherwise known as The Unit, this is the bathroom. Usually set in a scenic spot far from camp; often accompanied by a bad gossip magazine; always the most popular place in camp after morning coffee.

GUNNELS (GUNWALES) - The upper edge of the sides (the "railing") of a dory. What you grab for white knuckles.

HB – Head Boatman, the guide on a trip who gets paid an extra ten dollars a day to deal with all the headaches.

HIGH SIDE – To throw your body weight towards a wave that is trying to flip your boat. This has the effect of holding that side of the boat down so the boat won't flip. In theory.

HOLE - Where water in a rapid pours over an underwater obstacle, such as a rock or ledge. The resulting drop creates a void into which the water returns, upstream, rather that doing what most self-respecting water does, which is flow downstream. Boats, and their crew, which get caught in holes occasionally find themselves "re-circulated" with this upstream water, a process called "maytagging."

HYPOTHERMIA- Freezing to death, a potential problem with the very cold water of the Colorado.

INTERCHANGE - see EXCHANGE or HEADACHE

LEFT, RIGHT RUN - The correct side of the river to be on when running a rapid. As the water level changes with dam releases, so do the runs in rapids. For instance, at low water levels, a left run at Crystal is possible, even preferable. As the water rises, the left run "closes" and becomes dangerous, and the right run is the only option.

MANTLE - A rock-climbing move that gets you up onto ledges, by throwing one leg over. It's what you used to use to climb up onto walls or trees as a kid.

MARKERS - Many boatmen look at certain rocks in the river to tell them what the water level is at a particular rapid downstream, since the water level is continually changing and it's hard to keep track all the way down the river. For instance, if the Oracle Rock at National Canyon is three inches underwater, then the Slot at Lava Falls is open. Or maybe not.

MERC - Mercury brand outboard motor.

PAINTED DESERT - A region to the east of Grand Canyon that is a gathering of shale hills in fantastic colors and through which the Little Colorado River flows before beginning its path towards the Grand Canyon.

POUR-OVER – See DOMER or HOLE. Same idea only more of a ledge.

PRIVATE TRIP - A group of people who have obtained their own permit to go downstream, and are not paying a professional outfit to guide them. People used to wait almost two decades for a private permit, now they use a lottery system.

RIFFLE - A wannabe rapid.

RUN - The path through a rapid. "Bad Run" = "oops!" or "Oh, shit!" depending on how bad it was.

SIDE HATCH - The hatches on a dory that lie left and right of the place the boatman sits to row.

SNOUT RIG - A twenty-two-foot boat designed like a catamaran, with two inflated "snouts" held together by a very heavy frame, rowed with four-teen-foot oars. These boats are not known for grace and elegance. Perhaps their most admirable feature is that they are harder to flip than any other type of oar powered boat. As for actually making them go where you want them to, well, there are various opinions on that.

THOLE PIN – The vertical metal pin on the boat's frame to which the oar attaches for rowing with fixed oars. Provides a pivot point for the oar and an excellent handle for grabbing to drag yourself back in the boat after having been thrown out in a rapid.

THRILL BOAT – Georgie Clark would lash three eighteen-foot rafts side by side. The "thrill" came when the whole rig went sideways into a hole and one boat would flop over on top of another, a process called "pancaking."

TONGUE - The V-shaped slick of water that points downstream into a rapid, caused by the constriction of the channel at the head of the rapid. Usually the tongue points to the deepest and fastest water, and the best place to go in the rapid. Sometimes, though, as in the case of House Rock Rapid, the tongue leads you right where you don't want to be, which is, needless to say, a bummer.

TL – Trip Leader, see HEAD BOATMAN

VULCAN'S ANVIL - Mile 178, the landmark that tells you that Lava Falls is just around the corner. This is the remains of a volcanic neck that sticks up out of the river like a giant fist. It is a sacred place to the Hualapai Indians who live in the area.

WILLY WORLD - Nickname for Wilderness World, a company that ran trips until 1987, when it was bought and morphed into Canyon Explorations, now Canyon Expeditions.

ACKNOWLEDGMENTS

THIS BOOK WOULD NOT HAVE BEEN POSSIBLE without, first and foremost, the river guides of Grand Canyon. Their good humor and ability to make and tell a story from just about anything provided both the inspiration and the material for this collection. Thank you all for telling your stories.

I wish that I could have used every tale spun to me, for they were all entertaining and so revealing of this unique place and lifestyle. I received stories that would fill another volume, and could not include them here for reasons of space. I am grateful to all who contributed, and take comfort in knowing that many of those stories will continue to be retold around campfires in the canyon and elsewhere, which is, after all, where they truly belong.

As this volume was taking shape, I noticed that the storytellers were dominated by men. Several women told me that they had stories, but were less inclined to tell them in such a forum. I have worked with so many talented and experienced women on the river that I know they have volumes of their own tales to tell. Thank you, all of you, for the inspiration and encouragement that I have learned just from watching you make your own stories and keep them quietly to yourselves.

Equally as important, and as revealing of the talent and depth of the guide community are the photographs and artwork included in the book. I am endlessly impressed with the quality of these pieces, and all those I had to choose from. Thank you all for showing that boatmen tell stories with more than words.

My thanks also go to Red Lake Books for first publishing this book and getting it out to the world. It was our good fortune that Larry Stevens spent enough time as a guide to recognize good stories when he read them.

One of the hardest issues we all had to deal with in creating this book originally was the decision on a title. Many good titles found their way into my head and across my desk, some more colorful than others. I extend my thanks to Dan Marshall for the inspiration that became the final title. It truly fits the spirit of the stories, and can be taken many ways, as can any good boatman tale.

Mary Williams, fine boatman and graphic artist, took this project under her talented wing and gave it a new face and feeling. Her skill, humor and sense of design are evident in every page. And thanks to Katherine Spillman, another talented boatman and designer, for making the changes to the second printing. Thank you to author, naturalist and lovely soul, Rose Houk, for taking the time to proofread the manuscript and make sure we didn't break too many Chicago Manual of Style rules. Author and boatman Brad Dimock provided invaluable advice and humor about publishing, printing, design and all the other headaches associated with something like this, as did Hazel Clark of Vishnu Temple Press.

Thank you Ted, Joan, Bob and Nonny, who first took me down the river as a commercial passenger, and didn't laugh when I told you I wanted to come back to stay.

I am indebted to all the boatmen I have had the great fortune to work with over the years. You have all taught me as much about life as you have about the river.

Finally, my tremendous gratitude, appreciation and respect go out to all the people who work ceaselessly to take care of the canyon and the river and to keep all rivers running healthy and free.

Shoreline
Larry Stevens
1988

Information About Grand Canyon

Protection, Preservation, Education and Recreation

Grand Canyon Association
P.O. Box 399, Grand Canyon, AZ 86023
(928) 638-2481
www.grandcanyon.org

Grand Canyon Field Institute
P.O. Box 399, Grand Canyon, AZ 86023
(866) 471-4435
www.grandcanyon.org/fieldinstitute

Grand Canyon Monitoring and Research Center
2255 N. Gemini Drive, Flagstaff, AZ 86001
(928) 556-7094
www.gcmrc.gov

Grand Canyon National Park
P.O. Box 129, Grand Canyon, AZ 86023
www.nps.gov/grca

Grand Canyon Private Boaters Association
www.gcpba.org

Grand Canyon River Guides
P.O. Box 1934, Flagstaff, AZ 86002
(928) 773-1075
www.gcrg.org

Grand Canyon River Outfitters Association
www.gcroa.org

Grand Canyon Trust
2601 N. Fort Valley Rd, Flagstaff, AZ 86001
(928) 774-7488
www.grandcanyontrust.org

Grand Canyon Wildlands Council
P.O. Box 1594, Flagstaff, AZ 86002
(928) 556-9306
www.grandcanyonwildlands.org

Grand Canyon Youth
P.O. Box 23376, Flagstaff, AZ 86002
(928) 773-7921
www.gcyouth.org

Museum of Northern Arizona
3101 N. Fort Valley Rd., Flagstaff, AZ 86001
(928) 774-5213
www.musnaz.org

Whale Foundation
P.O. Box 855, Flagstaff, AZ 86002
(928) 774-9440
www.whalefoundation.org

CONTRIBUTOR BIOGRAPHIES

GEORGE BAIN first hiked the canyon when he was in college at Northern Arizona University. In the mid 1970s Grand Canyon hiking legend Harvey Butchart gave George and his climbing friends a list of about thirty buttes that he thought were unclimbed, and they "really went nuts" with that information. George began working commercially for Steve Glass, ARTA and Wilderness World in the late 1970s. In 1981 he decide to use his engineering degree to some good and went to work for an oil company in Farmington, New Mexico. George now works at W.L. Gore, in Flagstaff. He and his wife Janie introduced their son, Wesley, and their daughter, Lena, to river life early on and have enjoyed raising kids with a lot of river time.

JEFF BEHAN has guided in Grand Canyon since 1981 and remains active as a boatman and trip leader on science and NPS river planning trips. Jeff also works as an environmental policy analyst at the Institute for Natural Resources, and as an instructor in the Recreation Resource Planning program at Oregon State University. In addition to exploring Oregon rivers, Jeff enjoys mountain biking, hiking, and skiing with his wife Becky and tending to his organic vegetable garden.

ELIZABETH BLACK worked as a Grand Canyon river guide for Arizona Raft Adventures from 1986 to 1995, rowing and paddling. On every trip down the Colorado she took her art equipment, and gathered source material for paintings of the canyon, which she completes in her studio at home. She is married to Chris Brown, another AZRA guide, and now paints and gardens full time in Boulder, Colorado. More of her work can be seen at www.ElizabethBlackArt.com.

STEVE BLEDSOE had his first river adventure in 1964, when Mack Miller invited him and his dad to travel from Temple Bar into the Grand Canyon on his jet boat. He knew after that trip that he had to spend more time in the canyon. He was hired in 1968 as a boatman by Hatch River Expeditions, and in 1990 he began running boats for science trips. He retired from the river in 2002 with around four hundred trips. He now devotes his time to his other love, creating art. More of his art can be seen on his website at www.stevebledsoe.com.

LOWELL BRAXTON worked with ARTA in the late 1970s. He has rowed western rivers since the 1980s, and currently lives in Salt Lake City, where he works as a geologist for the state of Utah.

DUGALD BREMNER came to Grand Canyon in the early 1980s, working for Grand Canyon Expeditions and then later for Grand Canyon Dories. All the while he was developing his photography career and exploring the swift rivers and high mountains of the world. By 1996, he was shooting for *National Geographic Magazine* and *Outside Magazine*. He was at the peak of his career when he died suddenly in a kayaking accident in the high Sierra of California in 1997. He is remembered for his quick-witted humor and love of adventure. Dugald's photographs are handled through www.powerhousephoto.com.

MATHIEU BROWN is two parts canyon enthusiast and one part commercial boater, as evidenced by his haphazard boating career. In 1997 he started working trips from Diamond Creek to Lake Mead, and did his first full-length trip a year later. Following an unexplained diversion to Jackson, Wyoming as a river ranger, he returned to work with Arizona River Runners, after which he fell into a student position at Grand Canyon National Park. Although easily distracted, he continues work as a recreation and wilderness technician and has managed to labor seven consistent seasons for Grand Canyon Semester, an educational program jointly run between Northern Arizona University and Grand Canyon National Park. He remains privileged and lucky enough to still row a few trips a year.

GHIA CAMILLE has been working and playing on rivers for the last two decades, mostly in Utah and Arizona, but her adventures have taken her all over the country. She believes that being a mother is the most important job of her life. To pay the bills she works as a graphic designer. In her spare time she skis, rock climbs, river rafts, mountain bikes, spins wool, makes baskets and writes stories. Ghia lives in Mammoth Lakes, California.

TIM COOPER worked as a river ranger on the Middle Fork of the Salmon in Idaho before settling down in Grand Canyon where he drove motorized rafts a couple of seasons, conducting the fastest commercial trip offered through the entire canyon in the slowest motor boats ever designed. Burned out on that, but not Grand Canyon, he worked for another eleven years for Grand Canyon Dories, tapering off after the birth of his son Ryan in 1986. He now lives near Dolores, Colorado with his wife and former guide, Lori, and daughter and accomplished kayaker, Morgan. He currently pays out huge dough to keep son Ryan in school. He still writes sporadically, and uses the manipulative skills he learned on the river to earn a living.

OTE DALE has worked as a guide in Grand Canyon since 1975. After thirty years, she still rows six trips a year in her dory, the *Dark Canyon*. Ote lives and paints in Flagstaff, Arizona, and she shares the river with her husband Regan, and two children, Duffy and Alissa, all dory boatmen.

BRAD DIMOCK has been a boatman since the early 1970s in Grand Canyon, Utah, and around the world. He is the author of *Sunk Without a Sound: the Tragic Colorado River Honeymoon of Glen and Bessie Hyde*, and *The Very Hard Way: Bert Loper and the Colorado River,* available through Fretwater Press at www.fretwater.com.

DAVE EDWARDS began rowing for Arizona Raft Adventures in Grand Canyon in 1974, and has been a freelance photographer throughout those years. He has traveled extensively through Asia documenting and exploring native cultures, and is especially interested in Mongolia and China. Dave photographed the Kazakh eagle hunters of western Mongolia for the September, 1999 issue of *National Geographic Magazine,* and founded the Flagstaff International Relief Effort to bring clothing and medical supplies to Mongolia. Dave can be reached at www.davidedwardsphotography.com.

KENT ERSKINE worked as a river guide from 1970 to 1976 with ARTA and Grand Canyon Dories. Kent met his wife on a private trip in 1974 and they moved to Ashland, Oregon where they proceeded to raise children and sheep on their ranch. Over the years they have run a construction business, and a yarn and natural fiber clothing store, and published a magazine for wool growers around the world. And of course, dropped everything whenever they could get back down the canyon.

MATT FAHEY has worked in and loved the canyon since the early 1990s. He works with OARS when he's not exploring his other loves of surfing, kayaking, cameras, art and travel. When he's not on the river, he makes outdoor documentary films with his production company, Down By The River Productions (www.downbytheriverproductions.com).

KYLE GEORGE has been working for Arizona River Runners since 2000. In the off-season he does "the typical dirtbag thing:" traveling, surfing, climbing, biking, general exploration and photography. Visit his website at www.kylegeorgephotography.com.

GEOFF GOURLEY has worked in the canyon since 1983, for Wilderness World, Expeditions, and Canyon Explorations and Expeditions. Geoff is a free-lance photographer living in Flagstaff with his wife Susan, also a boatman in the canyon. Geoff's images can be seen at www.geoffgourley.com.

CREEK HANAUER is a resident of Forks of Salmon, California, where he is a senior whitewater kayak instructor at Otter Bar Kayak School, on the Cal-Salmon. He's been running the Colorado River since 1989, working as a kayak safety boater with Sleight Expeditions (now Grand Canyon Discovery) and AZRA. He is a volunteer river recreation consultant with the Salmon River Restoration Council, the forest community's environmental group, and the publisher/editor of *The River Voice*, an online newspaper/magazine that covers the Salmon River and mid-Klamath River communities.

TOM HANSEN has been a whitewater river guide through Grand Canyon, Cataract Canyon and on the Salmon River for more than thirty-six years, mostly on the Colorado River through Grand Canyon. His father, Russell Hansen, was one of the original founders of Tour West, Inc. a whitewater rafting company. As a consequence, Tom's first river trip through Grand Canyon was at the age of fifteen, and he was a licensed guide by the age of seventeen. Tom is currently a software consultant, but continues to guide river trips whenever possible. In response to the many requests for his photographs, he began his web site, www.canyonmemories.com.

CHARLY HEAVENRICH has been sharing the canyon experience with passengers as a guide, the author of *Dancing on the Edge: A Professional River Guide Shares the Life Changing Power of the Grand Canyon*, a photographer (*Grand Canyon: A Different View*) and a speaker since 1978. He has worked for Wilderness World, Canyon Explorations, Arizona Raft Adventures, and OARS. He is also a life coach, helping people go from where they are to where they want to be. Charly lives in Boulder, Colorado. He can be contacted at www.charlyheavenrich.com.

NANCY COKER HELIN did her first trip as a passenger in 1981, and has proceeded to be a part of the Grand Canyon community ever since as a boatman for OARS. The singer-songwriter has traveled to Ethiopia, Chile, Turkey and Alaska to run rivers and find inspiration for her songs. Nancy lives in Flagstaff where, among other things, she teaches voice and runs Professional River Outfitters with her husband, Bruce. Nancy's CD *River Running* is available through her company, Poppy Ray Music or cdbaby.com.

TOM JANECEK worked as a guide in the Grand Canyon from 1986 to 1996 for Wilderness River Adventures. Two sons and a career as a mechanical engineer have reduced his river time substantially, but he plans for a private trip with his family. Tom lives and works from Flagstaff, Arizona.

NATHAN JONES was a commercial river guide in Grand Canyon from 1979 through 1996. He currently lives in Salt Lake City, where he works on his photography.

SAM JONES has worked in the canyon for Colorado River and Trail Expeditions and Canyon Explorations and Expeditions for more than twenty years, the same amount of time that he's been painting southwestern landscapes. Clearly, there is a connection. Sam lives in Flagstaff, Arizona, where he continues to paint and guide.

Coby Jordan worked in Grand Canyon from 1979 to 1996, mostly as a boatman for Grand Canyon Dories. In 1983, his wooden boat experience landed him a job playing Powell expedition member William Dunn in the 1983 IMAX Grand Canyon movie.

Lisa Kearsley became acquainted with the Grand Canyon by spending summers camping on the North Rim while her father, a biology professor, studied Kaibab squirrels. She began running the Colorado in 1991, working for AZRA and ARR. She has worked for the National Park Service at Grand Canyon as an interpreter and as a researcher, primarily studying the effects of Glen Canyon Dam on river campsites. She also works as a guide on the San Juan River in Utah, and wrote and published *The San Juan River Guide*, a comprehensive guidebook for river runners, available at www.shivapress.com. Lisa lives in Flagstaff, Arizona.

Rebecca Lawton, former whitewater guide and river ranger, worked in Grand Canyon from 1976 to 1986. She is a geologist and the author of *Reading Water: Lessons from the River* (Capital Books). Her work has been published in journals and anthologies such as *Orion, THEMA, Walking the Twilight*, and the *Traveler's Tales* series, Visit her website at www.rebeccalawton.com.

Teresa Yates Matheson's experience with Grand Canyon began in 1985, as a volunteer on a Georgie Clark trip. From that point, her involvement with Grand Canyon has taken her into many avenues: from being a commercial motor, oar and paddling guide, to work in the science community. Teresa initially discovered the wintering population of bald eagles at Nankoweap Creek. She has been involved in studies of them, as well as humpback chub, trout, waterfowl, vegetation, aquatic insects, beach erosion and debris flows. She currently lives in Salt Lake City with her husband, Steve. She's on the river only part time while she studies for her bachelor's degree, but she'll be back to the river a lot more as soon as she's done.

Bob Melville worked in the canyon from 1975 to 1995 for Arizona Raft Adventures. He currently lives in Flagstaff, where he helps his wife Jan by doing the dishes, taking care of the dogs and keeping the house clean. Kind of like being a boatman on land.

SHANE MURPHY began guiding in Grand Canyon in 1986, and served as president of Grand Canyon River Guides in the mid-1990s. Murphy is an historian, writer and illustrator. His treatment of Sir Ernest Shackleton's 1914–1917 *Endurance* expedition to Antarctica is the most extensive on record, and he is the author of four works on expedition photographer Frank Hurley and his photos. Murphy was also a major contributor to *South With Endurance* (Simon & Schuster, 2001), a coffee table-sized (and priced) book. His latest compilation is *The Colorado River In Grand Canyon: An Interpretative Sketch*, an ephemeral guide to the riparian rocks, people, plants, critters and history found in Grand Canyon National Park. Murphy lives and writes from Rimrock, Arizona.

RAECHEL RUNNING first went down the Colorado when she was twelve years old. In the name of science, resource management, commercial, charter and a few private trips, she has swamped, bag hagged, rowed, motored, painted, and photographed throughout the seasons for more than ninety trips since 1990. She's worked primarily as a freelance guide and cook. She's been the camp hostess, menu planner, feng shui-ing kitchenlandia coordinator—the "Cocinera," whose Caribbean and Southwest cuisine specialties have turned menus upside down for Arizona River Runners, Tour West, Wilderness, AZRA, Hatch, OARS and Expeditions. Freelance photographer Raechel lives in Flagstaff, Arizona. Her work can be seen at www.rmrfotoarts.com.

JOEL RUSSELL started working in the business in 1995 as a driver for several river companies. Since then he has been everything from a driver to a boatman. He currently lives in Flagstaff, where he works for a small publishing company and spends as much time painting as possible. He tries to get back into the canyon as often as he can for inspiration.

CHRISTA SADLER has worked in the canyon since 1988. She also works as a wilderness guide, writer and earth science teacher. She lives in Flagstaff, Arizona and can be reached at www.this-earth.com or www.thisearthpress.com.

LEW STEIGER started out in 1971 with Fred and Carol Burke's Arizona River Runners. Wanting to row, he started freelancing in the late '70s and has since worked proudly—rowing and motoring—for all but a few of the

Grand Canyon companies. Rowing dories for Martin Litton, George Wendt, and Mike Denoyer has been a particular highlight, but honestly, every single trip has been a wonderful gift. Lew and his brother are film-makers in Prescott, Arizona.

LARRY STEVENS began working in the canyon in 1974, and has worked for the Museum of Northern Arizona, Wilderness World and Arizona Raft Adventures, among others. He has a doctorate in zoology from Northern Arizona University, and uses it as a freelance ecologist and science advisor for the Grand Canyon Wildlands Council. His recent work on seeps and springs and dragonfly biogeography has taken him all over North America with his company, Stevens Ecological Consulting, LLC.

MARIEKE TANEY has worked in the canyon since 1999, mostly for Canyon Expeditions. Marieke also works as a NOLS instructor and ski patroller, and she has taught outdoor leadership classes at Northern Arizona University. Marieke's love of the Grand Canyon and the Southwest has inspired her artwork and she hopes to write and illustrate her own children's book.

KATE THOMPSON has worked as a guide and scientist in Grand Canyon since 1990. Her love for rivers and all that embodies them constantly guides her photographic work. In 1998, she started her travel photography career while continuing her geoarcheology research and commercial boating. In 2001 she committed her greater love of photography to a full-time career and now resides in the small town of Dolores, Colorado. Her most recent clients include *Arizona Highways Magazine* and the Patagonia catalogue. Visit her at www.powerhousephoto.com.

SCOTT THYBONY writes books and articles for major magazines such as *National Geographic, Outside,* and *Smithsonian.* Long before receiving awards for his writing, he won the coveted Colorado River Jerry-Rigging Award for fixing a motor mount with beer cans and driftwood. He worked as a boatman for Canyoneers from 1972 to 1974 and returned in 1976 as a river ranger for the National Park Service.

ELLEN TIBBETTS was introduced to the Grand Canyon on weekend hikes while studying art at Northern Arizona University. The Grand Canyon seemed like a great place to be and in 1974, after four years of college and hiking, she began working for Martin Litton's Grand Canyon Dories. She continued working in the canyon until 1994, rowing the *Music Temple*. Today she lives in Flagstaff and teaches ceramics and other art classes at Coconino Community College.

VINCE WELCH fell under the spell of the canyon in 1978 while working for Grand Canyon Dories. His guiding career came to an abrupt halt in 1988 with the sale of the company and the birth of his son, Jake, the following year. Later, along came Gwen, his daughter. He is amazed (and thankful) to be happily married to Helen, who he met on a 1983 high-water trip which had been delayed a day and nearly postponed. Since his quick and clean exit from the canyon, he has taught school, become a full-time Mr. Mom and returned year after year to any river within reach. In 1998, he co-authored *The Doing of the Thing: the Brief, Brilliant Whitewater Career of Buzz Holmstrom*, available from Fretwater Press. He continues to write about rivers and mountains and everything in between.

MARY WILLIAMS has worked for Grand Canyon Dories since 1985. She is semi-retired from commercial guiding these days, and spends most of her time running her graphic design business and riding her horse. You can see her studio, staff, and portfolio at www.marywilliamsdesign.com. She lives with her husband, Chris, her dory, *Mille Crag Bend*, and assorted four-legged friends in Flagstaff, Arizona.

TYLER WILLIAMS moved to central Arizona with his family in 1977, when his father traded a career as professional football coach for the slower pace of cattle ranching. After college, Tyler lived out of his pickup truck as an itinerant river guide throughout the country. Tyler has written and photographed for *Paddler, Canoe & Kayak*, and *Back Country* magazines, among others. He has completed over a hundred multi-day hiking routes and paddled nearly two hundred rivers worldwide, including several first descents. His books on canyoneering and river running can be found at his website, www.funhogpress.com. Tyler lives in Flagstaff with his wife, Lisa, and dog, Kaibab.

ALLEN WILSON worked in the canyon from 1969 through 1976, for ARTA and the United States Geological Survey. On one of his first trips, they laid around on a beach watching the first man walk on the moon. Allen lives in Gold Beach, Oregon, with his wife, Terry. They ran a small river company there for eight years, but he now builds custom homes and websites.

PETE WINN has worked in Grand Canyon since 1969 for a variety of outfitters, but mostly for ARTA and AZRA, and also as a NPS river ranger. He took a time-out to do only private trips from 1982 to 2001. He lives in Grand Junction, Colorado, with his wife Cindy and his two children, Travis and Carmen, all of whom were or are currently Grand Canyon guides. In addition to his work as a geologist, he has been leading first descents of major rivers in Tibet and western China since 1994. More information and the trip journals are posted on his website at www.shangri-la-river-expeditions.com.

ABOUT THE EDITOR

CHRISTA SADLER'S LOVE OF THE COLORADO RIVER and Grand Canyon began at the age of twelve, when she rode a mule to the bottom of the canyon to have Thanksgiving dinner. Dreams of mule wrangling gave way to dreams of being a geologist when she took her first trip down the river in 1985: a six-day motor trip with Hatch River Expeditions. Despite the fact that Ted Hatch smiled politely and refused to consider her request to work for him, she went home to her graduate studies in geology at

the University of California at Santa Cruz, and proceeded to learn the basics of rowing on the Rogue River in Oregon. She worked for a season on the rivers of Oregon and northern California, and dreamed of coming back to the Colorado. In 1987 Christa came to Flagstaff to find a job on the river, although she told her parents it was to finish a master's degree in earth sciences at Northern Arizona University, the only legitimate excuse she could come up with. She did indeed finish her degree, as well as become a guide on the river, something she admits to planning her life around since finishing school.

In her attempt to avoid a desk job and stay outdoors in the most beautiful places she can find, Christa has worked on rivers throughout the Southwest and Alaska, and in Ecuador. She has worked as a sea kayak guide, naturalist and educator for several ecotourism companies in Mexico,

Alaska and on the Colorado Plateau. Her research in archeology, geology and paleontology has included several ridiculously hot summers searching for dinosaurs in the badlands of Montana, fighting off dust storms and overly curious camels in the Gobi Desert in Mongolia, and steering clear of annoyed marine iguanas in the Galapagos Islands.

Christa has taught introductory geology and paleontology at Northern Arizona University and Coconino Community College in Flagstaff and Prescott College, in Prescott, Arizona. She works as an instructor for the Grand Canyon Field Institute, and runs geology programs for park service personnel at Grand Canyon National Park. She also operates This Earth, a business that brings earth science programs to children and adults around the United States, and designs earth science exercises, programs and field trips for students grades K-12. Information about her programs is available at www.this-earth.com.

Her articles and photographs have appeared in numerous regional and national publications. She has worked as a reporter for the *Chilkat Valley News* in Haines, Alaska, and she is the author of *Life in Stone—Fossils of the Colorado Plateau,* published by the Grand Canyon Association. She is currently at work on a book about the fossil history of the Southwest during the beginning of the Age of Dinosaurs. Occasionally, she makes it home to Flagstaff to sleep.

Additional copies of this book can be ordered at www.thisearthpress.com.